40 · 0 · 40 · 80

UGRO-FINNISH

SCANDIN-AVIAN

RUSSIAN

ENGLISH

GERMAN

FRENCH

INDO-EUROPEAN

CAUCASIAN

ALTAIC

PORTUGUESE

SPAN-ISH

ITALIAN

TURKISH

GREEK

HAMITO-SEMITIC

HINDUSTANI

DRAVIDIAN

TAMIL

ARABIC

SUDANIC

ENGLISH

FRENCH

BANTU

ENGLISH

PORTUGUESE

HOTTENTOT

ENGLISH

NKIN

UOIS

SPANISH

ARAWAK

CHIBCHA

CARIB

ARAWAK

SPANISH

QUICHUA

COLLA

PORTUGUESE

TUPI

GUARANI

ARAUCANIAN

D1266655

LANGUAGE

LANGUAGE

A MODERN SYNTHESIS

Joshua Whatmough

PROFESSOR OF COMPARATIVE PHILOLOGY

IN HARVARD UNIVERSITY

ST MARTIN'S PRESS

NEW YORK

PREFACE

THIS book is directed at the interest, and it is great, of intelligent people, and they are many, in one or more of the several aspects of language; not at the experts in any of these aspects (or in any particular language), who may well be critical of the treatment of their specialties. It makes no claim to originality except in my theory of Selective Variation; it aims to bring together in a new synthesis current views about language developed in many different fields of knowledge. But it may be observed here that every new step that is taken in communication theory and in its practical applications—and such steps are now being taken fast and surely one after another—demonstrates that communication theory does correspond very neatly to language as well as to what is commonly called 'thought', and that it is neither mistaken nor too enthusiastic to transfer that mathematical theory to language. But of all this and of Selective Variation (a theory which I formed in 1941, and first mentioned in print in 1948, see *Actes du sixième Congrès international des Linguistes*, Paris, Juillet 1948, p. 348, a paper written in 1946) only time will tell; and I venture to hope it will not be so long a time as was needed for the acceptance of the theory of evolution. As to the possible objections that 'information' is defined in terms of probabilities, so also is language (p. 258); or that the Boltzmann theorem applies to a message, and not to a message-source, observe that in my account of H (of the Boltzmann formula), I do apply it to linguistic acts, that is to utterrances or acts of speech (*la parole*), and not to the abstraction LANGUAGE (*la langue*); and, finally, observe that full weight is given to redundancy. It may be said that the electric impulses of telephone, television, and radio, are not the same as linguistic acts; but these are all freely convertible from one to another, and back again. Moreover, it seems also that cerebral impulses are electric (or electronic); in fact, by a curious inversion, computators are popularly called 'electric brains' (or 'electronic brains'), when actually the human brain is an

v

electronic computator, if not a very good one for some operations (e.g. high-speed calculation), but an excellent one for others
(e.g. the composition of poetry, or every day talk).

If I mistake not, in recent times the initiative was taken in
the Harvard doctoral dissertation *Relative Frequency as a Determinant of Phonetic Change* (the important words are, of course,
'relative frequency' and 'determinant'), see *Harvard Studies in
Classical Philology* volume xl, 1929, p.1), the title of which
stressed my idea (see the footnote on p.3, *ibid.*) of the evolutionary significance of the undertaking, although the author of the
dissertation while accepting, as he in fact did, was always more
interested in his method (this, I feel sure, was his idea, and he
deserves full credit for it) as a descriptive technique, and for its
psychological implications, something to which he was passion-
ately devoted. A century ago, as I now learn from George
Boole's *Laws of Thought* (London, 1854, p.245) the method had
been used by the Rev. Charles Graves, Professor of Mathematics
in Trinity College, Dublin, in discovering the key to Ogam, and
was applied by Edward Hincks to deciphering cuneiform.
Graves verified his principle by constructing sequences table for
'all the European languages'. Again, if I mistake not, linguists
have been quite unaware of this anticipation of statistical
methods in linguistics. But I could never feel sure that my ideas
of 1927-1929, when that Harvard dissertation was being written,
and being discussed with me almost daily, that I could prove
my merely intuitive theory; that conviction was borne in upon
me as I heard a talk given in 1950 by Professor Robert M. Fano
of the Massachusetts Institute of Technology before the Institute for the Unity of Science, and then, almost at once, read
Shannon's papers (also put out in book form) on the mathematical theory of communication.

Some matters, which had to be omitted from this book are
developed in my forthcoming Sather Lectures of 1955 on *Poetic,
Scientific, and other Forms of Discourse* (University of California
Press, Berkeley and Los Angeles, 1956), especially an attempt
to put the 'qualitative' aspects of literary discourse (barely
mentioned on p. 210 below) on a scientific footing.

This book owes much to my own observations and reflection;
but like many books, it owes much also to others who have
written in these fields, and to discussions with colleagues and

friends, the experts, and—most of all—with some, namely the best, of my students, past or present, who have constantly led me to new, and, I hope, better efforts to wrestle with our common problems. I have read everything that I could lay my hands on that seemed to be pertinent; and I have drawn freely on stock examples familiar to all linguists, both from standard works and from articles in periodicals, especially *Word* and *Language*, but also some others, English and European. To Dr D. M. Mackay I am indebted for the brilliant concept of meaning as 'goal-directed activity'; and I have at times paraphrased my authorities, without, I hope, misrepresenting them. I am in the debt also of alert and thoughtful readers of the press; but most of all in the United States scholars owe much to enterprising men of business, and this book owes its very existence to the interest of one of these, for it owes to him the stimulus that at last impelled me to put these twelve chapters down on paper, an interest my thankfulness for which I can hardly express adequately. Dr Lawrence G. Jones, Dr Anthony G. Oettinger, and Mr Thomas D. Houchin, all of Harvard, and my wife, have read proofs, in whole or in part, and saved me from some errors.

Finally, the repeated use of one and the same example, notably that of temperature and of words meaning 'hot' or 'cold', may, I hope, serve as a clue to a single thread of argument that runs through this book.

J. Wh.

31st July 1955
Cambridge, Massachusetts

ACKNOWLEDGEMENTS

THE following works have been useful to me:

Bloch, B., and Trager, G., *Outline of Linguistic Analysis*, 1942
Bloomfield, L., *Language*, 1933
Cobb, S., *Foundations of Neuropsychiatry*, 1952
Goldstein, K., *Language and Language Disturbances*, 1948
Harris, Z. S., *Methods in Structural Linguistics*, 1951
Holloway, J., *Language and Intelligence*, 1951

Mandelbrot, B., Publications de l'Institut de Statistique, Université de Paris, vol. II, 1953, fasc. 1-2, pp. 2-123; *Contribution à la Théorie Mathématique des Jeux de Communication*

Pollock, T. C., *Nature of Literature in relation to Science and Language*, 1942

Potter, R. K., Kopp, G. A., and Green H. C., *Visible Speech*, 1947

Reichenbach, H., *Elements of Symbolic Logic*, 1947

Sapir, E., *Selected Writings*, edited by D. Mandelbaum, 1949

Shannon, C. E., and Weaver, W., *Mathematical Theory of Communication*, 1949

Troubetzkoy, N. S., *Principes de phonologie*, translated into French by J. Cantineau, 1949

Ullmann, S., *Words and Their Use*, 1951

Ullmann, S., *Précis de Semantique Française*, 1952

Wellek, R., and Warren, A., *Theory of Literature*, 1949

Yule, G. U., *Statistical Study of Literary Vocabulary*, 1944

Others that have become available, or came to my notice since this book was written in the winter of 1953 to 1954, will be considered in my forthcoming Sather Lectures; and in a book upon which I am now engaged (to be called *Language the Measure of Man*), in which also far more attention is paid to indeterminacy (cf. pp. 178, 203 below), especially in literary discourse.

I have profited greatly from the monographs of R. M. Fano, R. Jakobson, M. Joos, W. H. Huggins, and W. F. Twaddell; and from numerous articles, for offprints of which I am indebted in many cases to their authors, in particular W. E. Bull, Y. Bar-Hillel, J. B. Carroll, S. H. Chang, E. C. Cherry, C. D. Chrétien, N. Chomsky, P. Delattre, M. W. Essigman, H. Frei, C. H. Fries, T. Griggs, A. W. de Groot, R. A. Hall Jr., M. Hallé, E. P. Hamp, A. A. Hill, L. J. Hjelmslev, W. H. Huggins, S. Johansen, L. G. Jones, C. Kluckhohn, M. Kurath, R. H. Lees, J. C. R. Licklider, J. Lotz, R. I. McDavid, B. Mandelbrot, A. Martinet, V. Mathesius, C. N. Mooers, A. G. Oettinger, E. Pulgram, D. W. Reed, E. Reiffler, F. M. Rogers, P. J. Rulon, H. Spang-Hansen, H. L. Smith Jr., C. P. Smith, A. Stender-Pedersen, H. L. Stubbs, M. Swadesh, L. C. Tihany, G. L. Trager, W. F. Twaddell, R. Wells, R. Valin, F. Vilbig, J. P. Vinay, C. F. Voegelin, B. L. Whorf; and to papers written by a number of former or present students of mine, especially R. Abernathy, Mrs J. C. Chomsky, Miss F. M. Chude, R. J. Funke, Miss M. A. Handy, Miss M. Hill, E. H. Lenneberg, W. J. W. Lewis, W. F. Mackey, D. S. Marshall, L. E. Opdycke, H. A. Roe; as well as to articles in periodicals too numerous to name, but familiar to most linguists, the scope of which runs the entire gamut from the *Journal of the American Acoustical Society* to the *Modern Language Review* or the *Travaux du Cercle Linguistique de Copenhague*—both in subject matter and in spanning work done in two hemispheres.

CONTENTS

FIGURES

LANGUAGE

INTRODUCTION

THE study of language is of great antiquity. In the nineteenth century it participated in the evolutionary views then prevalent, and the result was the great achievement of historical and comparative linguistics, a methodology which was to language what the telescope had been to astronomy. Many valuable generalizations resulted, particularly the principle of regularity in change of sound; but attention was focused chiefly on the Indo-European languages as such, and on the details of their history, which were thoroughly explored. No general theory of language was sought except by a few individualists, whose scepticism prepared the way for the analytical method of the present century, a method stimulated also by the necessity of recording and describing native languages outside the Indo-European, Semitic, and other groups of languages which had long literary traditions and long traditions of exegesis. At the same time a new philosophical interest in language grew up, particularly that which regarded language as one of a few fundamental sets of symbolic forms. The question of functional relationships has thus become as prominent as that of historical connexions. In this field, still less than forty years old, international co-operation, which has fostered the development of all modern sciences, has been difficult and at times impossible for the new science of general linguistics, as a consequence of two world wars; but some solid results have accrued and some fundamental doctrines have been established; quite recently linguistics has been recognized as worthy of a place with the other subjects that are being actively pursued as contributing to the movement for the unity of science. Most striking of all is the still more recent application of symbolic logic and mathematics to linguistic problems, thus bringing linguistics into still closer relation with the exact sciences. Above all it has suddenly become clear that language seems to be orderly in its processes—far more orderly than had been supposed—and actually to be governed historically by pre-existing order of its own that constantly maintains and renews itself. In contrast, living organisms tend to go over into disorder, 'to approach the dangerous state of maximum entropy, which is death' (Schroedinger). Linguistic events, which are the conscious correlatives of cerebral activity, on the other hand, are statistically determined.

Take an example of a brief linguistic event. My boyhood was passed in the north of England, and the first general election that I remember was that of 1906, a Liberal landslide. My father was an ardent Liberal, and when he came home from a gathering of several thousand voters to whom the election results had been proclaimed in the Town Hall Square shortly after midnight of election day, my mother asked him 'Were there mony theer?' and he said 'Nobbut a tuthry'. This we all understood: 'Only two or three.' This also we all understood—a good crowd. The Lancashireman, like the New Englander, is fond of understatement. 'Three' is plural, that is more than two, which is dual number. So in common law, three is a crowd and may be moved on, as being likely to create a disturbance, by the police, without a warrant and without waiting for the Riot Act to be read. The old nursery rhyme has it 'One's none, two's some, three's a many, four's a little hundred'. In Tierra del Fuego, before the white man arrived, counting did not go beyond three. 'Where two or three are gathered together' (Matt. 18.20) the time is ripe for testimony; testimony of a different kind, to convict a murderer, called for two or three witnesses (Deut. 17.6; Numb. 35.30).

A man's will, to be valid, must have a witness or witnesses, that is, a third party—namely in addition to the testator himself and the beneficiary. That is what makes it his testament, an instrument that has a witness, in Latin *testis*. (The other meaning of *testis* is secondary: testicle, or a witness to virility.) But *testis* comes from old Latin *ter-stis* and this from *tri-stis* which meant 'third (person)', that is the witness, 'standing by' (Latin *stare*, from the same root as English *stand*). When he testifies, he *says* what he has *seen* done, the seal and signature of the testator—not hearsay; but 'see-say', and *see* and *say* also come from the one and the same root, for to 'say' is to make someone else to 'see' vicariously that which you have 'seen'. In a Greek tragedy three actors are enough to present the whole drama of life.

There is magic in the spoken word. It was because 'God said' let this and that be done, that it was done; or in the New Testament: 'In the beginning was the word.' The early Keltic peoples had a god of language called Ogmius (*ogam* being the name of their most ancient alphabet) who was identified with Hermes, the Greek god of speech; so had the Romans, a shadowy divinity called Aius Locutius (*aio* 'I say', *loquor* 'I speak'), 'sayer-speaker' (a doubled assertion, like the Chinese 'look-see'), the people of India a goddess Vagdevi (*vak-* 'word', cognate with Latin *vox*, and *devi* 'goddess' cognate with Latin *dea*), the ancient Egyptians a god Thoth (better Tehuti), and the Chinese a sacred turtle, who gave the gift of writing. In Homer writing is fraught with peril (σήματα λυγρά), and spoken words are winged (ἔπεα πτερόεντα)—either wing-swift, or, like a feather-tipped arrow, they reach their aim. A ban may be placed on writing, so that the sacred books of the Hindoo or the Moslem still are, and of the Gauls were, handed down by word of mouth; outside the sacred circle their contents might not be revealed even by word of mouth, so that silence becomes a golden virtue. The proper word is an open sesame; but the sacred name of God must not be spoken. My father addressed my mother by name when he was dying—he had always called her 'missis' both in addressing her and in referring to her, until that last half-hour. The mention of a person's name is felt somehow to weaken his defences against the outside world; the freedom with which given names are used in North America perhaps means that the old superstition is dead there. But the magic of language is not: a child can mobilize strong feelings with a word or two, a politician stir up pandemonium: *nobbut a tuthry*!

The phrase itself contains only two or three words. But those two or three give a glimpse of dialect compared with standard usage, of language at work, of change in language, in sound and in meaning, of language as an emotional outlet, of language and the law, language and religion.

An American learning to speak Arabic by the direct or conversational method once answered the question 'Where do you come from?' by saying *Iowa*, and the instructor told him that 'yes' could not be the answer to that question, the Arabic for 'yes' being *aiwa*. So the meaning of a word is not the sound of it, which may be more or less the same in different languages

LANGUAGE

with totally different meanings. Or the same meaning may be given by totally different sounds: *horse, pferd, cheval, misatim*; *house, casa, maison, domus*. But *bill* may be an account rendered, a piece of money, a boy's name, and a metal implement. How are such things sorted out and kept distinct? Or pairs like *it swings : its wings*, or French *un invalide : un nain valide*? Multiply the questions many times in every language:

> Alas, it's not the cares of State
> That prematurely age the great,
> It's angry pens a-gleaming at them
> And someone always screaming at them.
>
> The parting injunctions
> Of mothers and wives,
> Are one of those functions
> That poison their lives.
>
> The earth is used to bores,
> It heard, through ages long,
> The saurian's complacent roars,
> And the halting birth of song.
>
> Our restless tongues—their lust
> For action never dies.
> The noisiness of living dust
> Astonishes the skies.

It also astonishes anyone who stops to think for a moment of the miracle as well as the magic of language. During the last quarter of a century new methods of observation, new lines of attack, new collections of evidence, have combined to put the story of language in a new setting. The pages that follow tell this old story in a new way.

I

SCOPE AND METHOD

NEARLY everybody talks, many can read and write, and some
listen. Language is the most important meeting ground of the
sciences and of letters. An age in which words play a greater
role than any that has gone before calls for an examination and
interpretation of linguistic processes—for language about language—to the end of better understanding and mastery of itself.
Both the act of speaking or writing and the act of memory
are events. But they are not random. They have, as we say,
meaning; they are activities directed towards a goal, or goals,
achieved if at all by their own mediation, so that understanding
becomes a function of grammar. Modern computators demonstrate this peculiar feature of language in a peculiarly vivid
way. But the verbal behaviour of human beings has a self-
starter and controls its own output—the stream of speech in
which the successive words and sentences follow one another
without premeditation. Moreover these remarkable feats are
performed in such a way as to produce very extensive results
with the help of materials of quite limited range. Thus it has
been found that command of the 3000 most frequent words in
a continuous sample of 100,000 running English words gives an
understanding of 95 per cent of all the words, and that 2 per
cent more can be acquired by derivation from these; but that
a further 1 per cent increase can be attained only by the addition of 6000 additional words. Such statistical evidence raises
a number of interesting problems.

How, for example, is meaning in different kinds of discourse
related to the resources and structure of a language? And how
is such a structure formed? We have modern 'information'
theory of communication engineers, which is at least as much
concerned with conformation as with 'information' (that is, with

a measure of the restriction which habit, or structure, imposes
on freedom of choice). But not all language is informative in
the ordinary sense either. So much of language is emotive as
to inspire distrust, even in much of that part of it which pur-
ports to be informative. Moreover, in languages with a great
literary tradition, far more than mere structure is of compelling
interest. On the other hand, it has been maintained that even
in languages devoid of such a literature, say of the Hopi or
Shoshoni or Navaho, everything is really in the structure, in
the form, of the language—that its way of saying things or mere
grammar gives us the speaker's view of the universe, as contrasted with the totally different way in which scientific discourse says the same things, for example the causes of rain.
Can this be true? Again scientific discourse transcends, from its
own point of view, both a vernacular, devoid of the tradition
of literature other than folk-tales orally transmitted, and also
the literatures of the so-called 'great' languages. How far has
scientific discourse its own peculiar structure, and why cannot
it get on with ordinary discourse? What are the operative functional units to be isolated in the structure of a language? Or the
operative units of meaning? Are these identical in one and the
same language, or in more than one language, in all languages?
Are there any items that are universal? Is there any language
that comprehends, or seeks to comprehend, the world, and what
then is its structure? Does the structure of the one correspond
to the structure of the other, so that syntax is a model of the
universe? Or must there always be a selection of units of meaning as well as of units of form? In Neanderthal society just how
much was there to talk about? What, if any, are the limits to
the variety of things to be talked about, and to human capacity
to talk about them? Is knowledge itself coextensive with language? Or can anything be known that cannot be said? Does
the emergence of an abundance of grammatical forms, as in
early Indo-European languages, the age of inflexion, represent
a suddenly widened understanding, which was making unprecedented efforts to cope with previously guessed at, but very
involved relationships, which their modern representatives now
face with simpler linguistic devices? And the almost complete
absence of variety in grammatical forms, helped out by ample
gesture to indicate even fairly simple relationships, as in the

Aranta of Australia, does this represent a feral stage in which
not much is found to talk about? May 'thought' be not merely
sub-linguistic, but also non-linguistic, or both? What is the
relationship between a language and a culture? Does language
mould or reflect the culture, or do they react each constantly
upon the other? What about those words, in Lewis Carroll or
Edward Lear, which might have been structurally valid in English, but never occur elsewhere? Or the orders of words, in a
poet like Hopkins or prose writer like Joyce, which are not
structurally valid in English at all? These are some of the endless questions that present themselves.

This book is about language. Normally, all men and women,
except idiots and, unless they are carefully trained, except deaf-
mutes, join in this human babel before getting out of baby-
clothes; and there is nothing comes their way that they will
not talk about. Language touches everything, human and in-
human, in heaven and on earth, and beneath the earth, language
itself included. Language about language is called linguistics,
a vast and highly technical subject, yet only a very small part
of language. Since this book is about language, some attention
must be given to linguistics. But the book is not solely or
primarily about linguistics, but (to repeat) about language. Not
everything, however, can be got into one book, and the subject-
matter of this one must be selected; even the aspects of the
subject-matter must be selected, and also what is to be said
about each of them. The criterion of selection will be interest
and importance, not technical detail or exhaustiveness.

What is language? It is customary to begin with definitions.
But philosophically a definition comes at the end of an investigation. If we begin by defining language, that is because language has been investigated from more than one point of view
already. We might indeed be clear first about the nature of
a definition. To define is to set forth the proper or peculiar
qualities of an object, the features that give it its character and
quality. But to define is also to differentiate an object, to set
forth the features that distinguish it from other objects with
which it might be confused. Again a definition is not bound to
be permanent, but may be changed. The ancients regarded
vinegar as typical of acid substances, but vinegar is impure
acetic acid; acetic acid (the acid of vinegar) in modern chemistry

is $HC_2H_3O_2$, of which only one of the hydrogen (H) atoms has acid properties—an acid being a salt of hydrogen, in the language of chemistry a substance which gives a hydrogen ion in solution, or which neutralizes bases yielding water. In general, an acid is 'a molecule with a positive field which is capable of neutralizing a basic molecule having a "free" electron pair'. In ordinary conversation, of course, the term 'acid' is not restricted by the scientific definition.

Now, to define language with precision is far less easy than to define acid or other chemical terms. This is because many scientific inquirers are interested in language, philosophers, psychologists, physicists, logicians, literary critics, neurologists, sociologists, as well as linguists, to name no others. There is also, just now widespread interest in language and in meaning on the part of many intelligent men and women, no matter whether they regard an understanding of the nature and function of language as directly important for their daily work or not. No wonder, then, if many different definitions are made by different thinkers. But there need not be one, and only one, definition of language; and the different definitions advanced are not exclusive. They bring out different aspects of language, and supplement one another instead of excluding one another. Everything depends on the investigator's point of view and interest at the time that he makes his definition.

To many, language is the most important form of human communication, and this is the broadest way of regarding it. Certainly language is human, and human only. Insects, birds, and some mammals as well as man do communicate; but they do not talk. And language is normally, though not invariably, a form and a means of communication. Humans also use other means of communication, such as a red light, or a flag; but these are interpreted in language. 'Communication' means that an organism is affected by an external event and makes a reply to it. Clearly both the reply and the original event, in many cases itself also an utterance, are quite commonly what we understand by language: 'Is it raining?' (utterance) 'Not much' (response).

To others, language is first and foremost a form of symbolism. Here again we must stop to ask a question. What is a symbol? A symbol is a surrogate. We speak of mathematical symbols, for example x for any number, x^y for any number multiplied by itself any other number of times, i.e. x^y is the continued product of y x's, or x multiplied by itself $(y-1)$ times; Σ for any sum, and so on; or logical symbols, as a or b as variables in a statement or proposition, and then $\bar{a}$ to mean 'not a', $a \lor b$ for 'a or b', $\supset$ for implication as $a \supset b$ to mean 'a implies b', and so forth. But all these surrogates have one feature in common. There is nothing in the nature of things that gives them the meanings stated; that is something *we* have given them, by agreement or convention, so that the symbol acquires a certain arbitrary character. This is something quite different from a *sign*. A sign has a direct relation to its object, like water dripping from the trees as a sign of rain; but the *word* rain (which obviously is not rain, or a sign of rain, for I can say it indoors, or for that matter I can say it repeatedly, even outdoors, without getting wet) is a symbol of 'rain' or 'raining', as in our question *Is it raining? Not much!* or (to vary the event and therefore the response) *Not at all!*

Moreover, any consistent or coherent group of symbols, as in a language or dialect, is *systematic*. Like a family or society, it is not a merely accidental collection of stray individuals. The nature of symbols is such that to speak of an unsystematic symbolism is to fall into a contradiction in terms. Certainly linguistic symbols which are combined in such a way that the ties between them are unsystematic or are even bizarre—that is linguistic symbols unrelated to one another but merely juxtaposed—make nonsense; they cease to function as symbols. A haphazard jumble of symbols, say a pied text, is a mathematician's, or musician's, or a mere writer's or talker's nightmare —but still a nightmare. An isolated symbol, on the other hand, remains just that to all eternity. The symbol for implication implies nothing by itself but implication in the abstract, and there it must rest; probability is probability in relation to something. All higher order abstractions are symbolic—'justice', 'freedom', 'goodness', 'truth' and the like. Neither their content nor their form is directly or independently experienced, but only in relation to that which they symbolize; which is the reason why they are so much either distrusted or blindly worshipped, like the ideal of autonomy which destroyed the ancient Greek city-states.

But there remains one other factor even in this definition of language. Language is not only a systematic symbolism. Music is that, and also like language uses sound, and at times, as in singing, combines its own rhythm and melody with language. Language is a *verbal* systematic symbolism. That is to say, it makes use of verbal elements and structures, in brief of what we commonly call words and of their arrangements. It will be better to postpone for a while any definition of words, or of what, in some languages such as Eskimo, behave pretty much as words do in others such as English. For the present it will be enough to take an example, say 'table'. There we have a symbol of a certain object; the symbol is also a word; that is, it is a verbal symbol. So, in like manner, *and* or *beer* or *have* or *embryo* or *drunk* or *man*. Now when we have occasion to use such a verbal symbol, we do so in a systematic way. Thus the verbal symbols 'table and embryo have drunk beer,' placed in that sequence are so unsystematic in arrangement as to symbolize nothing, unless possibly dementia on the speaker's part; but 'the man has drunk beer,' by adhering to the system, retains the symbolic integrity of each symbol, and the arrangement enhances their symbolic values.

The same is true at each step; *table* is a symbol, *letab* is not. It is not even necessary to add that *elbat* or *letab* is not a symbol in English, implying that it is, or may be, in some other language. What we have said so far is true of languages, or of a language, as well as of language at large; for every case is a given case when you come to it, and this is true of languages as of everything else, from cabbages to kings. To raise the question of system or no-system of a symbol outside its own systematic symbolism is idle. How deep-seated this principle is may be seen by taking the following groups of Latin words:

saxum 'stone' but *sexum* (acc. sing.) 'sex', and *sex* 'six'
lacus 'lake' but *locus* 'place'
liquens 'clear' but *līquens* 'fluid', *lŏquens* 'speaking', and
liquans 'liquefying'.

Lucretius, like all the ancient atomists, was aware of all this, and fond of it as an illustration of his theories: *ignis* is 'fire', which may be had from *lignum* 'firewood' by disturbing or subtracting from or adding to the constituent particles of the words as well as of the substances! The principle may be illustrated from the system of any language whatever. It is astonishing how few of the primary units, that is the speech-sounds, will serve, and how little strain is put upon them, or upon the user, by quite severe demands for efficiency in their use. Even a child, or even a very dull adult, can easily make this powerful instrument serve all his needs.

But there are other ways of looking at language. One other way of putting what has just been said about the systematic character of linguistic symbolism is to say that language is a form of order, a pattern, a code. That is to say, at any given status of its history, a language is found to show a statistical regularity which may be put in terms of formulae that are concerned with classical probability of frequency of occurrence of the constituent elements, and of permitted combinations of them within the pattern of a particular language. Objectively, therefore, a language may be described as a body of physically discrete events in which relations of similarity occur in a statistically definable pattern. The sequence of events is governed by probabilities of occurrence; i.e. proceeds by probability, ranging from 0 to 1, in a series of mass phenomena showing repetitive events. The successive steps in the process are dependent also upon preceding steps. Finally, a sufficiently large sample of the sequence is representative of the whole, precisely because the events are repetitive. For example, in modern written English the occurrence of the symbol *q* guarantees that the symbol which follows it will be *u*; the symbol *th* in English may be followed by *a, e, i, o, u, r, w, y* but not by *l* (unless in borrowed words) or *x* or any of the other English alphabetic symbols. *Thx* would be a zero probability in genuinely English words; *tha* and the rest will always be less than 1. Even *th-* (as in *then*) is not followed by *r*, but only *th-* (as in *thin*); likewise English *shr-* occurs, but not *shl-*, or *pw-*: if you hear *pwivate* 'private' from a few speakers [w] is a variant, phonematically speaking, of [r]. The probability that *th* will be followed by *e* is considerably higher than that it will be followed by *u*. This is a very simple illustrative example.

In modern English, if a permissible sequence of symbols that makes a word, for example the series *f u r i o u s*, is followed by anything at all, then those following symbols are already pre-

scribed and limited; in this case they must be *l y* or *n e s s* (not
normally *e r* or *e s t*) and nothing else, for example not *th* (like
wide : *width*). In other words, the symbols *l y* or *n e s s*, in this
particular sequence, are determined by what went before.

But in all this, there is one feature of language that must
never be lost sight of. *Language is first and foremost a means of
transmitting information,* and its study a branch of the study
of symbols and of the signs and objects that they symbolize.
Language is made up of messages purposively produced in such
a way as to be decoded word-by-word in the easiest, i.e. most
economical, possible fashion. The length and arrangement of
linguistic structures such as words, the nature and relation of
speech-sounds (phonemes) one to another, the length and relation of constituent clauses in a sentence or period, all these have
evolved in such a way as to promote an economical, but powerful, means of communication.

Language is also a form of social behaviour. If all normal
humans talk, and only humans, they also talk to one another.
At the moment I am talking to my reader, as much as if I were
'on the air'; there is a greater time-lag in a printed book, as in a
recording, than there is in face-to-face talk, the telephone, or
direct, unrehearsed radio. A letter is written not to its writer,
but to his family or friends or business acquaintances, to his
tailor or grocer, to the tax-collector, and so forth. If I make
notes for my own subsequent use, then I am practically two
different persons, in different places or at different times, one
here and now, the other somewhere else in the future. Some
forms of language, shall we say those partially tabooed (but
often infuriating or laughable) varieties of language, profanity
and obscenity, have been made the objects of psychological
study. Perhaps it is a mistake to treat them solely as matters
of individual psychology. When language, or verbal behaviour,
is taken up by the psychologist, it is or should be as a matter
of social as well as of individual conduct. Linguistic phenomena
are conditioned by the social group, by circumstances which
are socially determined—both the linguistic patterns of the
community, and extralinguistic group habits, e.g. customs such
as taboo or courtesy or the like.

To say that language may be studied as a form of behaviour
by no means admits that the school of psychology known as

behaviourist is unreservedly supported by linguistics or by all
linguists, or that a behaviourist interpretation of linguistic
phenomena is the correct and only one. The serious objection
to behaviourism is that it fails to take adequate account of
intelligence. Intelligence consists in the power to make a new
departure instead of repeating the old habit, to take a new step.
A high degree of intelligence is always abnormal, and it occurs
in the individual. How can behaviourists explain any initial
success which they may themselves experience by their own
professed theory that initial success is to be explained only in
terms of chance and habit? A behaviourist who sets himself
the purpose of proving that purpose does not exist is in the
impossible position of starting himself into flight by tugging on
his own bootstraps; he seems not to have noticed that the more
frequently something has been tried, the less likely it is to recur
if it has been unsuccessful, so that an intelligent result calls for
deviation from normal habit. This is true also of language.
Even on the mathematical view, a striking utterance is found,
on inspection, to disturb commonplace encoding and decoding
processes, as in T. S. Eliot's 'The yellow fog' (not 'dog') 'that
rubs its back upon the window-panes'.

A notion of language that was common, at least by implication, in the nineteenth century, is held by nobody today, though
many of the old ways of expression are constantly met with.
We speak of mother languages, sister languages, dead and living
languages. These expressions clearly suggest the view of language as an organism. But a moment's reflection must always
have shown that the expressions are figurative only. Languages
do not intermarry and produce offspring; to talk of a 'family'
of languages means that a number of mutually unintelligible
languages all represent divergent forms that can be shown historically to go back to a common original, that they possess a
common stock of words, forms, sentence-structure, and speech-
sounds, all greatly modified in the course of time, the relationships of which one to another can be accounted for only on the
assumption that they represent a previous single, more-or-less
homogeneous, speech. Provided that this fact is clearly understood, there is little harm in talking about this or that 'family'
of languages.

But the whole matter was often put in the terms of a family-tree relationship. This idea was fostered in part by the evolutionary theories associated with the name of Darwin which were very much in the air in the middle of the nineteenth century. It was also encouraged by the work of a prominent philologist of the time, August Schleicher, who happened also to be a botanist, and was tempted to apply not only his scientific attitude of mind to his theorizing about language, which was all to the good, but also the current ideas of genetic relationships among plants or animals, which was misleading. Yet language certainly is an activity of living organisms, and through them shows remarkable power of adaptation to a changing environment.

But if language is not itself an organism, neither is it a mechanism. Many modern linguists are confirmed believers in a mechanist theory of language which shuns all mental interpretations and all mentalist terms. The theory of course claims to be objective. But it is difficult to admit the validity of the claim. For then we are asked to accept language about language about language about language . . . (and so on to infinity), and all of it starting from the hypothesis that language is nothing more than a matter of mechanical stimulus and response. If the theory were correct it would refute itself; for it would, on its own showing, be reduced to being a response or series of responses made by a certain linguist or linguists to certain stimuli, chiefly verbal. Such responses might tell us something about the linguist or linguists concerned and even about his or their use of language, but hardly anything about language as such. It is impossible to explain x by x; an unknown cannot be interpreted by itself. The mechanist theory aims at strictly scientific method, and therefore pretends to use only direct observation of communicating individuals; but in practice it leans heavily on indirect observation through records of all kinds. It tends also to restrict itself to observing and discussing the effects of language on the behaviour of the individual, notwithstanding the fact that verbal behaviour is essentially social. It is difficult to see how a mechanical theory of communication can ever escape the charge of solipsism: the mechanist always overlooks the fact that he himself, an organism like any other, is doing the observation, so that his much-vaunted objectivity is false.

As for the quaint notion that language arose from primitive facial gestures, and therefore does not differ fundamentally from other muscular behaviour, not only does the idea rest on nothing stronger than conjecture; it naively assumes the validity of an absurdly simple solution to an extremely complicated problem. A truly philosophical account of language must comprehend, for example, poetic as well as scientific discourse, the power of human intellect as well as the chit-chat of everyday conversation.

But it will not do to fly to the opposite extreme and regard language as pure intellection. In scientific discourse, in logic, a large part of the total utterance serves intellectual operations, in mathematics close to 100 per cent (a definite article, demonstrative pronoun, the substantive verb, short phrases or sentences, and the like here and there in a page of mathematics perhaps are supererogatory); in poetry and creative writing generally, in aesthetic discourse too, a high percentage may still be said to be concerned with intellect. But in ordinary conversation as much as 90 to 95 per cent of what we say is neutral, and the meaning is carried largely by the overtones of the remainder—say such words as 'friend', or 'enemy', that arouse the emotions. Even here there is still a crude correspondence between the structure of the utterance and the structure of experience. But in some commerical and political propaganda any such correspondence may be not seriously attempted at all. There is often a pretence at making the statements informative, but it is a pretence unworthy of human intellect. It is, however, precisely the intervention of the individual cerebral (or mental) event between stimulus and response that effectively rescues language from being an automatic mechanist affair, even when it proceeds from the mouth of a dictator.

Finally, it has been suggested that language is a relation, or (better) a means of establishing and sustaining relations between members of a community, large or small—a village or hamlet, or on a world-wide scale. This is another, and in a way a more concrete statement of what is meant by saying that language is a form of social behaviour. Think of a human being as a point on a plane; and of what he says as projected like a double cone with the point on the plane, the cones produced above and below the plane and the axes variable; suppose also a number of such points, each corresponding to a human being, close to-gether or more widely separated, as the case may be, on the plane. The cones will intersect. And the farther each cone is projected into space, the greater the volume of intersection. Even cones widely separated, people who are, if you like, 'poles apart', may be brought into contact by the spreading influence of what they say, especially if they use modern techniques of communication, including the light-swift radio. The members of a family, however, clan, village, city, or nation—the latter usually, if not always, having a single language—are bound together not less by language than by law and government; and, under modern conditions, more than by religion and some other institutions such as education or 'amusement'.

But no matter in which of these different ways we look at language, we shall always find that all languages have certain characteristics which make language what it is. For example, there is the high degree of convention that characterizes lin-guistic symbolism—its features are conventional rather than arbitrary, for they are evolutionary. Then again, every lan-guage has its pattern, to which it adheres consistently. Diverse as are the aspects of language, and even more varied as are actual language-patterns, and the national languages that are utterly incomprehensible, without learning, to their several groups of speakers, still there are universals, fundamental and intrinsic to language, that appear in every particular language that has been examined.

Very early in life each normal human being becomes aware of his own existence, conscious of self and of environment, and may continue so as long as he lives. Language is indeed part of this environment, and though we believe it to be a derivation from the background of human nature and experience, it has become relatively independent of the immediate environment. We may conveniently separate, therefore, from all other events (and their relations) those events which constitute that which is said about them.

The domain of this second kind of events, namely linguistic, is limitless; for clearly not only does it run the gamut from everyday conversational discourse to philosophy and mathe-matics, but there may be constructed a hierarchy of language in which we have language about language about language and so on—like a set of Chinese boxes. We distinguish, therefore, between (*a*) language at large and (*b*) language that is concerned with the interpretation of language and with logic; further we distinguish (*c*) language that is concerned with the description, history, and comparison of languages (linguistics); and (*d*) language which reports on sciences preliminary or auxiliary to the study of language (e.g. acoustics or phonetics) in the sense of linguistics proper (description, history, and comparison).

Any field of knowledge which is being actively cultivated may be expected to produce new crops, and in the field of linguistics spectacular results have been won in recent decades. In the eighties of the last century leading linguists insisted on strict historical method in tracing the relationship between, for example, Hindi *punch* 'five' (hence applied to a drink compounded of five ingredients) and English *five* and French *cinq*, all of which are the modern representatives of one and the same original word, which can be shown (by the same methods) to be connected with the English *fist* and *finger*, so that *five* has to do with counting on your fingers (and thumbs) or toes, five to each hand or foot. The theory which embodied the method was that historical changes or substitutions of sounds are absolutely regular and must be stated in terms which adhere strictly to this principle. This was definitely a new departure, and the leading spirits behind it were called 'new grammarians'. At that time there were hardly any other concepts behind the study of general linguistics.

Now we have new methods again, logical, psychological, physical, structural, statistical and mathematical, which are giving a tremendous impulse to the study and understanding of language.

II

LANGUAGES IN HISTORY

TAKE a glance at a good language map of Europe with its diversity of tongues. Here may be found side by side closely related languages or dialects, like Flemish and Dutch; more distantly related ones, like Danish and German; or not related at all, like German and Magyar. Related languages are sometimes geographically cut off completely from one another, say Magyar and Finnish, or Rumanian and Italian. Yet the cultural patterns of the peoples speaking these different tongues have much in common, a basic European twentieth-century mechanized civilization, and we are apt to associate marked differences of culture with languages that are themselves so different in structure as English and Paiute, or French and Chinese. It is commonly taken for granted that there is a direct relation between the culture of an ethnic group and the language that it speaks.

But generalization is just as risky in this matter as in comparisons between geographical contiguity and 'genetic' linguistic relationship, or in the assumption, now completely abandoned but very popular in the last century, that language is a criterion of 'race' or of nationality. For a single language belongs to the politically separate nations of Great Britain and the United States of America; and the Swiss Republic recognizes four languages (Romansch in the Graubünden, as well as the better known German, French and Italian). In the United States all 'races' speak the same language. Each case, therefore, must be examined separately, since transfer of language is neither theoretically more unlikely nor actually more rare an event than transfer of culture. The nature and degree of the relationship between a civilization and its language is a matter for determination and explanation in each situation against the entire background of history, every bit as much as geographical and historical linguistic relationships.

Much depends, in fact, upon historical events and forces that promote or hinder the prolonged and independent development or the rapid, and even sudden, diffusion, as the case may be, of language and dialects, as well as of civilizations and cultures. Our knowledge of language does not often extend beyond history, at least on a human, not to mention a geological or astronomical time-scale, judged by which all languages are both recent and virtually contemporaneous. The jumps and intrusions made by human beings, the historical activities of human groups in general, help us to understand the shadings of related dialects and languages into one another, or the sudden apparition of something alien; or to trace the focal or relict areas of linguistic expansion, or the total disappearance of a language and of everything related to it—such as has happened more than once in distant but still recorded history.

The distinction between kindred dialects and kindred languages is a matter of degree. The test is intelligibility. When communication is disturbed between speakers, we say that we have to do with related dialects; when it is completely broken, related languages. Thus speakers of standard English and German are mutually incomprehensible; but speakers of standard English and that variety of English known as 'Lowland Scots' understand one another well enough even though at times they may encounter difficulties. The idea of dialect is by no means modern; but the method of study that has been developed in recent times has greatly improved knowledge of many dialects, though it has not sharpened the concept itself. The techniques of personal interviews, and skilfully constructed questionnaires, elicit information concerning local usage from speakers of two or three generations, and the details are plotted on maps. Usually it is possible to draw lines connecting places in which the same pronunciations or the same items of vocabulary or other grammatical features are current, and these lines, when they lie in bundles, as generally happens, form the boundary of a dialect. The principle is not different from that of mapping frontiers of languages. Moreover, just as language frontiers are apt to march with national and political boundaries, dialect boundaries too are often associated with regional or historical lines of cleavage which are not primarily connected with language, for example ecclesiastical boundaries (of dioceses) in France, or county boundaries in England; or with routes of exploration and expansion taken by colonizers and early settlers, as in the United States.

Both historical and contemporaneous data of related dialects and languages lend themselves well to statistical study. The relationship usually comes out most clearly in what may be called 'basic' words—personal pronouns, the substantive verb 'to be', names of family relationships (the words for 'father', 'mother', 'brother', and the like), names of numerals and often of fauna and flora, and in characteristic structural features. Occasionally we meet a 'cross-genetic' situation, in which certain affinities appear between languages which cannot be shown to be historically cognate, for example, vowel harmony in a vast area of language stretching from Germany far into the continent of Asia.

Mere geographical contact is no assurance either of genetic relationship or agreement in type. The confused picture which is presented by the language map of Europe, as compared with that of the American continent, is the result of historical movements which can be traced in detail as far back as about 1000 B.C.; on the American continent, expansion of Western European languages, chiefly English, French, Spanish and Portuguese, is recent, and also into a continent that was rather sparsely populated.

Modern methods of transportation and communication may be expected to change profoundly the typical, historical cycle of events that has prevailed in the past. This has regularly been a cycle of expansion, culminating in the spread of a common language over a wide area, followed in due course by cleavage into separate dialects, and then the development of these into separate languages. Next the cycle is repeated. This process is seen in the spread of common Indo-European, which gave rise to separate languages such as Latin or Germanic; then these became the modern Western European languages that we know, both with far-flung extensions overseas outside the continent of Europe.

As a child Queen Victoria travelled in much the same way as did Julius Caesar. Since then we have had the steam locomotive, the internal combustion engine, and now jet propulsion.

The fast courier or navigator by sail has been displaced by telegraph, submarine cable, and now the radio message. Such changes as these, leading up to the electronic revolution in which we are living, are bound to affect the development and distribution of languages more in the future even than the forces which in the past have been powerful factors in the diffusion of languages such as migration (Indo-European), nomadism (Semitic), or seafaring (Austronesian), even mere fleetness of foot as with the American Indian—anything in short which confers mobility on man or rapidity and sureness in communication. In the past the spread of a language has often accompanied the spread of a religion, and sometimes a particular system of writing, or even a first acquaintance with the art of writing at all, has come with both language and religion, for example the Latin or Cyrillic alphabets in company with the spread of Latin or of a Slavonic tongue and of Christianity; of Pali with Buddhism; of Arabic with Mohammedanism.

Some effects of modern methods of communication are already apparent. But some five thousand years ago the spread of the early Indo-European languages would have been impossible without the much earlier domestication of the horse or without the invention of the wheel. The place from which these languages came is unknown. At the dawn of history we find them stretching from the Ganges valley to the Atlantic, and already so far differentiated as to be distinct languages. But there is no way of accounting for their complicated relations with one another except the doctrine that they represent divergent forms of a common original, precisely the process repeated at a later date in the emergence of certain Indo-European dialects, events of which the historical facts are known and undisputed. It is reasonable also to suppose that this common Indo-European original was spoken within the confines of a comparatively small and well-defined area, suitable for the development of a homogeneous form of speech. It is when communication is dislocated that direct cleavage sets in; and evidently there is no reason to believe that there was any direct, or large-scale, spoken communication between people living in Gaul and people living in Persia or India in the second millenium B.C.

A very minor dialect of Indo-European, that of a small community settled not far from the mouth of the river Tiber at the city Rome and in its immediate vicinity, was spread, mainly by conquest, over large parts of Europe where, particularly in the west, it took permanent root and survives to this day. In the same way, Germanic dialects from a small area in Jutland and northwestern Germany were transplanted to England, from which the resulting English has been carried since the fifteenth century to North America, South Africa, Australia and New Zealand, like the Spanish and Portuguese, that developed from the Latin of the Iberian peninsula, to Central and South America; and the French that was carried to Canada, Louisiana, and elsewhere. These familiar examples of the diffusion of languages, dependent chiefly upon migration and seafaring, are far from being unique. They are chosen as illustrations because they are well known. Even the Indo-European belt of languages in the Old World is not continuous. Nor does it include, or ever did, all the languages of Europe and of India as the name Indo-European might suggest—a name now intended though not by its first user Dr Thomas Young (in the *Quarterly Review*, no. 19, 1813, p. 255) to mark old geographical limits, east and west, of this particular family of languages. In ancient times, some Indo-European languages were spoken neither in India nor in Europe, for example Hittite and Phrygian in Asia Minor; and, in modern times, Armenian.

An example of migration in historic times, marked by a typical case of linguistic intrusion, is that of the Hungarians into central Europe, where they arrived about the beginning of the tenth century of the present era. Their language is totally unrelated to any of its immediate neighbours. A westward thrust of Slavonic, which seems not unlikely to come about during the second half of this century, carrying Russian as far west as Berlin, would not be the first such movement. In the Middle Ages speakers of Slavonic tongues reached the Elbe westwards, and the Balkans in a southerly direction where Bulgarian, and the Slovene and Serbo-Croat of Yugoslavia, were and are firmly established.

Expansion of one language often means restriction or suppression of another. Romance, Germanic, and Slavonic have all encroached, within the historic period, upon territory which while not densely populated was settled, if at all, by speakers

of Keltic—not only in France, but along the valleys of the
rivers Rhine and Danube, and in the greater part of central
and southern Germany and Austria. Some of them had crossed
into Asia Minor, where they are represented by the Galatians,
to the Keltic character of whose dialect we have the express
testimony of Jerome in the preface to his commentary on the
Epistle of Paul to the Galatians.

Western European civilization, a post-Renaissance and greatly
modified offshoot of which lies at the foundation of our own
twentieth-century civilization of the American continent, is at
bottom a Latinized Hellenism, with infusions of Hebraism and
north European elements such as Protestantism and Noncon-
formity, modified by political and philosophical liberalism, and
(more important still), nineteenth- and twentieth-century science. Its languages, notably English, French, German, Italian
and Spanish, have been the vehicles of that western European
tradition, and conspicuously of its educational tradition. But
such a tradition may be seriously fractured by violent happen-
ings—or even completely wiped out. A deep fracture has certainly occurred during the first half of this century and it may
in consequence be expected that the stress placed upon a knowledge of the great languages of western Europe in our educational
system will be diminished. There is no reason to believe that
such a consequence is in itself alarming. It can by no means
rob us of whatever inheritance we have already received as
participants in western European culture. The function of
language-learning in an educational program turns upon the
little understood fact that in language two divergent factors are
involved, namely habit (the way in which you say what you
have to say), and choice (what you choose to say); and on the
further considerations (1) that habit varies almost totally from
language to language—it is bound up with structural differences; but that choice varies much less—it is one index of the
social content of each language-community, and also of certain
common aspects of human life and experience on one and the
same planet; (2) that to recognize, and to be able to estimate
at their proper level, such differences (e.g. not to make mere
difference in linguistic habit a ground for prejudice or misunderstanding), is an important and necessary part in the training of every educated person in the modern world.

A language as divergent from English as Russian or Japanese would teach this lesson more effectively than the more familiar French or German. It ought not to be necessary to add to this that the learning of a language for a specific use of it in a specific programme of study, literary or scientific, or in some professional or like undertaking, is its own justification and needs no argument. What is maintained here is that many of the pleas that have to do with 'cultural tradition' or 'background', as advanced by teachers of languages, who are by no means disinterested parties, have little or no justification. Educational experience shows this; both for student and, alas, sometimes also for instructor, motivation is weak and results poor. Those who are convinced that to learn at least one ancient or modern language is a valuable educational experience—with a good teacher, who knows his business, it may be a major experience—should see to it that the experience is initiated not later than the age of ten, that it is continued uninterrupted for at least four years, and that it is given a fitting amount of time in the weekly time-schedule.

To learn to read Dante in the original may or may not be worth the effort—that depends. To be able to read Italian mathematicians or economists in the original may or may not be of capital importance—that depends. To be able to address, and to understand, a French professor at the Sorbonne may be of the utmost moment—that depends. But to say that no one can call himself educated without learning a foreign language is not true. Which of us does not know more than one man or woman of deep and genuine mental and moral cultivation and development who has no language but his mother tongue, whatever it may be?

If to learn a second language is to open the mind in the manner which the Harvard report on General Education calls taking a Copernican step, then there is implied a control and a penetration of the structure of the second language, and of the total content of works written in it, such as to make them your own, and few be they who do it ever, and none in two or three years of study. Nor is it really necessary to do so in order to know that there is not only the United States, the English language, and American activities in the world; there are other ways of escape from egocentricity or geocentricity, or learning to see man and the world as a whole, and far more pertinent than a year or two of baby French or baby German or beginner's Latin. To say that certain basic changes in a student's mind are produced by the learning of languages, and that this result can be achieved in this and in no other way, is contradicted by the entire history of education, indeed by all experience.

This by the way. In addition to the genetic and typological classifications of languages, it is possible to group languages together on a quasi-geographical and cultural basis, for example a western, or better, western and central European area. There is enough that is common to the civilization of all the inhabitants of this area to make it profitable to study their linguistic tradition also as a unit, even though a language map, distinguishing unrelated languages by the use of different colours, gives the impression of a patchwork quilt; and especially to study their languages against the background of their political, social, religious and, in general, their entire cultural history. The old 'Classical' training was just such an 'area and language' study —the ancient Mediterranean world, with its two great and well understood languages and their literatures, the history, systems of government, philosophy, economic structure, and material remains of the people who spoke them, their ventures in colonial expansion and imperialism. A survey of the languages of the world, enumerated in accordance with such principles, is likely to be more useful, to others than linguistic specialists, even than the more scientific genetic classification. The typological classification has never yet achieved any rigour, though it may be on the point of doing so, but has had to be content with selecting an outstanding feature or two and making them the ground for putting a given language into this or that group, prefixing, inflexional, holophrastic, or what not, it being always admitted that the language might simultaneously but less prominently show other features characteristic of a different grouping.

Material so complex and of such varied age as linguistic evidence, if it is to be kept under any sort of control, must be classified one way or another, granted that to comprehend the working and function of language is far more important than mere classification, the itch for which is now less urgent than in the past century. A geographical grouping such as follows is

not strictly a classification at all, but a means of bringing together languages that are culturally and historically associated.
Even the so-called 'typological' classification, which depends
on linguistic structure, is far from being clear-cut, and the
'genetic' classification leaves much to be desired except for the
purposes of historical and comparative method. The observation that 'for a long period of science, the Aristotelian impulse to
classify took precedence over the modern impulse to search for
the manner of working of a phenomenon,' has been as true of
linguistics as of botany and biology; how language works, and
how it has come to be what it is are essentially modern questions.

(1) *Western and Central Europe, together with their expansion
     overseas*:

    (a) Western Europe, from the Atlantic eastwards to a line
        drawn through Königsberg and Trieste

Here we have long-established and long-recognized more or
less standardized, national languages, that began as languages
of a city or smallish region which later became pre-eminent,
usually the capital city and its environs, for example Paris and
the Île-de-France, from which French was extended to the
national boundaries through the forces of national government,
and of a civilization and literature the influence of which also
was (and is) nationwide. Local usage is by no means completely
suppressed, as anyone who has travelled in Provence will know;
the standard usage is, as it were, superimposed. Here and there
are small but marked enclaves, such as Basque, believed to be
a survival of an older linguistic stratum, or Breton—an intrusion from Britain. In Corsica not the French idiom, but Italian,
is chiefly current.

Until recently western Europe was unaffected by a linguistic
'politik'. The pan-Germanism that would have followed Hitler's
success had begun to manifest itself, however, before the out-
break of war in 1939, notably in the use that was made of it in
the case both of the Sudeten and the free-state of Danzig. There
are, in fact, in this area two countries with more than one
nationally recognized language, namely Belgium and Switzerland, which show clearly that one law and one government may
be administered effectively in more than one language—provided that the number is not too large—a fact that deserves to

be considered by those who devise so-called 'international' languages.

(b) Central Europe

But in central Europe the situation has been different. Here is a wide zone running from Finland to the Balkans in many parts of which the linguistic problem is desperate and was grievously exacerbated by nationalistic sentiment between the two world wars. Speakers of different languages within the same political frontiers in theory were given equal recognition (e.g. Magyar in Hungary), but they have often been out of sympathy with one another and the language of a substantial minority, though in theory recognized, might in practice find its rights severely restricted. The vexed state of affairs in Czechoslovakia or Yugoslavia, each with three languages in use, tended to make those newly established nations (after 1918) hotbeds of linguistic dissension. The language of the city, for example of Vienna or Prague, might not be that of the countryside. Or there would be considerable linguistic enclaves (for example Slavonic in eastern Germany) within the national frontier. The urban language was that of a long written and cultural tradition, but not always the official language; for, between 1918 and 1940, appeal to the principle of self-determination enabled a rural majority to prevail in a decision determined by popular vote, and disputes were frequent in this modern tower of Babel. In contrast with western Europe, with its fairly stable conditions down to 1939—conditions which had been accompanied by the growth of prosperity and civilization, and inferred agreement, apart from a few rare and unimportant exceptions such as Wales, between state and language—in central Europe the linguistic and political frontier again and again were at variance. This state of affairs may now once more be coming to an end, for the time being at any rate and possibly for a long time to come, as a result of the renewed Slavonic expansion westwards, and of the Soviet determination to impose Russian wherever it goes.

(2) Eastern Europe:

So far as the ancient Mediterranean world influenced the eastern part of Europe, it was through a Byzantine Hellenism, a fact that may help to explain some of the less attractive features of its public life as they appear to western eyes. The area is largely that of the Soviet Socialist Republics in Europe, virtually that of the old Russian Empire, including the Baltic lands, Finland, Poland and Bessarabia. Theoretically these are independent, each with its own language, for example Lithuanian, which is not Slavonic. Again we have to deal with languages of minorities, beside several varieties of Russian— Great Russian, White Russian, and 'Little' Russian—which is the language of the vast majority. Even when it is a question not of 'national' but of local languages, still equal rights are granted, at least in theory. But a forceful linguistic propaganda machine has been set up, with Russian as the second language, wherever it is not the mother tongue, for such purposes as education and political indoctrination. This applies also to the languages of the Soviet republics in Asia, where there is great diversity of language. And it is certain that such a policy, if it is firmly applied and long enough maintained, will bring about the object aimed at—the conversion of the inhabitants of the Soviet Union to Russian ways of thought and civilization.

Extended at its northern and southern ends this area may be regarded as comprehending, at least as a matter of geographical fit, not only the languages of the Caucasus, including Stalin's mother tongue Georgian (Malenkov has Altaic Kirghiz as well as Russian; Georgian, like Basque, is possibly a relic of an early linguistic stratum); but also Turkish (in Asia Minor) and Armenian; and, in the north, Samoyede, a member of the same family as the Finnish dialects which it adjoins to the west, and extending as far east as the Tunguska and Khatanga rivers.

(3) *The Middle East, together with Baluchistan and Afghanistan :*

The experiment of teaching Hebrew in the schools in Israel, like that of reviving Irish in the Irish Free State, is contrary to the whole of linguistic history, and even to the present actual trend. It remains to be seen whether historic linguistic events are reversible, even on a small scale, any more than biological. Until quite recently Arabic was the recognized language in Palestine, as in more than half of the territory loosely grouped together under the name of 'Middle East'. Arabic is the language of Islam, a militant faith, and at the period of its most vigorous expansion, military conquest and religious conversion —not always forcible, but usually forcible if not willing—went hand in hand. Mohammedanism has spread beyond the limits of Arabic as a spoken tongue, and Arabic itself has ceased now to be spoken in some countries, for example Spain, where it once seemed likely to be permanently established. But Arabic is still expanding in Africa, particularly at the expense of Sudanese. It is the language, in one form or another, of the Sudan and of Egypt, of Syria, the Lebanon, Jordan, as well as of Arabia itself. Even in Persia, which was conquered by the Arabs in the middle of the seventh century, the official language was Arabic for long after the national revival that began three centuries later, and the modern Persian which is now the recognized language of Iran was profoundly influenced by Arabic.

Iranian dialects, of Indo-European origin, have survived from ancient times in villages and small townships of the region from the Caspian to the Indian frontier; and in the Pamirs dialects of Persian proper and some related dialects as Kurdish, Pashtu (in Afghanistan) and Baluchi, also have maintained their hold.

The reader should bear in mind some recent changes in political subdivisions. Pakistan falls into eastern and western Pakistan, the latter being made up of Baluchistan, the Western Punjab, the old North West Provinces of India, Sind and some princely states; the former largely East Bengal. These two parts of Pakistan are separated by some 1000 miles of intervening territory. Religion, not language, is the criterion; in fact, notwithstanding well-meant but disruptive attempts to establish Hindi for 'India' (in the new political sense), India (geographically so called) has no common language for interlingual purposes. As these lines were being written news came that a new state of Andhra has been created to accommodate speakers of the Dravidian Telugu. Wiser counsel might deplore these separatist tendencies unless and until they are offset by some genuine means of interlingual communication, not necessarily English, or any single language. Already the government of India has appointed a commission to consider the problem on a national scale, before linguistic cleavage leads to the formation of more 'splinter states'.

The wide dispersal of Arabic inevitably has fostered the

growth of a number of dialects with local variations of pronunciation and vocabulary, and a greatly simplified grammatical
system as compared with Classical and literary Arabic. But
they remain dialects of one and the same language, and recourse
is commonly made to the traditional Classical pronunciation,
especially for education; the impression is that, unlike Latin
and Sanskrit, Arabic has not given rise to independent languages; and that even the modern dialects, at least of cultivated
speakers, diverge less from one another and from the classical
standard than (for example) French from Latin or Bengali from
Sanskrit. It is easy, however, to be deceived in such a matter
when productive national literatures are rather meagrely cultivated, so that the written materials upon which, in the absence
of detailed accounts of the vernaculars, opinion is necessarily
founded, tend to adhere to the classical literary norm. It is this
common written standard, used in a very restricted way in
countries of whose population more than 90 per cent is illiterate,
that fosters a notion of intelligibility not at all sustained by a
close comparison of, say, the Moroccan vernacular with the
Arabic spoken in southern Arabia on the Persian Gulf. If it is
true that there is a somewhat more persistent fixity in modern
Arabic generally than is found in European languages generally,
as compared with the same languages some fourteen centuries
ago, the reason is probably to be found in the more rapid and
more penetrating changes in the respective civilizations, which
in Europe have encouraged, even demanded, linguistic innovation and been in turn encouraged by it. Change in language
marches with change in the social, economic, political and technical environment. Except in large cities, an Arab community
of 1940 showed more likeness to one of A.D. 640 than can be
found in comparable communities of the same dates in any
European country. But the events of the last decade are dis-
rupting this state of affairs at an increasingly accelerated pace.

(4) *India with Tibet :*

Few countries have a greater diversity of language than India
and Pakistan—despite the recent political separation, geographically they form a unit. Two main groups of languages, totally
unrelated, provide the old linguistic make-up of India: (1) Indo
European and (2) Dravidian and Munda. Munda is now found

chiefly in the eastern Himalayas and in isolated regions in the
Central Provinces. It may formerly have extended to the Bay
of Bengal, and presumably with Dravidian it constitutes the
chief linguistic substratum of India, anterior to the arrival of
speakers of Indo-European. Dravidian is spoken largely in the
eastern provinces of the Deccan, but there is a notable related
dialect, Brahui, in Baluchistan. Tamil in the province of Madras
is the best-known of the Dravidian dialects; it has a literature
composed in an archaic form of the language no longer intelligible to uneducated speakers.

The remainder of the Indian continent speaks one or other of
a large number of recent dialects of Indo-European origin, descended through middle Indic from the ancient dialects represented by classical Sanskrit and the much older variety of
Sanskrit known from the Vedas, or by the more popular Prakrit
and Pali or other derivative dialects. The names indicate the
locality in most cases—Punjabi, Sindhi, Bengali, Gujerati,
Marathi, and Hindustani (Hindi). Modern Romany is a hodge-
podge of scraps of language picked up by the Gypsies during
their long sojourns and journeys westward from India, but its
original core was undoubtedly an Indic vernacular.

Historically Burma has had close association with India from
a date not precisely determined, but according to native tradition the royal lineage derives from the ancient Buddhist kings
of India. As with Tibet, the strength of Buddhism reflects this
old cultural link. But linguistically Tibetan and Burmese belong
to the same Sinitic group of languages as Chinese and Tai
(Siamese), and Burmese was perhaps introduced as a consequence of a vast Indo-Chinese migration from western China.
It is written in a script that comes from India, and the literary
tradition also combines this dual strain, partly Pali, partly
native Burmese.

(5) *The Far Eastern Area :*

This region includes more than the Japanese and Chinese
which everyone thinks of as 'Far Eastern'. The close historic
cultural ties between China and Japan notwithstanding, there
is no genetic relationship between the two languages, and the
term 'Chinese' covers a great variety of divergent dialects. Even
the ancient literature is pronounced quite differently in different

provinces, the true ancient pronunciation being long ago totally lost.

In addition to these two, note also Tai (Siamese), related to Chinese and Tibetan; Korean, perhaps akin to Japanese; Ainu, spoken on Sakhalin and other islands to the north of Japan; the great belt of Mongolian and Tungusian (to the north of Chinese), which is connected with the Turkic languages further west, and with Yakut to the North, reaching through Siberia to the Arctic. This stretch of Turkic languages, spanning 120° of longitude from Asia Minor to the Sea of Japan and South China Sea, is bisected by a narrow strip of Indo-European, namely Slavonic which has followed the Russian penetration of Siberia and adjoins the Trans-Siberian Railway all the way to Vladivostok, with spurs of Slavonic-speaking settlements north and south.

There are also broken patches of other languages—Mon-Khmer in Annam and Assam down to the Malay Straits; Yukaghir, Chukchi and Koryak in the northeastern corner of Siberia, grouped together with Kamchadal and Gilyak, as 'Hyperborean'—a mere geographical label, not intended to imply linguistic relationship; and finally, Eskimo which, linked by Aleut across the Bering Sea, reappears on the coast of Alaska.

(6) *The 'Pacific' Language Area* (including *Australasia*) :

This is really more than that, for it runs from Madagascar to Easter Island, through 210° of longitude. But in this great stretch there are several geographical sub-groups; and, if Madagascar be set aside, the Malay-Polynesian or Austronesian classification attains a unity of sorts. Some recent guesses that settlers in these islands had come from the west coast of South America ought to imply ultimate linguistic relations, but such are far from obvious. That seafaring played a large part in their distribution is nevertheless quite clear.

Other names for the Pacific area are Austronesian or Malay-Polynesian, subdivided broadly into Indonesian (which includes, among others, Tagalog in the Philippines, Malagasy in Madagascar, Malay in the Malay peninsula); Melanesian (e.g. Fiji); Micronesian (e.g. in the Marshall Islands and Carolines); Polynesian (e.g. in Samoa and Hawaii, Maori in New Zealand, now with a strong infusion of English); the extinct Tasmanian; Aranta in Australia, which has practically no formally distinctive 'parts of speech'; and Papuan in New Guinea.

(7) *Africa :*

The huge African continent, hardly any better known in the equatorial belt than Austronesia, shows as great diversity as the continent of Asia. The ancient stratum of Hamitic languages, to which Egyptian belonged, is represented in modern times by Coptic, the liturgical language of the Christian church in Upper Egypt, now no longer spoken, and has been largely overlaid by Arabic. It survives in a number of modern north African dialects such as Berber and Tuareg, which reaches out into the Sahara. Hamitic was carried along the course of the Nile and down the west coast of the Red Sea, presumably before the spread of Arabic. It survives in a number of modern dialects, for example Somali, and forms the substratum of the Semitic Ethiopic, which it adjoins (as Cushitic) both north and south.

There runs across Africa from the Atlantic almost to the Indian Ocean, just north of the equator, a great belt of dialects known comprehensively as 'Sudanese' since geographically they are grouped with the remnants of non-Hamitic dialects of the Sudan where Arabic tends to become more and more dominant. But actually they are little known; even the estimate of their total is given in merely round numbers, and it is both asserted and denied that these make a related 'family' of dialects.

South of the equator is a massive group of Bantu or Kaffir (Arabic *kafir* 'infidel') languages, characterized by a prefixing method of word formation. The word *Bantu* itself, like *Navaho*, means 'men' i.e. 'the people'. It is a collective form, contrasted with *mantu* 'man' (individual, animate) and *kintu* 'thing' (inanimate); *ngamantu*·is 'with the man', *ngabantu* 'with the men'. Hottentot and Bushman are contracting under stress of the unequal struggle with the white man of the Cape, like languages of the Australian blackfellow; and though they may escape the native Tasmanian's fate of total extinction, they seem unlikely to make the splendid recovery from the impact of western European civilization that distinguishes the Maori of New Zealand. The Cape itself, and some of the inland territories like the

Orange Free State and Rhodesia have their Indo-European languages, English and Afrikaans. The latter is a derivative of Dutch (better Netherlandish) introduced by Dutch traders and kept alive by their Boer descendants. At one time it seemed likely to sink to the status of a socially and politically 'inferior' (i.e. substandard) language. But during the twentieth century it has gained new vigour, has now a growing literature of distinction and originality, and it is recognized on an equal footing with English politically and educationally and in the law courts. Whether the current attempts to make it supreme will succeed, remains to be seen.

(8) *Amerindian:*

This name is used to describe the native languages of the American continent. It is once more a geographical label and implies nothing or little about strict linguistic 'kinship'. Except on the northern fringe (Eskimo), and in certain parts of South America, as Brazil, and particularly along the Amazon Valley, and of course in the Indian reservations, these languages have been overlaid everywhere with one or other of the Indo-European languages of western Europe. There is no present likelihood that their status will be much improved, or that their speakers will become numerous or influential enough to put their languages, important as they are to American anthropologists and historians and linguists, into the main current of modern civilizations. There are over one thousand mutually unintelligible American Indian languages, grouped into some hundred and fifty different families.

The real interest of the language situation on the American continent lies in the fact that two minor Indo-European dialects, one of which was of no significance politically or culturally so recently as two thousand years ago, have taken over, almost in their entirety, these two great land masses. This is, linguistically speaking, a simpler, and more forward-looking, prospect than is found in any other continent. Both Asia and Africa are by comparison excessively complex; Europe is largely Indo-European, it is true, but there also variety of language is an impediment to easy large-scale communication.

III

LANGUAGES IN THE PRESENT

To a naive speaker of but one language, and especially to an adult but uneducated speaker, everything but his own tongue is likely to strike him as somehow unreasonable—either absurdly funny or extraordinarily accomplished. Anecdotes abound, about the way in which the French call a cabbage a 'shoe' (chou), or of the Cockney who was amazed at the way in which mere children in Paris talk French so fluently. Such a naive observer, if he were presented with each and every spoken language of the globe in this present year of 1955 would be lost in amazement. Speakers of different languages are incomprehensible to one another—you do not immediately understand Russian or Chinese merely by listening to it—and, on the surface, the differences seem total, thoroughgoing, and fundamental. Mere occasional agreements, besides being superficial and, as the expert knows, accidental, like French *feu* and German *Feuer* (both meaning 'fire'), or Greek *theos* and Latin *deus* (both meaning 'God'), are no help to your naive listener in comprehending so much even as a single sentence.

Yet this first impression is in part false; and the falsity well below the surface. Obviously, every linguistic group, no matter how small or far-flung—contrast the Romansch of the Canton of the Grisons in Switzerland with the widespread Spanish, both being derived from Latin—uses an extremely involved system of linguistic devices for its own purposes, and this complexity pervades the entire system—sound-types and combinations of sound-types, words and methods of forming them, orders of arrangement, and even meanings, though in this last feature there is just as obviously more in common. Modern English rarely uses *dildo*, the name of an object called *mava'tca* (an instrument of female masturbation) in the American Indian

35

Paiute southern dialect, or ὄλισβος in classical Greek, and perhaps *gillo* in Latin; or Aranta may have no word for the physicist's *neutron*; but there is no difficulty in saying 'two and two make four, and neither five nor three' in English, Greek, Latin, Paiute or Aranta. Everyday things like names of parts of the body, or of day and night, things that are of universal human experience, invariably find their linguistic expression. The great differences appear in the expression itself, not in the things expressed.

Even here a closer inspection shows how far the first impression of irreconcilable speech elements is from the fact. In the first place, it is, biologically speaking, precisely the same human vocal organs, namely from the lungs up and out, that are used for making those noises which, by virtue of selection (that is, not all, but only a small parcel of the total inventory of all speech-sounds known to be possible for these organs), and even more by virtue of their combinations and permutations, give rise to the patterning peculiar to this or that language. How economical, and yet precise, these devices are, and also their written counterparts, may easily be discovered by anyone who tries to use other devices, such as clapping the hands, which also make a noise, or gesturing as by pointing in the direction of distant objects instead of naming them by spoken or written word. The very fact that the same human being may learn to speak more than one language, and in some cases extremely diverse languages, shows that, notwithstanding the diversity, there is a common physical basis for the production of phonemes, that is of distinctive speech-sounds.

The point is to be pressed still further. The total number of actual phonemes, the world over, is found upon examination to make a very limited number of classes. We distinguish between sounds which are partially or completely stopped at some point between the larynx and the lips (these are known as obstruents), e.g. $p:k$, or $f:\chi$, the Scotsman's *ch* in *loch*, and combinations of them such as the German *pf*; and among such sounds we distinguish further according to the point at which the stoppage occurs, i.e. from front to back labial, dental, palatal, velar, glottal, and laryngeal; or depending on whether or not the sound is accompanied by the vibration of the vocal chords (e.g. $p:b$); or accompanied or not by a puff of breath (e.g. English initial *p*, but not English *p* after *s*). Then we have the class known as resonants (e.g. *l*, *m*); and the class, not in itself large, but of sounds that occur very frequently, known as vowels (*i* as in *bit*, *e* as in *let*), the chief characteristic of which (as a class) is that the voice-sound is modified by the position of the tongue, but without any kind of stoppage—acoustically vowels are also distinguished by differences in fundamental tone and in the distribution of overtones. There are also such features as palatalization (e.g. in Russian), pitch (e.g. in Chinese), length and stress; or of classes of speech-sound that are not widely distributed, for example the clicks (suction sounds, like the smack of a kiss) used as phonemes in some African languages. But all this is a trivial limitation to the statements that the number of classes is quite small, and that most of them are represented in nearly every language. More important, any given language has only a limited number of phonemes, some of them quite common, almost universal, e.g. *a* or *i* or *n* or *s*. There are said to be dialects which show no *s*, but this is a most unusual state of affairs. In other words, phonemes are normally quite clearly distinctive. If the number of them were abnormally large or abnormally small, many distinctions could not be marked. Consider the extreme possibility in either direction; a language which had only one speech-sound, no less than a language which had an infinitely large number of speech-sounds, would be unable to function as a language at all, would be more like the babbling of congenital idiots or the jumbled noises of the jungle.

In the patterning that goes into the making of words, and into their orders of arrangement, the deviation between languages is great—think of German or Latin order as compared with English. Those who maintain that from the structure of syntax, in the sense of the logical positivist, we can learn about the structure of the universe are hard put to it to prove their point, and though they sometimes speak of the assimilation of 'civilized' languages, they are hardly talking about the same thing as linguists when they speak of 'syntax'. What is true, is that scientific discourse has freed itself far more from conventional linguistic bonds, that is from subservience to local semantic patterns, than any other kind of discourse. But in the sense in which the terms are ordinarily used, patterning and order show great, almost limitless, variety in different languages as compared one with another.

Nevertheless every language has a definite and strictly delimited grammatical system. Such a system is apt to be more complex the more 'primitive' the culture of the society that uses it. Most of the societies which share twentieth-century western mechanized civilization, on the other hand, have drastically reduced their grammatical apparatus to mere remnants of irregularities, that is alternants, such as English *foot* : *feet* or *good* : *better*; *if he be elected* has long since given way to *if he is elected*. This is inevitable, for the simpler the language instrument—within limits—the more effective it is. Contrast the English 'he is running' or 'he runs' (i.e. 'he is a runner') with Hopi *wari* for the former (provided that 'he' is within your field of vision) and *warikngwe* for the latter (when you are not present to watch 'him' run). The logical categories which a language implies may differ widely; but, whatever categories have been, as it were, selected for treatment, they are expressed consistently by means of a strictly limited number of grammatical devices.

A few such categories seem to be fundamental to language. The distinction between naming an object or situation and predicating something about it, even if only its existence ('I am' or 'I am that I am') seems to be universal. That the actual form of word may be the same, e.g. English *love* noun, but also *love* verb, for both categories, makes no difference; it is always one or the other in a given context. Again, relative position of the actors in the drama of life (e.g. *here*, i.e. 'I', *there*, i.e. 'you', *away over yonder*, perhaps even out of sight, i.e. 'he, they') gives rise to the three persons of grammar (first, second, and third) and of Greek tragedy, if not of Christian theology. Distinctions of time of action, kind of action; of number; of locality; of animate and inanimate existence—all these and many others are involved, more or less obviously, in the grammatical devices concerned with tense (present, past, future) and aspect (inceptive, perfective, aorist); of number (singular, dual, plural); of case (e.g. accusative of the end of motion 'he goes *home*' or locative 'he is *at home*'); and of gender (masculine, feminine, neuter). These examples have been chosen from English as illustrative of the way in which language must actualize, by means of spoken symbols, the perception of objects and situations external to the speaker or hearer or to both, but relevant to their experience. The more precise distinctions made by grammatical terminology, or trivial quibbling about whether English has cases, are of no serious moment here.

Many modern students of language are apt to ignore the question of the content of meaning of a grammatical feature, and concentrate upon the form of its linguistic expression. There are two important devices in wide use, derivational and relational. Thus, in English, *manly* 'brave' beside *man* uses a derivational process by adding *-ly* to *man*; but in *books* as compared with *book* the addition of *-s* merely alters the relation of number (many of a kind as compared with one of a kind) but not otherwise the content of meaning, whereas *-ly* modifies the content of meaning of the derivative *manly* as compared with the simple 'non-derivative' word *man*.

These two devices, through the process of selective variation, consistently carried out as is the way of language, lead to results which characterize languages usefully, if not rigourously. The derivational device tends in general to be more concrete than the relational (think for example of some of the abstractions involved in the varieties of meaning of the genitive case in Latin, e.g. possession, or authorship, as the case may be, in *patris liber* 'my father's book'), and a thoroughgoing use of the derivational method tends to the rise of unwieldy compounds which may be laughable, like those in the comedies of Aristophanes or Plautus, or part and parcel of a regular and normal grammatical process, as when Sanskrit describes (in a single word) a river as 'wave-agitation-loquacious-bird-row-girdle-stringed' where English would say of the river that 'its girdle-string is a row of birds, loquacious because of the agitation of the waves'. The relational process either favours the growth of inflexion, as when *-en* in *oxen*, which is historically not a plural ending at all, came to be so used (e.g. *brethren*), especially in German, where a large class of nouns forms the plural in *-en*; or going still further, favours analysis, which uses a separate word (English *he was going*) for each part of the total perception, in contrast with synthesis (as in Latin *ibat* 'he was going').

On the basis of these and similar differences a rough-and-ready but convenient typology of languages has been constructed. It depends on the degree to which transitions between

successive bounded semantic entities, commonly called words,
are marked, and therefore realized, by speakers of the language.
Thus Chinese is said to employ an 'isolating' procedure, by
which each unit of meaning, or 'concept', is separately uttered,
usually as a monosyllable, and may also be separately written
by means of an ideogram, or highly stylized picture. For instance, a picture thought to have been originally something like
the 'pupil of the eye' has the value 'child, baby, dolly'; in English (which also in some measure uses the isolating procedure)
the corresponding symbol is the word *pupil*, which has both
meanings (*a*) 'a young person', and (*b*) the 'pupil' of the eye.
In Chinese, therefore, features of structure may, in accord with
this isolating linguistic method and its ideographic devices of
writing, dispense with such contrasts as *I*: *me* or *he*: *him*. Thus
wo pú p'à t'ā (here ‾ means level tone, ´ rising tone, ˇ 'dipping'
tone, and ˋ falling tone) is literally 'me not fear him', i.e. *I do
not fear him*, but *t'ā pú p'à wŏ* means *he does not fear me*. Since
English is in part like Chinese it is not difficult to construct a
rebus in which 'I' might be the picture of an *eye* (for the sound
is the same), but in which it is difficult, if not impossible, to
devise a similar symbol for 'him'.

The reason for that difficulty is that English has a small
amount of what we call inflexion still preserved in its pronouns.
Old English had far more, rather like Latin. In Latin we find
a thoroughgoing use of inflexion, i.e. the use of endings and
similar formants to convey relationships, e.g. of possession in
patris liber, 'my father's book', or plurality (occurrence in number) in *patrum libri* 'the fathers' books'. Evidently there is
nothing in *-um* as contrasted with *-is* that means either possession
or number specifically. Both concepts are done up each time
into a single bundle, but the two bundles have nothing common
to them in form. How inadequate this system may be is clear
from the consideration that, in an appropriate context, *libri*
might also denote single occurrence of the genitive relationship
'of the book'. It is hard to imagine how such perplexities might
be indicated in writing without a syllabary or an alphabet. But
Chinese has developed ideograms to designate so-called 'empty
words' or particles, which serve to mark a class of phrase (such
as genitive or possessive); thus in Chinese *tši* 'child' has come to
mean 'little' in the formation of a quasi-diminutive; and like-

wise *tši* 'place', i.e. within the sphere of activity (of the preceding concept) has come to mean possession (i.e. to function like a genitive). In other words Chinese still uses chiefly, and at one time seems to have used exclusively, free-standing monosyllabic forms. Languages which use an inflexional procedure have a highly complex morphological pattern, such as classical Greek *apothnēiskei* 'he is an unconscionable long time a-dying', but *apethane* 'he died', and *tethnēke* 'he is dead' (something like English *he is singing, he sang, he has sung*, but conveyed by the opposition *-nēi-* : *-an-* : *-nē-*, within the single word; or like Arabic *yaqtulu* 'he is killing', *qatala* 'he killed', *qutīla* 'he was killed', with the opposition *qt* : *qat* : *qut*). In Greek and Arabic, contrasts of relation, which in Chinese are expressed by 'full-words' and 'empty-words' (particles, or markers), and in English are usually expressed by separate words, are indicated by inflexion.

In addition to these two, inflexional and isolating, structures, there are also the so-called 'agglutinating' and 'polysynthetic' structures. Of the latter Eskimo, spoken in Alaska as well as in the Hudson Bay region, in Labrador and Greenland, and Aztec (Mexico) are stock examples. In pre-Columbian times Aztec used picture writing; Aleut was reduced to picture writing even in the last century, so fitting does picture writing seem for a language in which the transitions between articulate units of meaning are not very clearly designated or symbolized, perhaps not even so clearly actualized or perceived by the speakers themselves as in languages with a long tradition of writing both in the sense of ability to read and write (i.e. of literacy) and in the sense of literature. Picture writing can indeed be used for such languages, and attempts have from time to time been made in this direction, always without success, for example by Bishop Wilkins in 1668 (*Real Character or Logograms*), more recently by Neurath (*Basic by Isotype*), as if one wrote T42 and read it 'Tea for Two'. But such devices are vague and altogether ambiguous, unless accompanied by words, as in those popular magazines which are nearly all pictures, so that advertising and 'feature' articles are all but indistinguishable; or in talking pictures, where the picture without voice now seems empty and feeble. Besides, unless one is dealing with widely understood conventions (say a blue bell to indicate a public telephone) differences in language always return to impede interpretation.

Division of an utterance into 'words' is primarily a matter of linguistic structure; in written form this comes to be indicated conventionally by unoccupied intervals of white paper, as the result of reflection on the part of the speakers or of grammarians, and, where literacy is widespread, of teaching in the 'grammar' school. Valid as such descriptive identifying devices as inflexion, amalgamation, isolation, or polysynthesis may be in their proper place, we are really more concerned with the transition from one unit to the next, as when e.g. *'impossibilities'* or *'a'* (in 'a book' and the like) or *'an'* (e.g. in 'an ant') having been said, nothing more can be said except by beginning a new permissible sequence of phonemes, i.e. a new 'word'. So far as it is possible to reduce such a fluctuating matter to order at all, it seems most promising to proceed on the assumption that there is a constant relationship (k) equal to the product of the ranking (r) of a unit of utterance as determined by its complexity of form, and its ranking in frequency (f) of occurrence (i.e. $r \times f = k$). One may say that there is an inverse relationship between frequency of occurrence and the comparative perspicuity that accompanies the utilization of a speech-utterance. *'The'* is frequent and brief and may be dispensed with altogether (as in Russian); *antidisestablishmentarianisms'*, if it occurs at all except as an artificial sample, is rare, lengthy, and hard (for some people impossible) to take in. The device of polysynthesis is on the whole disfavoured; and even if sooner or later 'should of' (*should have*) or 'wayamin' (*wait a minute*) and the like come to be accepted, then also, sooner or later, the process which they imply is either made universal or put a stop to. The ideal seems to be, as usual, the golden middle way, somewhere between the extremes of monosyllabication and polysynthesis. English is not at all a bad approximation to such a goal; alphabetic and syllabic writing are not bad approximations to the same goal in writing.

So far it may have seemed as if there were a real substance, language. Actually this is not so—there are only languages. And even here is a paradox—we speak as if there were real substances, languages, French, English, Japanese, Chinese and the rest. Actually this is not so—there are only groups of people, human societies that speak (and write) these languages. Their utterances and their acts of writing are physical events, each string of which from the moment of its initiation to its end is a continuum. 'Language', is not a part of nature, linguistic events are; and also, at first remove, those events which the linguistic events, speech-acts, or utterances, whichever they may be called, symbolize. The 'language' that anyone knows is, physically speaking, at the utmost the residue of traces of his lifetime of experience left as a series of 'routings' and junctions in the nervous pathways of his brain, to form a statistical storehouse of memory, a cerebral assembly of patterns and of links between them, which provide for the controls and impulses that govern his acts of speech each time he 'opens his mouth'. The mystery of all this lies in the matching with the actualities which they symbolize, and with one another, of (1) the speech-acts, the phenomena with which the linguist deals; (2) the structural forms which these acts may variously take in different languages, sometimes with almost complete agreement both historically and semantically (I = Latin *ego*), usually with far less or none at all; and (3) the written or printed marks. Language is the vocal actualization of the tendency to see realities symbolically, and to express them both abstractly and economically; and it confers a freedom of choice in usage that may range from the banal to the sublime.

Usually a complex of form plus content differs enormously from language to language. In English we say 'cabbage', in French 'chou', but 'mon petit chou' is not 'my little cabbage'; in English we say 'shoe', in French we say 'chaussure' or possibly 'soulier' or 'botte'; but 'à propos de bottes' is 'totally irrelevant', which in Latin was 'nihil ad rem' and in ancient Athens 'nothing to do with Dionysus'. Not only that, we may not say in standard English 'cabbitch' or 'shoon' (plural) or 'irroolivant',* still less 'cap-itch' or 'shine' or 'a hooligan' without changing the meaning; further deviations would be simply not English, as 'coobage' or 'tchan' or 'oolalavant', i.e. they are sequences which do not occur. In any language you 'play the rules of the game' by sticking to the habits of that language, to the 'rules' of its grammar. This usage is fixed by the habitual speech-habits of the speakers, who in this way remain in communication with one another. But what I have to say about a

* A frequent blunder is *irrevalent* (OED), and may therefore in time cease to be a blunder.

cabbage (I bought it; or I threw it, when rotten, at somebody's head), or a shoe (I shined my shoes; or this is where the shoe pinched), or irrelevance and relevance (he is not to be restrained by mere irrelevance; what he says has a distant relevance to the case) are matters of personal expression, of individual decision, within the limits of my own discrimination, or of the occasion, and of the endurance of my audience; I may even choose to say nothing at all. The facts of habit and rule in linguistic behaviour (as distinguished from choice) are at bottom concerned with meaning and its expression, in short with linguistic symbolism, and are fundamental to the acquisition of any language at any stage of life; your mother tongue in infancy, or a new language if you go to live abroad in youth or maturity. A fuller understanding of the nature of grammatical rules than many now have, would be greatly to the advantage of both teachers and students of foreign languages. The ideal is to acquire, as nearly and as fully as possible, the total experiential environment of native speakers; to set forth the characteristics of a language is, ideally, just that. Hence in acquiring a new language, the student should, like native speakers, begin early (say at the age of seven or eight), in the foreign country itself, and learn as steadily and uninterruptedly as native children (who have spent four years doing little else). That is the way bilingual and multilingual speakers are made, for few people of mature age, having overlearned a single language, are able even to hear a foreign language, and since they fail to observe all or most of its spoken features, they certainly will never be able to reproduce them with their own vocal apparatus. Speaking comes before reading, reading before writing. A failure to observe these self-evident truths vitiates much elementary language-teaching to the extent of making it all but worthless.

A way of speaking is apt to be deep-seated, and what seems to be an innovation is often nothing of the kind. The expression 'fellow-traveller' (in its literal sense) is recorded as far back as 1665; its application to a peculiar political situation of modern times is new. But a geologist who has to solve problems preliminary to current attempts of engineers and construction men to build roads, airfields, and other facilities in the Arctic finds himself at work in a new sub-science and proposing a new name for it. Such new terms are usually fashioned, on accepted patterns, from Greek and Latin, and usually do not disturb even the pattern of the 'standard average western European', e.g. in textbooks on geology *cryopedology* 'the science of frozen-ground' (like *geology* 'the science of earth'), and with it a string of new terms, some of which (e.g. *congelifract* 'a fragment produced by frost-splitting', *pergelisol* 'perennially frozen ground') are not yet to be found even in standard dictionaries of English.

Within the territory of a language, wide deviations of dialect may be found, for example in the English of the United States largely, but by no means solely, of vocabulary; of England more often in speech-sounds or word-forms as well. Such deviations disturb communication, they do not completely disrupt it. And they are, in all known languages, past and present, a constant feature, like archaisms (e.g. in religious or legal terminology), innovations (e.g. in scientific discourse), and some other well-marked types of variants, just as prominent in everyday discourse as in the specialized terminology of any of the natural sciences.

Thus the device of compounding, which in English is commonplace with nouns (*firehouse*), but not with verbs, appears also in verbs in Southern Paiute, which has a compound *eat-stand* in the sense of 'to eat while standing' and even a verb *several-travel* 'to give birth while travelling'. In the same way Chinese has verbal forms in which the two parts of the compound elucidate the meaning by a kind of repetition or reduplication, a type made familiar to Americans by its imitation *look-see*, although in Chinese this redundancy or tautology arose from the needs of the peculiar system of writing, which is not the case in English. Paiute again, like other American Indian dialects, has distinctive forms of verb to correspond to the distinction of meaning between whether an object is visible or not with regard to what is predicated of it, a distinction not as a rule considered necessary in English; when it is a necessary part of the expression, then it is made articulate by a separate word. Even some of the distinctions of kind of action, known to grammarians as 'aspects', that normally appear in the verbal forms of Russian and other languages, if expressed at all in English are expressed by different devices; we say 'she burst into tears' to indicate the sudden onset of an activity, though the meaning might not be obvious to a non-speaker of English

who had learned the meaning of 'burst'. Names of numbers
and counting are apt to show devices strange to our society
which deals in billions, granted most of its members may well
have little comprehension of just what a billion amounts to.
In Paiute even 100 is 'just 10 and another' (i.e. ten times ten)
and, as also in many other languages, the only primary names
of numbers are those of *one*, *two*, *three*, all the rest being derivative from those three. Or consider features such as stress in
modern English, which may be distinctive as in *contráct* (verb)
but *cóntract* (noun), and hence recently *contáct* as well as *cóntact*.
In Hindustani nasalization of vowels, such as is familiar to us
in French, performs the same function, which in classical Greek
was a matter of pitch, e.g. *nómòs* 'law' and *nòmós* 'pasture',
depending on which is high (-ó-) and which low (-ò-), and in
Latin a matter of quantity, e.g. *décŏra* (short o) 'ornaments'
(neuter plural of the noun *decus*) and *decŏra* 'adorned' (fem.
sing., adjective), though both pitch in Greek and stress in Latin
had become partly congruous with vowel quantity, a further
refinement that reinforced the expression, by means of these
devices, of distinction in meaning.

   In Finnish and Hungarian, the well-known phenomenon of
vowel-harmony (like German *lang* 'long' but *länger* 'longer', in
which *ä* approaches the *e* or *-er*, precisely as in Old English,
e.g. *lang*, *lengra* 'long, longer', a device which, so-to-speak, 'no
lenger' appeals to us), is unusually developed. Thus Hungarian
has *állok* 'I stand' (in which *á* goes with *o*), but *beszélek* 'I speak'
(in which *é* is matched by *e* in *-ek*, not *-ok*, in the ending). The
same feature is characteristic also of Turkish, thus *baba-lar-
um-dan* 'from our fathers' with so-called 'heavy' (better, 'back')
vowels (*a*, *u*, *a*) but *dede-ler-in-den* 'from their grandfathers',
with so-called 'light' (better, 'front') vowels (*e*, *i*, *e*). These
examples reveal also another feature, namely extreme perspi-
cacity of structure: *ler* (or *lar*) is plural not only in the noun
but in the verb, as if we used a rebus '2' meaning plural. Contrast German *der Sprachen* 'of the languages' or Latin *patrum*
'of the fathers', in the *-en* and *-um* of which, who shall say what
part gives the plural meaning and what the genitive meaning,
any more than what in *-is* of *patris* ('of the father') gives the
genitive and what the singular meaning? To return to the
Ugro-Finnish languages, we may note as prominent features co-

ordinative word-building (as if we say 1 + 1 = 2), e.g. the juxta-position of *maa* 'earth' + *'ilma* 'sky' gives *maailma* 'world'; or the use of the same item of vocabulary both as denominating (English *love*, a noun) and predicating (*love*, a verb, as in *I love*), thus Hungarian *fagy*, which is either 'frost' or 'it freezes', de-pending on the context. This is a widespread phenomenon, e.g. in Hopi *rehpi* 'flash'! i.e. 'it lightened' as well as in the old Indo-European languages, for Latin *pluit* 'it rains' stands for an older *pluiti* (* means a form recovered by comparison, but not actually attested); but this *pluiti* was an old *ti*-noun (like *hos-ti-s* 'stranger, foe') and meant 'rain there'!

A language said to be of extremely 'archaic' type is that of the central Australian native tribe called the Aranta, who were recently on the point of extinction, some 300 souls in 1930, although they had numbered about 2,000,000 in 1900. Their linguistic usage is undoubtedly quite atypical, if recent surveys of the languages of the world give anything like adequate speci-mens. It is not, therefore, clear that the term 'archaic' is justi-fied, with its suggestion that Aranta is something as near to typical languages of the Stone Age peoples as their civilization would appear to be. Nevertheless it seems likely that the char-acter of Aranta, what it is called upon to express and what not, must be intimately related with the kind of life that the people have led and lead. It would be hazardous to conjecture that this kind of life is a reversal to a feral level of civilization.

As a symbolism their language is helped out continually by the use of gestures, to the number of over 400 in the list com-piled by one observer, which may not be complete. Thus, an utterance relating the fact of death may be tabooed and replaced in its entirety by signs. Aranta structure is much less elaborate than that of the simplest of the Indo-European languages. It has only three distinctive vowels (*a, i, u*); vocables regularly end in a vowel, and except in a number of borrowed words this vowel is regularly -*a*. The consonant system is almost as poor (*p, t, k; m, n, ng; l, r; w, y;* and *tš,* i.e. like the *ch* of English *church*), and does not double consonants in a true phonological sense (such as Latin *uellit* 'he plucks' contrasted with *uelit* 'let him wish'). There are no distinctive parts of speech as we know them; or, rather, the meanings that we assign to parts of speech and to grammatical categories are not formally distinguished;

apparent 'formative' elements are really root-words of quite
concrete meaning. The language serves to express states and
actions (being and coming into being), but not objects except
so far as they may be regarded as participating in a state of
being or of action. There is nothing in common between the
technical language of flight navigation of the crew of a jet plane
and the Aranta:

alkira unkwanala tnaruparuma

'we fly to the heavens' (the sentence is taken from the eagle-
totem song), which more literally construed is 'sky in our bones
we go round and round'.

Unfamiliar to us in a different way is the structure of a language such as Eskimo in which the impression is given that
the smallest significant unit of utterance is not a word or phrase
(that is a unit with clearly defined limits or pauses before and
after it), but an entire sentence. This is not quite the case; it is,
however, true that there are used in such languages elements of
expression which to us would be free standing words, yet never
begin an utterance, but are bound into a complex with a preceding part of the utterance. These elements of expression are
not mere insignificant particles, but are semantically important,
such as the object of the verb. The clear distinction which
standard English gives of the transition or bridge that intervenes between the end of one word and the beginning of the
next is missing from a language like Eskimo. The procedure is
commonly known as 'polysynthesis', but pushed to an extreme,
the term is misleading. The situation is rather that certain
units of expression are given by word-stems without inflexional
endings, all being set side by side in a string or complex not
unlike the substandard English of 'comic' strips: *whadyamean*
'What do you mean?' *yashouldofwaiamin* 'you should have
waited a minute', with similar phonetic fusion. Adjectives,
nouns, appositional units, direct object are soldered into one
unit along with the main verb. Thus, in the Chukchi of the
extreme Siberian far east, *g-ača-kaa-nmi-len* 'the big reindeer
one has killed' (i.e. has been killed) is a single unit not analyz-
able into words in the same way as the English equivalent.

In this book we are not concerned with such departures from
true speech as the so-called whistle 'languages' of Mazateco of

Oaxaca, Mexico, and of the Canary Islands. In Mazateco only males whistle, but the women understand, and though the whistling is evidently a very precise symbolism (within its limits) it is as evidently secondary to, or derivative from, the actual spoken language, and in fact the whistling often has identical tonal patterns with spoken words and phrases. In tone languages, for example Chinese, pitch is a distinctive feature that serves to keep apart four or five forms which otherwise would be identical (homonyms). Nor shall we appeal to the peculiar features that are apt to appear in a creolized language (i.e. a language which is based on a pidgin variety of standard usage and has then become the only language of a speech community), for instance Taki-Taki (in Dutch Guiana), the character of which may be observed in such an example as *wan presi di en kari sotwatrasey* 'a place which they call Saltwaterside'.

There now exist more or less standardized questionnaires designed to elicit utterances upon which are based descriptions, not only of unknown or all but unknown languages, say the native languages of central America or the west coast of Africa, but also of the peculiarities of dialect in the 'great' langauges, say of American English in New England, along the Atlantic seaboard, in the South or West, or in the great Midlands area, which may be illustrated by such varieties of expression as *shivaree, horning, tin-panning* all meaning a noisy celebration after a wedding, or (in the South) *dogbit* 'bitten by a dog'. Even a matter such as punctuation, which corresponds or should correspond rather closely to the natural pauses and phrasing of the spoken language, has been made the subject of such an inquiry in the European languages—English, German, French, Italian, Dutch, Danish, Lettish, Finnish, Rumanian, Polish and others.

And it must be added that studies of the kind described contributed much to language instruction during the war when it became necessary to teach men in the armed forces a modicum of say, Italian or German or Japanese, and to teach it in a hurry. The results were not by any means a perfect command of a second language; but the same techniques may well be applied to the more leisurely procedures of peacetime. Things which English-speaking students often find vexatious and perplexing, such as the intricacies of the conjugation of the German verb, may easily be illuminated, and made some degree easier, for the mature student as well as for youngsters in school, by an intelligent application of the methods and results of linguistic analysis, in which the traditional grammars and techniques are often circuitous or cumbrous, sometimes misleading and occasionally faulty.

IV

BILINGUAL, MULTILINGUAL, AND INTERLINGUAL COMMUNICATION

THE survival of so many languages in the world, estimated to be close to 3000—and large enough, though far smaller in number, if only the important ones are counted—is something of an anachronism in an age of electronic revolution and jet-propulsion, unless the age, by creating a totally new symbolism for everyday use, does away with the obstacles to communication that everyday language barriers create. Meanwhile the age-old solutions of bilingual or polyglot, and absorption of one language by another, proceed at their snail-like pace. We have superimposed or adjacent languages (superstratum, substratum, and adstratum); borrowing; 'creolized' languages; and bilingual or multilingual speakers—the last likely to know 'all' languages and to have nothing to say in any of them. Lexical items, words in effect, unlike syntax or pronunciation, are relatively independent, especially the names of cultural objects, such as new inventions, which travel easily and rapidly; but not the basic words that deal with fundamental concepts—the substantive verb 'to be', personal pronouns, numerals, names of family kinship ('father', 'mother', 'brother' and the like). There is no difficulty when dealing say with the mutual relationships of French and English, in distinguishing those words which are borrowed, even though the percentage is high, around 50 per cent of the whole, in the English general vocabulary, but barely more than 5 per cent of the basic items. The rest are all concerned with the more incidental and adventitious things and ideas with which man tends to surround himself, and a high proportion of these are items of cultural, learned, or scientific vocabulary.

In the past, the need for communication between speakers of

different languages—invader and invaded, traders, travellers, scholars, and scientists—has not been acute, except at the highest levels of policy, and for that purpose the representatives of different linguistic groups have usually been highly trained. If not, misunderstanding obviously must follow; but that is not the real crux, for even when verbal understanding and all that goes with it has been quite adequate, the actual problems to which solutions were being sought have too often led to the exercise of force. The more peaceful methods and ends of commerce and science, when those who practise them are left to themselves, are always reached in the long run, and reached quite effectively, but it is apt to be a very long run. Religions, like nations, often burst their bounds, and here too the gift of tongues has proved inadequate, so that missionary zeal may become militant. When different nations voluntarily share a large store of words in common, they have also a common civilization, and often a common cultural inheritance.

To the extent that the entire human race may be said—in the words of more than one of the great religions—to be 'the children of one Father', and even more to the extent that a common civilization spreads among all the peoples of the earth, to that extent a common language may be expected to spread, at first as an auxiliary language, over and above the vernacular, and in the end perhaps displacing it altogether. Moreover, if the ease and certainty of modern telecommunications remain even as effective as they now are, or still more if they are improved and perfected, then the forces which in the past have led to the dissolution of a common language into manifold dialects, and these in their turn into separate national languages, will be greatly mitigated and perhaps cease altogether. It is the exacerbated nationalism of the times that chiefly hampers interlingual communication, not technical difficulty. Rarely is either of two languages—to limit consideration to two only—learned as well, even in childhood, as either one would have been if the child had confined himself to only one of them. This defect is at a minimum in countries such as Belgium, where two languages exist with equal prestige side by side. But in a continent whose people speak for all practical purposes one and only one language, students of high school age instinctively reject what strikes them almost as abnormal behaviour.

To translate fluently from one language to another, is to transfer a message from one code into another, exactly as if it were being put into a 'secret' code, except that it is done more rapidly if less accurately. Translation (i.e. the use of interpreters) is the means that is still most frequently resorted to, slow, cumbrous, expensive, misleading and sometimes even dangerous as it is. There is now some prospect that electronic computators, using digital coding (i.e. the use of a code that consists of the digits 0, 1, 2, 3, 4, 5, 6, 7, 8, 9) may be successfully used in turning one code (language), at least in its written or alphabetic form, into another code (language) in *its* written or alphabetic form. So far results are limited in scope and performance. Meanwhile we must be content with the means at our disposal, though the dangers consequent upon failure of communication are now greater and even alarming. Resort to violence, a not infrequent result of misunderstanding in the widest sense, like the Socratic identification of evil with ignorance, is condemned among individuals as barbaric and uncivilized; not yet among groups of people, nations and their alliances. Even in peaceful endeavours, communication, which is technically quick and easy over great distances if sender and receiver both speak the same language, is apt to be frustrated if they do not.

Take any large airfield to which aircraft belonging to different nations may come either in emergency or in the ordinary course of commerce and transportation, of which human beings also are common objects. Here some means of interlingual communication is clearly necessary. One ingenious solution that has been proposed is to assign dissyllabic spoken names to the digits 1 through 9, built up from arrangements of three syllables only, namely *ma, ki*, and *su*, pronounced like English *Ma, key*, ·and *Sue*. These names would be learned with these values (1 to 9) by all flight and ground personnel, no matter what their native language, thus *mama* 'one', *maki* 'two', *masu* 'three', and so on (*kima, kiki, kisu; suma, suki, susu* for 'four' to 'nine'). Then an arbitrary code book might be prepared, translated both ways for each language needing it, for example Numerals into Japanese words and phrases, Japanese words and phrases into Numerals, so that the same sequence of digits would have not merely a bilingual, but actually a world-wide interlingual value. For example, with reference to ground conditions, say some obstacle, 'equipment working beside the strip' or its (say) Japanese equivalent might be coded '3333' i.e. *masumasumasumasu*. The objections are obvious; not only the inevitable and perhaps dangerous, possibly disastrous, delay involved in the use of a code, especially in combining words and phrases, or in repetition of a statement, but also the fact that numbers relating to distance, time, height, and many other factors involved in the most ordinary and routine conditions of flight would lead to confusion, unless the numeral has a warning signal, or the coding is automatic.

The unlimited symbolic values required for effective communication, which language so readily gives, rule out everything but genuine interlingual communication, what is commonly called 'an international language', an inaccurate term, since a language may be in use already in the normal, but yet restricted meaning of international (e.g. English in Canada or the United States, but not for example usually or normally in the Argentine), and again one nation, or a union of nations, may have two or more normally and officially recognized languages (e.g. Belgium or Switzerland, or the U.S.S.R.). We now get serious attempts to build an 'international' language for specific purposes, such as aviation. This has already got as far as tackling problems incident to instrument flight, and promises well. But it uses English. To be sure, any language that plays or comes to play a similar part in world affairs may be used, and presumably is used, for example Russian as a solvent for speakers of the manifold languages of the U.S.S.R. Such goings-on are apt to be well monitored, except under conditions where a friendly reception may be assumed. But the use of a single language for interlingual communication can be successful, only if it is accompanied by favourable non-linguistic conditions. This has always been true; 'international' languages do not become operative as the result of well-meaning efforts, no matter how satisfactory in theory, on the part of linguists; or of statesmen, no matter how forceful. The use of a common language follows the course of events.

The role played in the past by partial world-languages such as Aramaic, Greek, Latin, or such as French in the recent past, or Arabic or English in the present, is possible only when the political or commercial or other non-linguistic conditions, e.g. large-scale migration or conquest or colonial expansion, have favoured a particular language, which then goes ahead just as far as the interests which favour it allow or encourage, but no farther. Evidently one language depends on 'one world', not 'one world' on one language; unfortunately only a small part of the population of the world has so far any interest whatever in the matter, and even that interest largely academic. To proceed on the opposite assumption is wasted effort, as has appeared again and again whenever real interests—or even imaginary ones, stimulated by the emotions of national prestige—have been at stake. At an international gathering of Esperantists in 1938, Italian delegates objected to the presence of Abyssinian delegates, and walked out when they were seated.

The form of discourse now proposed by the U.S. Civil Aeronautics Administration as an international language for instrument flight is a variety of specialized English with a minimum vocabulary of its own. It is significant of the trend of events that many foreign commercial airlines are willing to sacrifice national pride to safety and to commercial interest. In the same way scientific interests at large are served by the sacrifice of national prestige, and summaries in English or French are presented of original contributions written in other languages, Russian, Chinese, and the rest. In the great seats of science and learning one constantly hears foreign pronunciations that testify to the cosmopolitan character of modern scientific work. If man is now actually and at last shrinking from employing his destructive weapons upon a foe, because he fears the result for himself, we may be presented with the ironic climax that the one great unifying feature of mankind, his unique power of speech, must in international conflicts take the place of mere masses of men, or sheer weight of metal, or destructive 'scientific' devices of whatever kind. The necessary non-linguistic conditions will have come about in the least expected way, and the combative instincts of man will be restricted to fighting with words through mass communication media such as newspapers and radio broadcasting, or television.

Something not unlike this is happening in the adoption of English for scientific and commercial purposes. So far as aviation is concerned it has already produced a highly technical language based on English, with a restricted vocabulary of 800 words to be employed for radiotelephone communications connected with instrument flight. This is not to be confused with 'Basic' English. The 'language' may be used from the ground throughout the world in any and all language areas, and also universally from air to ground; its 800 words were selected on the basis of frequency counts, and its syntactic rules are few and simple. It is intended to be 'clear and intelligible against background noise, easy to learn and easy to pronounce, and also structurally simple and consistent'. These requirements are not easily met; noise disfavours fricative consonants like s or f; it also disfavours short words. In building this ILA (International Language for Aviation), its authors had international co-operation; they collected recordings in the cockpit in North America and over long transoceanic and international routes, they made two-way recordings on the ground in the United States, South America, five European countries, and one far-Eastern country. The product has been tested experimentally and is being tested now both in actual use and in further experiments, with the aim of improving the proposed wording (i.e. phrases) and vocabulary of ILA. The acquisition even of this restricted kind of English, with something approaching uniformity of pronunciation, is a very short step toward a unified cultural language, auxiliary to national tongues. Such a language is likely to contain elements from more than one language. The trend, a slow trend, seems to be toward a world vocabulary; but not yet toward a world-wide uniformity of pronunciation or of grammar. Such a world language as these would give may come with a world government, presumably of the federated kind, and even it may have to wait for a long time, content with the recognition of four or five regional languages, thus approximating the position of a nation like Switzerland with its four languages and federated government.

Especially in the diffusion of scientific and technical terminology progress is being made by speakers of different languages in regard to particular terms; and there is good hope of greater endeavour aimed at producing more uniform terminologies within the several sciences for international use. The International Organization for Standardization has concerned itself with directives for the creation of vocabularies and with rules for naming concepts independently of individual languages. The United Nations Educational, Scientific, and Cultural Organization has set itself the task of trying to overcome, in the field of the social, as well as of the exact and natural sciences, difficulties of language by means of standardizing scientific terminology. Over a thousand interlingual technical dictionaries, representing forty-five languages, have been prepared. The International Auxiliary Language Association has issued an Interlingua-English dictionary of 27,000 international words, Interlingua being the name of the constructed or artificial language which the Association has fostered; it also issues booklets illustrating the structure of Interlingua through articles of general interest on current scientific progress; pronunciation, a major stumbling block, is usually explained by written devices. For this purpose phonograph records are far better; and these call for a super-human speaker, a very godhead, to be acceptable the world over! But it should not be beyond human ingenuity to make and to keep international 'words' independent of any national or artificial grammatical system which would disturb their form. As for meaning, beside the world-wide understanding of words such as *orange, automobile, induction, transformer*, there are in existence a large number of monolingual technical vocabularies, like that issued by the University of Wales (Termau Technegol), arranged by subject and based on the Universal Decimal Classi-, fication (UDC) which is now under the care of the International Federation of Documentation (FID); its several classificatory sections, drawn up in different languages, constitute in practice bilingual or multilingual dictionaries of technical or specialized fields.

There is, or was, an Interlingua division of Science Service, which issues an Interlingua edition of *Science News Letter*; the following sentence is quoted as a specimen:

Le modificationes de aeroconstruction que has rendite possibile le velocitates supersonic recentements attingite per pilotas stato-unitese, esseva dictate per le resultatos de analyses a methodos photographic del undas de compression que se manifesta in le vicinitate del 'barriera' sonic.

There are two questions to be asked here: the above quotation is within the comprehension of a Western educated and intelligent adult who is capable of understanding scientific reports such as appear in good newspapers and magazines; but do not

Interlingua statements of a more highly technical character
defeat such a reader just as much as if they were written in his
native language? And, second, how much could an adult, intelligent, educated Oriental comprehend of such a statement as
that just quoted, unless his education had been not only scientific
but also occidental?

It might theoretically be argued that the historic steps which
have been taken in the development of the hundreds of languages now spoken could be reversed, and a common language
emerge which still would serve modern needs. Proposals to use
Latin, say in Western Europe, seem to imply this idea. In fact,
linguistic development is not naturally reversible. But since
language is a form of behaviour, it is susceptible to deliberate
modification and to transference and transmission from one
human individual or group by teaching and learning. We must
not be hasty, for it is hard to tell clearly in what direction man
himself is tending. If the course of events once sets definitely
in the direction of a single world-wide culture, that is a universal
acceptance of a single, though complex, analysis of man and of
nature, and of what we do to man and nature, and what man
and nature do to us (in brief, a world-wide 'cybernetics'), then
it will be relatively easy to move the corresponding world
language in the same direction. Without this prior development, the way seems to be barred, except to superlinguistic
symbolism.

Among specialists the difficulties of interlingual communication are not so great as they themselves sometimes contend. Any
scientist who can read English, French, German and Italian
will find that over 90 per cent of scientific publication is not
unintelligible to him on linguistic grounds. Moreover the number of people who know one or more of these languages in
addition to a mother tongue—no matter what it be—is far
larger than the number of people knowing any language other
than these four as a second language. The number of speakers
of English (or Spanish) as a first language is very large. So is
the number to whom Russian or written Chinese is a first language, but in the case of Chinese it is the written form (not the
spoken) that unifies; and in the case of Russian, this does not
mean all the inhabitants of the U.S.S.R., in many parts of
which a would-be scientist or scholar, if he wants to advance

his knowledge, must first learn Russian (as a second language), and then, astonishing as it may seem, often learns English in addition.

Linguists who have paid attention to the matter are agreed that certain criteria must be met by any satisfactory interlingua, such as relative ease of pronunciation for all speakers, a simple and flexible structure, unambiguous translation, the use of existing interlingual words (largely, but not solely, scientific and socio-political), and of existing logical developments in current linguistic trends, together with the development of an adequate but simple system of both longhand and shorthand writing, spoken intelligibility on the telephone, radio, and phonograph (whether discs or magnetic tape). They also agree that English does meet most of these requirements, the most notable exception being its quite inadequate system of orthography. The *de facto* position of English as an almost world-wide language cannot be ascribed solely to the fact that it has a great many attractive progressive qualities, but the fact of their existence is not to be denied. It is not to be denied either that its antiquarian spelling is a great stumbling block to further progress; and that the most serious obstacle to the introduction of a better orthographic system is, after sheer inertia, the economic one that all previously printed English books and papers would immediately become outdated unless (for some generations at least) those who wish to read as well as to speak English are prepared to learn the old as well as the new system, with some resultant confusion. It is not important that purely English exclamations and expletives have travelled around the world ('Hurrah!' belonged at first, characteristically enough, to the British Navy; and *goddam* seems to be universal too); or that most international ports of call (New Orleans is a good example) have, at least along the waterfront, terms adopted from the ends of the earth (Chinese, West African, Arabic, Indian, both east and west, as well as the more obvious French, Provençal, Spanish, Portuguese, and English); for an interlingua needs more than expletives and exclamations, and its scope is very narrow if it is restricted to a mere jumble of linguistic odds and ends, which are not truly interlingual in the same way as world-wide scientific and socio-political terminology. The real difficulty is that the vast majority of the inhabitants of the earth still are not the least interested in the creation or use of an interlingua, have never even heard of such a thing.

The experience of the United States in the adoption of a single language by large numbers of foreign speakers (or at least by their children), who were themselves initially not only alien but in many cases also hostile to it in varying degrees, suggests that self-interest and economic advantage may prove powerful factors in guiding the course of linguistic events. In the sciences we have a rapidly crystallizing form of discourse, scientific constructs, the language that interprets the world around us; politics also, on an international level, uses 'a common vocabulary, built up over generations and encrusted with evocative associations, which serves to give a certain order to the chaotic experiences and impressions confronted by men'.

Bilingual speakers range all the way from a theoretical native-like ability in two languages to an almost passive and imperfect knowledge of a second language, confined to an aural and visual knowledge, rather like the better product of school and college. Existing evidence about the much disputed advantage or disadvantage of bilingualism seems to indicate that if the situation is 'naturally' bilingual (e.g. in Wales or Quebec) little harm, beyond some retardation, and great advantage ensues from the knowledge of two languages. But when the actual conditions of life are such that numbers of individuals and their descendants must use two different languages, unless they are literate in both, the usual product is a 'creolized' language, not really a fusion of both, but a debased form of one. Such languages tend to be restricted in scope, and the speakers of them restricted in numbers. Their fate has in the past been not to spread, but gradually to die out and disappear. Speakers of geographically contiguous languages do not become 'creolized', although they may, under conditions in which one of them is socially or politically regarded as having greater prestige, exert unequal influence—the 'superior' upon the 'inferior', as for example Finnish, which has been influenced by Swedish in certain features of syntax, and Esthonian by German, although some centuries ago Finnish and Esthonian were almost identical.

Or in a bilingual situation, one of the two languages may prevail, given appropriate political conditions. Historically this has usually meant conquest, but it is not always the language of the conqueror that prevails. Since a spoken tongue is not the perfectly stable system that descriptive linguistic analysts postulate, bilingual speakers must use a 'turbulent' system, when both languages enjoy equal or nearly equal prestige, until one or other language is definitely absorbed; the bilingual speaker has a conception of the pattern of both languages which differs from that of the monolingual speaker of either. The new system that emerges is usually very different, since it must re-establish its own equilibrium. Thus, in the thirteenth century in England the children of the Norman nobility often spoke English as their first language, and the conquered were still trying to learn French. In the end English, not a 'mixed' or creolized language, emerged as the mother tongue for all. But it was a very different English from that of the English speakers whose island William the Conqueror had invaded in 1066.

It is unusual for the different sexes to be differentiated linguistically, like the Caribs whose women, being war captives, spoke their ancestral Arawak and taught it to their daughters (but not to their sons), or like Burmese children of mixed marriages between Burmese women and Chinese men, the boys learning to speak Chinese and the girls Burmese.

If a single speaker has two languages, the degree of adherence to the respective patterns of the two is directly proportional to the degree of agreement in both, e.g. high in Czech and Slovak, low in German and Magyar, and inversely proportional to the cultural or political status of the speaker. The Magyar of an educated Magyar speaker is characterized by a large number of German words; his German, however, shows many pattern-borrowings, especially in forms and syntax but also in sound from Magyar. Borrowings from English into Icelandic in North America (not uncommon in Manitoba and North Dakota) must go into one of the three grammatical genders of Icelandic. English *gang* is usually feminine in Canadian French, but in France it is masculine; in France it has chiefly a criminal, in Canada a social, connotation. The reason for this divergence seems to be that in France the word was learned through written media, in Canada through spoken American English.

In Belgium some native speakers of Flemish may be sent to schools where French is used, go to live in French-speaking districts or areas, marry into French families and lose their

Flemish all but entirely. This is not unlike the linguistic situation of many 'second-generation immigrants' in North America. It is, therefore, at least theoretically possible that a generation of men will come that has actually abandoned its ancestral languages in favor of a dominant world language. Or the linguistic conditions of the Middle Ages, when a small educated elite used Latin as an interlingua, may conceivably be repeated for English within the next few centuries.

If English is to be such a language of an elite, gradually occupying the vacuum that unintelligibility creates among the nations of the world, then 'Basic' English so-called (British, American, Scientific, International, Commercial) may well be a useful valve, so to speak, through which to let in the pressure slowly; that is as an easy initiation to Standard English. A simplified Russian seems unlikely in view of the complexity of standard Russian, compared with which even medieval or modern Latin is perspicuous. Sooner or later the effects of the technological revolution in the midst of which we are living are likely to drive us to a restricted interlingua. During the Korean War services of worship were conducted in the Presbyterian Labor Temple in New York in English, Korean, and Spanish. But partial solvents of a compounded act of worship such as a proposal made in August 1953 for the use of Yiddish among Jews of different nationalities, like Latin for the use of the Roman clergy, effect no solution at all, unless the world begins by adopting a common faith, a contingency far less likely than its adoption of a common civilization and government.

Unity is at best delayed by demands for linguistic autonomy such as evoked last year the new state of Andhra, the people of which speak Telugu, and which was detached from a quite newly established state of Madras! Not much more practical is a French proposal for the institution of a common second language among nations to be determined by a world-wide referendum, the choice being between French, English, Spanish, and, if the Soviet Union is willing to participate, Russian; a similar plan is to have French taught compulsorily to all children in the United States, the British Islands and in the British Commonwealth; and English in France and the French Union.

Other schemes also require that literacy is first achieved on a wide scale, and the work of missionaries in many parts of the non-Christian world has shown that this is by no means impossible, even though the Christian church has often discouraged literacy in the past—especially when popular command over a liturgy, and even Holy Writ, has been at stake. In recent years the armed services have been greatly concerned over the interlingual problem. They call from time to time for officer candidates who have, or are qualified to acquire, an idiomatic knowledge, both spoken and written, of the language, customs, habits, culture and physical characteristics of people in one or more foreign countries; and have taken active steps by setting up schools in which all ranks, from privates to colonels, are trained to obtain such a knowledge, at least of the language. Ideally the learning of a second language approximates as closely as possible the natural conditions of learning the first— talking, with abundant repetition and memory training to fix the new pattern, and this from morning to night; writing and reading second; and then both together with use of original texts, not manufactured 'baby' texts, the authors of which give a strong impression of feeble-mindedness to any intelligent child of twelve. It is not possible to acquit education authorities of the charge of neglect solely on the ground that intensive language instruction, occupying fifty to sixty hours a week of study of one language, is incompatible with the objectives of a well-conceived education.

Wherever there is the will to learn, methods, media and the organization of education are of secondary importance. In 1949 schools in Linz, Austria, actually used American department store and mail-order catalogues for teaching the children of displaced persons from sixteen different nations elementary English, a humble beginning from which classes in natural history and geography were taught afterwards in English; mathematics in particular, like music, must always start from normal linguistic symbolism, as a gateway to the understanding of its own peculiar symbolism. For *intralingual* purposes (i.e. communication within a single language) every language is a good language for those who actually use it. For *interlingual* use a choice will have to be made.

When there are many bilingual speakers, especially along a linguistic frontier, a limited number of items from such adstrata may be effectively fused without damage, particularly in local names or technical or trade names, e.g. *port* (wine) *of Oporto*, *guerrilla* ('war') *warfare, un amaro* ('bitter') *bitters*. These are hybrid tautologies. Similarly *greyhound* (Icelandic and English), or *reindeer* (Norse and English), *Châteaudun* (Latin *castellum* and Gaulish *dunum*, both meaning 'fortress'), *Donville* (Keltic and Romance), *Tundorf* (Low German and High German; *tun* 'town', *don* and *dunum* are all the same word, the notion of a fortified settlement coming to mean any human settlement— a town or village), *Rock of Gibraltar* (English *rock* and Arabic *jebel* 'rocky hill'), *Mon-gibello* (in Sicily, Italian *monte* and Arabic *jebel*), *Howdmon* (in Scotland, Scots and French 'high' [sc. mountain]-mountain), *Linguaglossa* (in Sicily, Latin and Greek), *Lleyn Peninsula* (Welsh and English), *Lletty Inn* (also Welsh and English). Many of these are appellatives, which, being used with some special reference, par excellence, have become proper names. During the Russian-Turkish war of 1878, the Russian army besieged a Turkish fortress (Turk. *kalè* 'fortress') called *Soukhoum-Kalè;* in the Russian official communiqués the French *redoute* was added, but the Russian soldiers treated this word which they did not know was French and did not understand, as part of the name and added further as an explanation in Russian *krepost'* 'fortress,' thus producing the conglomerate *krepost'-redoute-Soukhoum-Kalè* ('the fortress, fortress, fortress Soukhoum'), fortress being named three times—in Russian, in French, and in Turkish. An interlingua built in this way would take an eternity of time for the reading of a book of moderate size.

When a new language (superstratum) is imposed upon speakers of an older (substratum), usually the superstratum achieves mastery. In such situations,.there is apt to be large-scale influence exerted on the survivor in vocabulary; far less in sound pattern or in the structure of words and sentences.

A wilful attempt to amalgamate incongruent linguistic patterns is to be found in some modern writers (notably James Joyce). Naturally the result is vexatious, and it takes a wilful reader to attempt to cope with such an abuse of language. Language and dialect (including the individual dialect or idiolect) are symbols of social and national attitudes. As a linguistic venture, the muddle of *Finnegans Wake* is not to be taken seriously. Its language is basically English; there are some seventeen others freely introduced. Most of these belong to the Indo-European group, in its ancient or modern forms. It is barely necessary to say that the result is unintelligible to most speakers and readers of modern English without recourse to a learned glossary. A statistical analysis* reveals an abnormally low coefficient of correlation, i.e. of association or similarity, among those Indo-European languages on which, or on his memory of which, Joyce drew. The discrete units fail to give a coherent sequence. So the 'nonsense' words of Lewis Carroll might have been English so far as linguistic pattern goes. But no language uses all its resources of patterning with full efficiency, or anything like it. The strain imposed upon human powers of comprehension would be too great.

The babel of the twentieth century is the product of history; mankind is still noteworthy more for disorder than for good order in the conduct of its affairs. The individual speaker gives only an individual rendering of a particular language. But there are many historic examples of the formation and spread of a common language, the characteristics of which point the way to a better fashioned and better controlled language, with geographical limits not less than those of the globe itself.

* See Appendix 1

V

WORDS AND MEANINGS

SUNRISE and sunset, the changing seasons, a river flowing to the sea, the annual burst of growth in plants and trees, all these seem to be automatic. But a cat 'knows' when it is hungry or hurt, and there is no telling where the line between knowing and not knowing is to be drawn in the scale of creation. The psychologist Gustav Theodor Fechner seriously ascribed rudimentary awareness to trees and rocks, a poet's fancy reads 'sermons in the running brooks,' and the things which man has made, such as locomotives or ships, are popularly credited by their designers, and by the mechanics who care for them, with the power of 'knowing' what they are doing. This is going too far. Machines and other artifacts do not suffer pain, or feel pleasure, though it is not difficult at times so to imagine. But still, wear and tear is a sort of 'memory'.

Meaning in language is little understood because of the dearth of intelligent and searching discussion. This is the result of the bogey which meaning has become in the eyes of structural linguists, who forget or are unaware of modern scientific tests of meaning and feel that metaphysics still must hold sway. Action, of both human beings and other animals, often involves 'meaning': the activity tells what the situation 'means', for example putting on or off warm clothing, or reading a thermometer. Human beings often take only the second kind of activity— of pronouncing appropriate words. Thus an utterance is part of the performance of a 'mechanism' devised to define, delimit, formulate, identify and evaluate an external act or expression in regard to our consciousness.

It is absurd to recoil from the use of the word mechanism here. A machine is a contrivance or artifact made by man, and as such an extension of mind, and subject to the human mind.

What the human mind has done the human mind, *ex hypothesi*, can cope with. Hence meaning may be regarded as activity or expression directed to a goal. As such it is subject to purpose and control (cybernetics), not something to which man is servile, but something by which he may both interpret and modify his environment.

Thus, to a communications engineer, if a seeks a goal x, and the existing state of a and its environment e together is y, then the statement '$x = a + e$' designates the goal of a, which will act in such a way as to assimilate x to y by minimizing the interval between them. Some effector must be capable of influencing the state y, and it must be controlled by a receptor. Information about the state of xy is fed back from the field of activity to the receptor to activate the effector. Thus a thermostat in a furnace is such an effector, which can read xy on a temperate scale, and initiate or suppress activity in obedience to the expansion and contraction of a heat-sensitive substance in the mechanism and to the coincidence of the position of a rising and falling liquid in a tube with marks on the scale and with electrical switches arranged in a suitable circuit, all of which may be adjusted to suit the need of day or night time. This is just like a human being putting on or taking off clothing to control his bodily sensation of cold or warmth; or saying 'I am cold' or 'I am warm' as the case may be.

All in all, there is feedback, circulation of information, performed by a machine that combines a statistically defined pattern of activity with relations of probabilities—exactly what we believe of language. Perhaps the human brain is more like such a network for computing and controlling probabilities of transition in the language structure than it is like a warehouse or storage drum. Its network and activity will have been built up by experience with the outside world and with other human beings in their speaking and other activities, until it learns to identify, recognize, reproduce, and recombine the linguistic units in an effective way.

The principles of verifiability as a first step between utterance and experience; and next, of logical connectibility between utterances, and of communicability to other humans in such a way that their response is appropriate, are of prime importance. The successive units in the utterance (words) are a continuum (perhaps not in real time), with border or transition marks between them.

These borders must be made clear at certain points in order to facilitate understanding—regular arrangements of order, identifiable forms, categories, and parts of speech; but not the smallest units, the phonemes or speech-sounds, which are only distinctive, not significant. It is precisely because bounded units can be separately identified by initial and final patterns (e.g. *play*, *help* with *pl-* initial, *-lp* final) or statistical internal probabilities, that goal-directed activity is possible at all, instead of mere random sequences—a word is, from this point or view, a cohesive sequence of phonemes the arrangement of which is determined by strong internal probabilities, in accordance with the structural pattern of each particular language. It may be found that the mere reverse order is also governed by probabilities, and even is also a permissible sequence—but not the meaning, for this is a matter of convention, e.g. *top: pot, God: dog*, nor the reverse order of morphomes or words, which is unintelligible. Hence dictionary meaning may be stated in terms of definition—synonym or homonym; in terms of form (morphology) and syntax (arrangement), but not in terms of phonology (speech-sounds) except by distinguishing meanings as the same or not the same (*fop, hop, lop, mop, pop, sop, top, wop; or bog, cog, dog, fog, hog, jog, log*).

Restricting ourselves to human consciousness, and to one particular way in which it is activated, we may say that language makes overt in uniform patterns the attitude of the members of a given speech-community toward the sum total of conditions under which it lives, both natural and as transformed by the activity and hand of man. There is a combination of external phenomena and of human responses to them, that is of the perceptible universe, human and non-human, together with the constant interaction of the one upon the other and all the products of this interaction, including man's sensations. The attitude is far from uniform the world over. Think how different the attitude toward an apparently automatic or natural phenomenon of rain must be if one community dances to procure it, another prays for it in church, and a third 'seeds' the clouds by bombarding them with pellets scattered from an airplane, the pellets being so constituted (by man him-

self) as to cause the moisture in the clouds to condense and fall
to the earth as drops of water. The expression of these attitudes
varies from a laboratory in a university community to a
drought-stricken community in a village church or to an Indian
tribe going through its ritual dances. Yet all of them 'mean'
the same thing; and the thing 'means' the same to men, the
'idea' of rain being the totality of conditions which enter into
consciousness by a reactivation of the memory-traces of former
experience on a particular occasion, together with novel interconnexions that may have arisen since that occasion. 'Meaning'
is what you do about a situation; what does it 'mean' to you?
The question is answered by what you do, either by word of
mouth, pen and ink, mere cerebral activity (provoked by perception and sensation), or by some more overt performances.

Structural contrast, e.g. of *go* contrasted with *went*, implies
that at some point the meaning of *go* (namely present) is different from that of *went* (past), as well as the form. And so with
boy and *boys*, and hence *-s* has a semantic as well as the formal
value which distinguishes the two utterances *boy* and *boys* one
from the other. The linguist in fact shortens his labour of
description, as well as perfects the results of it, by an appeal,
more or less concealed, to meaning.

From the very outset the assumption is made that meaning
exists in forms, those fragments of utterance that recur again
and again in the stream of speech, either completely or partly
identical on each occurrence, e.g. *the boy came home, the boys
came home,* two utterances which together guarantee the correctness of isolating *boy* and *boys* as forms. Since *-s* also recurs
in this way, not only in *boys* but also in *dogs* (beside *dog*), *-s*
also is isolated as a form, with a meaning. On the other
hand, recurrent minimal speech-sounds, technically known as
phonemes (e.g. English *b, p, d, t,* or *m, n,* or *e, o*), do not have
meaning in themselves, but serve only to distinguish between
meanings, as *pin: bin*. Certainly perception of linguistic meaning is not obtained through such small segments of utterance
as single speech-sounds.

We are apt to take it for granted that the meaning of a
linguistic item such as a word, of the items, that is, which
makers of dictionaries isolate from the stream of speech and
record, is something capable of strict definition. In cases of

doubt or dispute we appeal to the dictionary. But disagreement is frequent among speakers, not unknown among dictionaries, and we are never quite sure in our daily dealings
with one another. 'Do you understand me?' asks the lover of
his lass in Stevenson, and continues 'I should think it highly
improbable.' In logic and mathematics only is it possible to
assign a strictly defined, rigid, and unchanging meaning to a
symbol. In language this is, fortunately, not so, and cannot
be so.

In symbolic logic meaning attaches to a proposition, not to
a single word, for the reason that only a proposition can be
true or false. Moreover a proposition that cannot be verified
as true or false is meaningless. But in ordinary discourse a
single word may have its symbolic value when standing alone,
and this is distinguished as word-meaning from sentence-mean-
ing. Words of ordinary language correspond to percepts or
experiences of rather vague definition—hence the disputes
about 'meanings'; in fact the very attempt to furnish a definition itself involves an addition to the linguistic usage. The
more you try to 'explain' an original message, the more impossible it becomes to do so, even in terms of communication
engineering. But how does a speaker convince himself in the
first place that he knows what a word means? Logically and
linguistically, that is to say in semantic terms, what happens is
that the same word occurs in different environments (this is
the way in which the linguist identifies it in the first place),
and we say that we understand the meaning of the word if we
know how to use it, or how it is used by others, in sentences of
different environments. Thus one may say 'The ass was carrying two panniers'; or again 'He's a silly ass.' As it happens
there is in English also the word 'arse', the pronunciation of
which for many speakers is indistinguishable from that of ass,
and this additional complication is resolved in the same way,
i.e. by usage in different environments. The procedure is to
set side by side sentences in which only one word or form is
different, then to ask ourselves whether and how the meaning is
changed, or not, by substituting the different word. For example *donkey* may be substituted for ass in two of the above
statements, but not for the word 'arse' in any environment in
which it might be appropriate. Nevertheless an ass or donkey

is a quadruped, a man is a biped, and in the utterance 'He's a silly ass (or donkey)' the word ass is not used with just the same connotation as in 'The ass (or donkey) was carrying two panniers.' Contrast, as well as agreement, is to be looked for in the use of the same word in different environments, and also of different words in environments otherwise the same.

In logic and mathematics the statement that the same symbol always has the same meaning is largely true. Yet even there, +(to take an example) is not quite the same in arithmetic and in logarithms,* and new discoveries bring new meanings. But in linguistics, identity of meaning is only a convenient fiction, set up for use in analysis. The naughty child who says 'I'm hungry' just after supper simply because he does not want to go to bed, is not hungry in the same sense as a beggar or a tired labourer. But we assume that the meaning is the same in order to be able to identify the word as one and the same word wherever it occurs in the use of the language, notwithstanding that the meaning is not identical in every context or situation. We know also that vast changes of meaning may occur in the use of a word as time goes by. French *tête* means 'head', but its Latin original *testa* means 'pot', and for 'head' Latin used *caput*. A French boy in school would rarely translate *caput* by anything but *tête* (seldom by chef), and *testa* never by *tête*. So the assertion that a word not only can stand alone, but has a unique or constant meaning, is a fiction. From a literal belief in this fiction trouble and difficulty often result, notably in law or religion, but also in ordinary everyday life.

Language, however, must strive toward equilibrium in meaning as in all its features, in order to serve the needs of communication. But a language is never a completely stable system until it ceases to be spoken altogether. It is, or rather, its equilibrium is such that a very slight impact will disturb the equilibrium seriously. Complete stability is not attainable in normal linguistic situations, nor even desirable. If symbolic logic aims at it, or scientific discourse, like law or religion, professes to attain it, this is a delusion. In logic stability is achieved only at the cost of inhibiting change, which sooner or later will burst the bounds of any system of logic. This is the reason why the Aristotelian system, which had become com-

* Since the process of reasoning are not the same.

pletely rigid, is finally being abandoned under conditions which are totally different from those in which the system was framed and which it was intended to serve. In the natural sciences, in law, and in religion, the use of normal language, whether a vernacular or a petrified legal or religious language, e.g. Sanskrit, Coptic, Old Church Slavonic, or Latin, will constantly demand new definition and exegesis. The sciences, like modern logic, and like mathematics, must prefer formulae and special symbols, since the vernacular is inadequate.

But take government and politics, in which the influence of unchanged names for changing institutions is profound. Bancroft, Archbishop of Canterbury from 1604 to 1610, speaks of 'the freest and most absolute of monarchies', in which the apparent contradiction between 'free' and 'absolute' is modern, and has led to misinterpretations of the rights of the constitutional monarch; in Bancroft's time the monarch was 'free' in relation to all foreign potentates, and 'absolute' implies not arbitrary but merely the absence of a superior; supreme but not (in the modern sense) arbitrary power. At the same date 'commonwealth' and even 'republic' were not incompatible with 'monarchy', and the definition of the former 'dominions and territories' of the king, in the Commonwealth Act of 1650, that these 'are and ought to be subject and dependent on England' (i.e. not on any monarch, but on the representatives of the People in Parliament), later on led to such misunderstanding that 'the subsequent break-up of the old colonial empire may be traced back, so far as the causes were constitutional, directly to this new definition'. In the time of the Tudors the wording had been 'this realm and other his Grace's dominions, seignories, and countries,' a definition which Parliament would not have sustained even in the worst of Hanoverian times, any more than in Stuart.

In private law, too, what one lawyer has called the 'disorderly conduct of words' makes for constant difficulty, no matter how carefully a document may be drawn. A Scottish testator, by naming in his will the National Society (instead of the Scottish National Society) for the Prevention of Cruelty to Children nullified his own intentions, names being identified with things. A word is a frequent source of mistake—in law spelled with a capital M.

That a word may have more than one referend (i.e. that to which it is to be referred) is well known. Then we have homonyms, e.g. *rank* both 'order' and 'foul, offensive'; or *wright*, *right*, *write*, *rite* where writing helps to distinguish. This state of affairs makes puns possible. But it also makes distinction of meanings necessary. Again, two words may have, more or less, the same meaning (synonyms). Or be opposed in meaning (antonyms). If no appeal to an outward referend is possible, to a physical object, experience, event, or experiment—i.e. an operational or, so to speak, laboratory definition—then, within linguistic description, the setting up of pairs of homonyms, synonyms, and antonyms in both identical and different contexts, is the best technique for classifying those linguistic symbols known as words in terms of their semantic relationship. This is what all speakers and writers do unconsciously in actual practice. In other words, there is a high degree of determinacy in the permitted sequences of words (as well as of sounds), at least of all words except those which are all but empty of distinctive meaning, such as the definite article *the*, or the ending -*ly* in adverbs, which also may be dispensed with ('Go slow'), since their frequency is high and semantic content correspondingly low.

A satisfactory technique of applying statistical methods to problems of meaning is still to be devised. It has been discovered that the number of different cultural meanings (m) of a word tends to be directly proportional to the square root of the relative frequency (F) of its occurrence, i.e.

$$m = F^{\frac{1}{2}}$$

This was found by plotting logarithmically the average number of different meanings (as ascertained by a previously made *semantic* count) of the 20,000 most frequently occurring words (as ascertained by previously made *frequency* counts) against the logarithm of the respective frequency-rank of the words. Words of low frequency of occurrence (e.g. the theoretically possible *antidisestablishmentarianisms*) or of great frequency of occurrence (e.g. *a*, *the*), precisely as they have extremes of size as well as of frequency, have little deviation of meaning; those of average occurrence (e.g. *spring*) may have as many as four or five dictionary meanings, and even more individual meanings, some quite possibly bizarre. Recent semantic studies modelled on information theory promise some notion of amounts of 'information' in symbols.

Etymological definition is not very helpful in dealing with current meanings. When we speak of *atomic fission*, we combine one word that means etymologically 'indivisible' with another which means, also etymologically, 'division'. Here scientific discovery has reversed the meanings completely. Ostensive definition (i.e. by producing a specimen of what you are talking about, say a persimmon) may be impossible. In discussing the ancient Greek idea of δική ('justice'), we have no opportunity to observe Greek legal and political procedure in operation, so that operational definition is out of the question. Verbal or lexical definition (dictionary meaning) loses heavily, particularly whenever translation is involved, and pages of commentary, so far from restoring the loss, only distort the meaning by adding to it. A technique still in its infancy, but not impossible to perfect, would give a minimum definition of the content of meaning of an utterance in terms of the permitted sequences of forms (or words) which determine its occurrence. In this procedure, meaning would be a unit to be calculated. For example the utterance *We were now on the doorstep, and then the dog barked and wagged its tail* assures us that the *hog* (or *fog*, or *frog*, or *bog, cog, jog, log,*) *barked and wagged its tail* will not occur (except possibly *fog* in T. S. Eliot); or *seal, fox, hyena*, or *gun barked and wagged its tail*. The principle of such an investigation would be statistical, i.e. use the body of theory known as Markoff processes, in which the probabilities of occurrence depend step-by-step each on the preceding events; and this has been proved to be the case in language. The theory is well adapted to handle a significant but difficult aspect of meaning, namely the influence of context or situation. Any linguistic unit may be described in functional terms, and meaning is a function of a linguistic form. A functional definition should give a statement of the environments in which the form in question occurs. Contexts such as (1) *O, my offence is X, it smells to heaven* and (2) *The X is but the guinea stamp, A man's a man for a' that* determine the occurrence of the English morphome-word *rank*; that is the definition is given by contrast or agreement with other English words or mor-

phomes*, the occurrence of which in both of these same contexts
is altogether unlikely, e.g. *gross, standard, sweet, measure, nobility,
title, fetid, aromatic,* or the like.

It may be said that neither Shakespeare nor Burns ran
through these alternatives. But that is precisely what they did,
and did automatically. Between the input of linguistic symbolism, as a member of a speech-community grows up and gets
control of his native speech, and his output of talk or writing
in the same language, specifically of creative (scientific or poetic)
work, there intervenes a medium of invention or discovery,
the precise nature of which, other than that it is subconscious
or perhaps rather superconscious, is still unknown. Some maintain that this cerebral activity is verbal, others just as dog-
matically that it is not. We shall not know the answer to this
question until the investigation of electric waves which accompany cerebral processes (electroencephalography) has developed
a far more delicate and refined technique. There is no reason
why this should not happen. Meanwhile we may observe that
attempts so far carried on to discover whether mathematicians,
for example, do their thinking with or without the help of
verbal symbolization, are hopelessly introspective, useless, and
unconvincing.

But imagine a very simple case: a man leaves London,
England, with instructions to report at a certain address in
(say) Winchester, Massachusetts. No one in his senses would
give such instructions to a horse or a dog. Yet the man does it,
without a verbal recital, even to himself, of what steps he will
take to reach his destination. He may, now and again, make
verbal inquiry; but he solves his problem of 'goal-directed
activity' not at all as he would work out on paper a problem in
algebra; and he does it without conscious internal verbal argument.

Verbal or not, cerebral activity is sometimes such that the
output differs from the input, and differs considerably. A different recombination or switching among existing available items
produces an unexpected result. And sometimes the result is
successful. The new invention or discovery, the new insight,

---

* A morphome is a minimum significant form, e.g. *rank* which may be
analysed into speech-sounds, but not into forms; *rank* thus is both a word
(being bounded) and a form, or morphome-word.

are individual recombinations, but they are cumulative throughout human evolution and presumably will continue to be so.
All this involves meaning.

Functional definition of meaning, arrived at statistically,
would be totally different from a verbal (dictionary) or referential definition, and much more exact. The quantitative criterion, it is suggested, might be established by some electrical
apparatus, such as an autocorrelator, or some scanning device.
There is less novelty about what has been called 'semantic
differential,' that is an objective measure of connotative meaning aimed at not by linguists but by psychologists. The method
rests chiefly on the assumption that polar opposites delimit an
experiential continuum within which a particular concept is
allocated, e.g. *character* described within the continuum *rough*
... *smooth*. The problem here is to devise a means whereby
the direction and position of a given semantic unit can be
measured.

It has long been realized that around a nuclear meaning a
number of peripheral meanings may cluster, e.g. *spring* of which
all the varieties of meaning appear to be peripheral to the single
meaning of 'jump, leap, bound'. Again expression of intent may
be not overt; language is used emotively, with the idea of
producing action ('My country, right or wrong'), as well as
dynamically (in the formation of opinion 'Murder is wrong',
'Thou shalt not kill') or informatively ('Murder is a hanging
matter') and as an emotional outlet, like much of the language
of religion (though this also partakes of magic), and much everyday profanity and obscenity of utterance. But none of this
really comes to grips with the 'meaning' of meaning.

To return to 'goal-directed activity' as a correlate of meaning.
This idea, curiously enough, stems from observing mentality
or mindlike behaviour in machines. Observe that an artifact,
a machine if you will, can be designed to play a game of chess
with reasonably frequent success against a human opponent;
'in principle such a machine may be said to engage in logical
dialogue, and no barrier of principle prevents the field of
dialogue, from covering other topics than chess.' Again, a
reasoning mechanism based on the calculus of probability has
been envisaged, and in principle no doubt could be designed,
which would behave very much like the threshold control (sub-

or superconsciousness) with which neurologists are familiar, and which has provoked the use of introspection, with all its unconvincing assumptions and denials, in the attempt to discover how the human brain modifies verbal input to produce the often quite different, but still verbal, output that we find in the work of all creative thinkers, scientists, philosophers, artists and composers. We may think of two or more interlocked networks, corresponding to the nervous fibers and synapses of the brain, not only those which pro-present and handle information in the shape of discrete symbols, but those which control the information in relation to the intermediating probabilities to be associated with them. The interpretation of a concept in the terms of the functioning of a mechanism of this kind, using statistical data, precisely as language itself does, comes very close to what is usually meant by 'thinking', even by 'invention' or 'discovery'. And this is far closer to the 'meaning of meaning' than anything hitherto suggested. It also allows for semantic shift.

This further problem is to define a quantitative scale of perspicuousness which would permit significant evaluations of the status of the semantic content of a particular linguistic form at a particular time and place (and hence to trace the process of semantic shift) in a definite manner. It is clear from investigations of meaning conducted so far, that the evaluations must be based upon statistics of frequency of occurrence. For example: in French, as it has emerged from Latin, we have *pas* both (1) a noun 'step' (Latin accusative *passum*) and (2) a negative particle meaning '*not, no*' (*pas de tout* 'not at all'), usually associated with the negative *ne* (*on ne voit pas* 'it is not clear,' lit. 'one does not see'). The shift seems to have started in expressions like *ne marcher pas* 'to go not a step' i.e. 'not to go.' But why did the shift take place at all? When did it take place, and why did it take place at just that time? What were the controlling or determining factors? Answers to these questions are promised, it would seem, better by statistical investigations than by any others.

We need more precise criteria for semantic classification than mere consensus or majority rule, especially so far as concerns historic shift. At first glance, finding (A) Latin *testa* 'potsherd' and (B) French *tête* 'head', we might suppose neither of these two classes of objects nor their names to have anything in common. But historical and comparative method satisfies both the phonetic relationship (with Fr. *ê* from Latin *-es-* before *-t-*), and the high probability of this particular semantic shift as demonstrated by the actual use of human skulls as drinking cups, by modern Tibetans and Kaffirs, or by the ancient Gauls in Italy. But in the transition from (A) to (B) there would be an intermediate stage (C) in which either meaning might appear, with a gradual decreasing frequency of (A) and a rising one of (B) until the transition was completed:

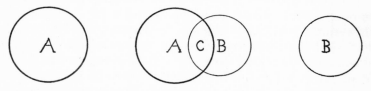

But (B) starts as merely peripheral to (A)

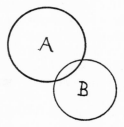

—presumably a soldier's jocular use of the word, as when on the stage a speaker in Aristophanes refers to his head as his 'brain pan'. Now the meaning and occurrence of *caput* 'head' had become so frequent as to be commonplace, but *testa* 'pot' was much rarer, and the contextual linking of the two was quite small in republican Latin. A frequency count has been made, and the proportion is 12 *caput*:1 *testa*. Then the superficial external similarity of the two objects enables them to be associated one with another, at first occasionally and then more frequently, until the delicate equilibria of frequency, rank, conspicuousness, size and meaning relationships were restored. What has happened is that the peripheral meaning of *testa* (low frequency) has attached itself to the nuclear meaning of *caput*

(high frequency), thanks to the association of similarity of shape or circumstances (say on the battlefield), and then usurped it. It is very noteworthy that we have the testimony of Livy to the use of skulls as drinking cups by the Gaulish Senones about 210 BC, which accords well with the date of Plautus from whose Latin the frequency count was made.

A semantic change is not complete until it has entered majority usage, consciously or not, as the signal to indicate the meaning intended in the particular instance. The process is gradual, and the problem is to discern what factors delimit a shift like Latin 'step' (*passum*) to French 'not' (*pas*), or 'thing' (*rem*) to 'nothing' (*rien*). There may be expected a direct relationship between the contextual semantic determinacy and the development of a specialized environment to resolve the ambiguity. If the determinacy is excessively high, the semantic content is low to such a point that the unit affected may become zero without loss, like English -*ly* : *Go slow*. But to drop the negative would be to reverse the meaning—something a maiden is strictly advised not to do, '*Never* say Yes when you ought to say No'; hence the only recourse is to reinforce the negative by repeating it, and the so-called double negative is a commonplace. Frequent in Old English, it was simplified on 'logical' grounds in modern English, only to return again and again in popular usage: *He ain't took nothing*. So when *ne* was enfeebled, it was revivified by the addition of *pas* or *rien* just as English uses 'not a jot', 'not an iota' as more forthright than 'not' or 'no' or 'nothing'.

A form that takes a semantic jump without recovering equilibrium falls into oblivion. This explains the disappearance of many a jocular slang expression after a sudden popularity. Frequency of usage is too high so long as the jocular basis for the semantic extension remains present, there is constant overuse, the slang utterance becomes 'tired' and the form is lost; but if the jocular basis is put into the background, the repetition is strong enough to entrench the form (hitherto of low frequency) in its extended or shifted meaning but not so strong as to destroy it. This is precisely what happened to *testa* 'pot' in becoming *tête* 'head'.

Another possible way of attack upon meaning is that of axiomatic and logistic, once the data are systematized. This is proving greatly superior to elaborate, but unfruitful, *ad hoc* classifications, and promises far better for meaning than mere labels attached to semantic categories long since recognized (so-called 'semiotic'). Historic change of meaning may be narrowed in scope, as in French *toit* 'roof' from Latin *tectum* 'covered'; expanded, as in *fee*, properly a payment in kind, or barter, namely cattle, cf. German *Vich* and Latin *pecu* 'head of cattle'; transferred, as in *sinister* from 'left-handed' to 'unlucky, ill-directed'; extracted from a phrase by segmentation, as when the phrase (Greek) *ecclesia kyriake* 'assembly of people devoted to the Lord' gave rise both to French *église* 'church' and English *church*; borrowed from another language, like the Gothic *gahlaifa* from Latin *companio* 'sharing bread', i.e. 'companion'; euphemistic, e.g. *cemetery*, which is etymologically 'resting place' or Christian Latin *refrigerium* 'place of refreshment' (i.e. life after death), since death and all that goes with it is subject in the usage of most people either to magic and taboo, through fear, or to pious hope for something better to follow it; in a similar way meaning may, so to speak, deteriorate, e.g. *knave* which used to mean 'boy' (cf. German *Knabe*), boys being proverbially always in mischief; less commonly it may appreciate in content, as in the title of nobility *Count* from Latin *comes* 'companion' (i.e. a member of an imperial commander's staff, an aide); or the emotional value of an utterance may exceed and displace an older definition, as in the Italian *cattivo* French *chétif* 'good for nothing' from Latin *captivus* 'captive,' 'prisoner of war,' since your enemies are always wicked, especially if you can capture a few of them. The stock epithets of poetry commonly show just this process. A trend that has recently become more pronounced in modern English is to create a new word from a string of initials of all the words of a phrase, and then the new word carries the meaning of the entire phrase, e.g. *Unesco* or *snafu*. These regularly follow the permitted linguistic patterns.

In addition to a lexical meaning which a dictionary gives for a word, a grammatical unit may have its own appropriate meaning, like that of the subjunctive mood in the older Indo-European languages, in which it designates possibility, or natural likelihood, a mild futurity, ideal certainty, command or its opposite (prohibition), will or intent, among other meanings;

and syntactic meaning, where the meaning is conveyed by features of arrangement in habitual patterns, like French *deux cents* (200) but *cent deux* (102). Such habitual patterns of counting cause confusion with dial telephones daily; *eighteen* is dialed 810; *quatre vingts* is dialed 420. 'The man bit the dog' is not the same as 'The dog bit the man.' Here we approach the logical notion of sentence meaning, i.e. the meaning of a proposition, as distinguished from word or phrase meaning.

Some shifts of meaning are due to environmental conditions. Both *discipline* and *mathematics* etymologically are defined as 'learning', but the things which Roman and Greek youth 'learned', were very different—the one stressed military, the other intellectual achievement. Specific meaning may be distinguished from general, as in *brush* (of a fox), *scutt* (of a rabbit) as compared with *tail* (in general). Not all 'mahogany' is mahogany. A frequent variety of meaning is the distinction between common and particular application as *smith* and *Smith*, *town* in general and (*down*) *town* particular (for one man Boston, for another New York), a *new town* and *Newton* (Mass.), which is also *Villeneuve, Villanova, Neapolis, Novaya Zemlya* (new earth, at least), *Illiberris* (Iberian), *Neustadt*, and *Carthage* (Punic). The shift is usually from general to particular, e.g. *father* (anybody's) to 'Father did not come home last night' (the speaker's), although historically it also may go the other way. Both an oak and a beech tree (Greek φηγός 'oak', but Latin *fagus* and English *beech* are both 'beech') may have the same name as 'providing food' (acorns or beech mast); yet also an oak may be called in Greek δρῦς, Welsh *derw* 'oak', as furnishing hard timber (Lat. *durus* 'hard'). Here the appellative adjective comes historically ahead of the name. Few words are exempt from this kind of shifting relationship, namely those which admit only the particular application, something of unique occurrence, as *God, I, Popocatepetl;* and those which have only common applications, as *here, now, if, why;* it is impossible to misinterpret 'now'. These two types of words hardly ever undergo change of meaning. The meaning of *here* and *now* is general, not particular, since it may apply to any given case in which it is appropriate, and every case is a given case when you come to it. Even proper nouns begin as appellatives and the printer's habit of using upper case initials (*Smith : smith, Wright :*

wright, Lincoln 'the colony at the pool,' cf. Welsh *llyn* 'pool')
only emphasizes this fact, by issuing a warning to the reader.

Non-linguistic environment may change meaning. Is *car*
flat or Pullman? Automobile or streetcar? Or, recently in
New Orleans, and in a famous moving picture, called Desire?
Usually we learn only one specific meaning at a time, that is
in context, like the Sunday School child who interpreted *blessings* in

> Count your many blessings, name them one by one,
> And it will surprise you what the Lord has done

as 'children', since his own mother had more than once called
him a blessing. As in all learning, corrective apperception sets
in later—by consulting a dictionary, if all else fails. But actually most of us know far more meanings of words, and recognize
them, than we ourselves employ, except in the case of the very
learned. Analogy plays a large part, e.g. *press* passes from
pressure, printing press, daily newspaper, to that amorphous
concept 'the influence of the press'. So *leaf* is not only the leaf
of a tree, but also of a book, to leaf through a book, and gold
leaf. Time and space are assimilated in *long*, sound and colour
in *bright, clear, chromatic*, human and plant life in *mother* (a
boy's mother, mother in the production of vinegar or port
wine), and Welsh has both *modrydaf* 'swarm of bees' and *modryb*
'aunt' (i.e. a deceased wife's sister, who plays the role of mother),
just as Albanian has *motrε* 'sister' (the same situation from the
husband's point of view, not the children's) and Lithuanian
even *motĕ* 'wife', which suggest not only that a mother is
normally a wife, and a wife a mother, but also that marriage
with a deceased wife's sister was neither impossible nor forbidden—all these words being cognates of our English *mother*,
Latin *mater*. Depreciation is severe in *whore*, cognate with
Latin *carus* 'dear', i.e. 'girl friend'. But if a lover calls his
love a *peach*, or a disappointed husband his wife a *lemon*, here
words of low frequency of occurrence and also of higher semantic
content, having become emotionally overcharged, have displaced the commonplace 'girl' or 'woman' which are too frequent
to have much content, exactly like *caput* 'head' which yielded
to *testa* 'pot', or like German *Kopf* (older *cupa*, borrowed from
Latin, 'cup, barrel') instead of *head* (Old English *heafod*, Old

High German *haupit*, modern German *haupt* 'top', cognate with Latin *caput*).

Language is the means by which man symbolizes and orders his concepts of his universe. This is important for meaning. It was, in fact, the invention of a unit of speech such as the word, with its corresponding unit of meaning, that was the first step in the evolution of true language as distinguished from the mere mimicry of onomatopoeia. The correspondence depends upon convention, not upon any supposed inherent tie between sound and meaning. This misunderstanding of the nature of language is easily disproved by etymological investigation of words supposed to show such a tie, for historically there is wide divergence between the forms held to contain a given element of meaning and their actual historic shape. Thus *sl-* in English is supposed to be derogatory by virtue of its very sound! But actually *sl-* has no such universally inherent meaning either in English in particular or in language in general. Words that have initial *sl-* in English come in part from Old French *escl-* and Latin *excl-*, or else they are of unknown or dubious origin, or are merely onomatopoetic and therefore not truly linguistic. On the other hand, meaning may be derived from a particular field of experience and its symbolization, like the concepts *time, space, mass, velocity;* or *mana, taboo, nirvana, polyandry, hara-kiri, shampoo, shaman, shogun, harem, tepee, topee, teocalli, maté, saké, boomerang, assagai*. These are fairly simple and concrete examples, with a few abstractions. A conceptual dictionary of all the languages of the world would show how important 'field' linguistics is, and what its limitations are. Thus English *corn, a-corn* (*a-: oak*), *kernel, grain* (Latin *granum*) all go together; and the cognate words corresponding to English *corn* mean peas in Lithuania, barley in Sweden, rye in Germany, and *corn* itself means wheat in England, oats in Scotland, maize in North America; the ultimate Indo-European concept was 'matured, ripened,' but the Sanskrit cognate *jīrna-* means 'old, wornout' and the Greek cognate γέρων 'old man' has been borrowed to give *geriatry!*

Concepts previously known only in a given 'field' may spread far beyond its boundaries, notably in recent times. The West has become cognizant of many concepts from the Orient, and the Orient from the West. The words themselves may be borrowed, as in the wholesale incorporation of scientific terminology (usually of Greek or Latin origin) from western European languages not only into Chinese, Japanese or Hindi, but also into Russian, where to the native-born an American technician seemed to know all the 'hard' Russian words, but not the commonplace or 'easy' ones. Add to these 'travelling' words, for new or spreading concepts, the native ones of each field for more or less universal concepts—for we all live on the same planet in the same broadly identical physical environment of earth and sky and sea, of heat and cold, time and space. Meaning, which symbolizes our awareness of this cosmic environment, is correspondingly complex, and so are its records—books and magazines, printed or microfilmed, magnetic tape, the storage drums (a variety of infallible memory) of mechanical computators and, very soon, mechanical translators (for meaning is translation). The strange words that a language adopts are adapted to its own phonematic and other patterns—in English *shaman* or *tea* are not uttered with the genuine Tungusian or Chinese pronunciation. Here is the marvel of language, its unlimited capacity for coping with meaning. Each language operates with a very small number of speech-sounds as compared with the number of formative elements that it uses, and these are fewer than its total number of words, which is less than the total number of meanings. Arrangement and re-arrangement in sequence permits endless variety. Meaning in the end is limited only by the universe itself and by man's ability to comprehend it. The scope of human knowledge is theoretically unlimited. A finer synthesis, a sharpening and refinement, of the unique biological instrument, language, is perhaps a next possible step, by a new means of symbolization; or it may not be achieved short of some new evolutionary mutation. To the extent that knowledge and wisdom are felt to be limited by language, this handicap now presents itself as a challenge to be met. The importance of science is less in its material boons than in its universality, in the large area of agreement that it has achieved; the fact that it has risen above particular languages to a form of discourse that may become common to all, and be incorporated into them. Modern theory is well adapted to estimating the degree and extent of the validity of propositions, and perhaps even of giving them direc-

tion. If successful such power of direction will be a dangerous
implement in the hands of the maleficent, and correspondingly
good in those of the beneficent. Some linguists in the past,
Max Müller for example, have held that we are bound hand and
foot by linguistic habit, that our model of the universe is merely
our language, English or Navaho as the case may be. It has
even been asserted that scientific theory is nothing more than
a mere recept from a standard average western European language, as if even the faintest atomic explosion should go off in
English, but the largest be mere imagination in Navaho! The
local, not to say parochial, features of meaning are all too
easily stressed to a point at which language becomes an instrument for positive misunderstanding. There is a specious half-
truth, but no more, in the view that meaning is controlled by
the very grammatical structure of a particular language. It
seems more likely that in standard average European the
structure of language has been made to correspond with what
the speakers of it have discovered about their universe, and
that what they believe about it depends not only upon the
structure of the universe itself but on free inquiry. Taboo and
the dead hand of tradition lead directly to where the Hopi and
Navaho are.

VI

THE USES OF LANGUAGE

IN the Philippines two speakers of Tagalog sometimes disguise their speech by re-distributing its normal constituent elements to such a degree as to prevent others from understanding. Thus a young woman will warn her lover 'Be quiet, your mother (or my husband) is coming.' This would be impossible if it were not that speech is a highly conventional affair. Usually the conventions are uniform within a group of speakers. The learning of these conventions—hundreds of them—constitutes the learning of a language. Children normally manage this astonishing feat within the first two or three years of life.

Many observations have been made of the successive steps of indiscriminate babbling, then of forming vowel sounds and consonants, singly and in groups, of narrowing down a wide repertoire of these to the ones that are habitual in the child's surroundings—the talk of parents and other relatives or older children; and so of acquiring more or less standard patterns in the orders of arrangements, until the day comes when there emerges an articulate word 'mine!' (in seizing a toy) or phrase 'all gone', clearly enough to be intelligible. The rewards of success are rich, and expiratory units, which become effective working responses, spontaneous and meaningful almost overnight, are reinforced by other successful experiences—both linguistic and extralinguistic, such as getting a drink of water or milk just by asking for it. Then vocabulary and the capacity to use it grow rapidly. The situation of learning a second language, if it must be learned, is not essentially different.

Talking comes first, then reading and writing. Written symbolism is yet once more removed from that which is symbolized than linguistic, already several times removed. It is built now-a-days on a foundation of talking. Historically the two were unrelated in origin, and the union of writing with speech, thousands of years ago, was as great an achievement in its day as the union of speech with waves of electricity in the twentieth century. Unconscious analysis, by opposing words that differ in but one written unit (e.g. *pin, tin, bin, din,* or *pin, pan, pen,* or *pin: pig* and *din:dig*) helps the association of written and spoken units. The old-fashioned copybook, with the cat sitting on the mat and eating fish from a dish, was not far wide of the mark. A flash of comprehension is followed by repeated practice and expanding range, until only the rare traps that a traditional spelling sets for the blunderers remain. But from those few who cannot or will not learn to read, a good deal of enlightenment and joy must forever remain shut off; to them, in any civilized community, one half of life is as a book sealed with seven seals.

Like the colours of the spectrum merging into one another from the extremes of ultraviolet to infrared, different uses of language overlap and merge into one another, running all the way from everyday conversational discourse, through law and religion, liturgy and homily, poetry, science and philosophy, to logic and mathematics. Words of high frequency of occurrence in the flow of ordinary conversation are neutral in value. But there are strong and high-pitched overtones in the remainder that call the tune. These are the words the emotional extent of which far outruns the strict semantic content, and these are the words that are most apt to semantic shifts. We saw how Italian *cattivo* means 'naughty' and French *chétif* 'good-for-naught'; but 'naughty' itself is literally 'good-for-nothing' as in the 'very naughty figs' of a wild fig-tree in the King James version of the Bible. 'Enemy' is at first merely 'unfriendly' (*inimicus*), and 'friend' was 'one whom you love' (here there has been a diminution of content), a 'beloved' is 'highly appraised, pleasing, believed in' (English *believe* and *lief*, Latin *libet* 'it pleases' and *libido* are all cognate). That which is 'dear' to one's heart is also 'dear' to one's pocket, 'highly valued, high in price,' and at the same time is one's very 'own'—at least one's own folk are 'dear', and Greek φίλος 'dear, friend' is also one's 'own', as in φίλον κάρα 'one's own head' (not 'dear head', which is nonsense!). These words are all highly charged emotionally, and if a purist had been at hand at the time when

the emotional content began to burst the precise semantic
bounds, he would certainly have condemned the new meaning
as a misuse of every one of them. The merely designative use
of language has in each case become appraisive, and judgement
has invaded the area of assertion.

Attempts to name all possible varieties of discourse lead only
to a medley of novel terminology. Four primary varieties are
readily distinguishable, and furnish a broad classification into
which most of spoken and written discourse fits. Any utterance
may be (1) *informative*, referential, concerned with setting forth
the facts of a situation. Much of the language of technology,
of the sciences, and of large areas of education is of this kind.
Education is always in particular danger of descending into a
traditional set of mere linguistic habits, repeated decade after
decade. In general the story of man's origin as it appears at
the beginning of the book of Genesis has been replaced by a
very different account. We no longer teach that the world is
flat, or that the atom is indivisible (which is the etymological
meaning of the word), or that light is a matter exclusively
either of waves or of particles, passing through the 'ether'. But
for long ages in the past scientific discovery was at a low ebb
and technological application uncalled for, so that such semantic
and pragmatic aspects of language as these remained relatively
unaffected generation after generation. Even in quite simple
matters, shifting definitions would give the lie to everything
around us, and make communication impossibly difficult; a
word, e.g. 'cat', implies a stable relation between the spoken or
written symbol and the object designated. In such matters
'truth' is the general rule. We could never learn to talk at all
if one and the same animate object were named in succession
cat, elephant, giraffe, or man. When the front legs of a horse
appear round a corner, we do not expect them to be followed
by the back ones of a cow. In England 'murder is a hanging
matter' still, and the people are so informed. A certain Mrs
Maybrick was adjudged guilty of having murdered her husband
and one may say so, without going on to explain how she
escaped the hangman. Lizzie Borden was adjudged not guilty,
and 'history' does not say that she took an axe and gave her
father forty whacks, and the rest of it.

But much of our talk goes beyond mere factual statement.

Informal education in our daily dealings with one another from infancy, as well as some areas of formal education, undertakes to direct thought and conduct, to inculcate morality, which is not a technique but a matter of social organization for man's survival and well-being even on the lowest level of opinion; on a higher judgement, which human experience tends to confirm and therefore seeks to justify, morality is a necessary condition for the development of his character and the fulfilment of his being. Here language, even when it claims to be informative (e.g. in economic theory, not to mention law or religion) verges upon dynamic and emotive uses; sometimes in formal, more commonly outside the formal teaching of the schools, it frankly passes over into such uses.

(2) By the *dynamic* use of language is meant the use of it in the formation and organization of opinion—the political manifesto, a party platform, all kinds of propaganda and advertising, the speeches of a leader in any walk of life from a Roosevelt or Churchill to a Messiah or a country preacher. Action does not always or necessarily follow: we are exhorted to 'love our neighbours as ourselves,' but do not. Nor is action always inhibited: 'murder is wrong'—no doubt, but it occurs daily. Nevertheless a nation may be led to its ruin by the sheer rhetoric of a Hitler or Mussolini, once words are translated into deeds.

Here we have reached (3) the *emotive* use of language, language directed to move others to action. (Distinguish *emotional* language, which makes overt the emotions of the speaker or writer.) 'My country, right or wrong' obtains results at least as often as 'Thou shalt not kill.' All the planning of industry and public life, from engineering to ethics, from the organized subdivision of labour to the appeal to individual conscience, from a blueprint for an assembly line to a five-minute talk or morning prayer in school or college chapel, contains much emotive discourse (again, not the same as emotional, even though it may and sometimes does become emotional). Such discourse is very powerful in bringing about action, and in some societies is wrapped up with magic, for it is important not only to utter effective, but also to refrain from uttering ineffective or mischievous words. Such utterances, therefore, come to be reserved to the priest or medicine man; the crowd is admonished to

silence (as in Horace's *fauete linguis* 'utter only favourable words',
i.e. say nothing); the liturgy may not be translated into the
vernacular or into an alien tongue; only the manager or his
deputy the foreman may give orders, lest confusion ensue.

There remains (4) *aesthetic* discourse, manifested chiefly but
not solely in poetry and other deliberately cultivated styles.
This is at bottom more a matter of form than of content.
Content may be put into any form whatever. But features of
style turn constantly both on the actual linguistic form and on
the arrangement or order of the successive units of an utterance:
'books in the running brooks, sermons in stones' is unexpected
in its order, and the would-be correction that transposes stones
and books turns the utterance into purely informative discourse.
The physicist's statement of the wave length of light that is
reported in what we call 'red' is not the same linguistic component as the dynamic or emotive red of politics, red of the
traffic light, red of 'red-light district,' or even the red of the
poet's 'red, red rose.' Here more than information, opinion,
or even action is involved; we have perception and appraisal of
an abstract and subjective kind: the 'beauty of holiness' in
the Psalmist (and in Cicero), 'the poet's hopeless woe' as
Tennyson tells the grief of Catullus *atque in perpetuom, frater,
aue atque uale* 'for ever and ever, my brother, good-bye,' these
are not the mediating, informative discourse even of didactic
poetry, but both express and stir the heart, not the head, move
our feelings, not our fingers. It is not a discussion of the worth
or significance of intangibles, but the presentation of them, not
through the content, which may easily be given the most prosaic
form, but in the linguistic units and in their arrangements.
Again and again we shall find these features of selection and
variation running all through language, like the warp and woof
that make the pattern of a fabric. Linguistic pattern too may
range from a humdrum weave of everyday conversation to
the most intricate shapes of a Homer or Shakespeare. This is
what style is—the selection of particular linguistic units and
the variation in their arrangements. Even syntax, both contemporary and historically, springs from these features of selection that are the framework, the structure, of language.

These different uses of language are not always sharply distinguished, for they may overlap. The inconsistency of response

—contrast the scientist's and the poet's account of one and the same natural phenomenon—is inherent in linguistic symbolism. If language were invariable in its responses, it would be static, and totally inadequate to any but the most simple and concrete situation. There is a fundamental weakness in that doctrine of 'general semantics' which seeks to reduce language to the purely referential use, taking notice of its dynamic and emotive and aesthetic values only to reject them. Timely as warning against the misuse of language is, it augurs ill that insistence upon a merely referential criterion makes so wide an appeal as it does. The nature of language is not to be changed by any such restriction upon it.

At each step in an utterance there is a binary opposition— this speech sound or that, this form or that, this word or that, this order, inflexion, tone, emphasis or that? The pattern of every utterance is determined in every language by precisely this device, the method of successive oppositions. Nor can the utterance be delayed; for to delay is to reduce the units of utterance to a succession of zero-elements.

Broadly, language is expressive in all its varieties. Linguistic expression manifests, that is it makes public or overt, but not necessarily explicit, what would otherwise be private; it also distinguishes experiences and their residues which would otherwise be undifferentiated. At the same time it may tell us something about the speaker, about his state of mind or body. Not only the actual content, but differences in the expression are significant. A symbol s (the utterance, act of speech) may be said to express r (the referend, that which s symbolizes), if there is a regulated relation between what can be said of s and what can be said of r. Thus language may be an emotional outlet, a mere routine 'good morning' at a low level; or, in the less articulate majority of mankind, those explosions of profanity or obscenity which are not primarily referential; or the overcharged rodomontade of an Othello. Deep-seated or sudden emotion—fear, anger, pity, love—on reaching a certain pitch, is apt to burst forth at the readiest way out, and in many situations there is an immediate outlet in a cry or shout, and perhaps no other.

Or the expression may be of a social character. To pass an acquaintance in the street without a word is regarded as unsociable, and in some communities as unnatural. Casual encounters lead to small talk about the weather long before politics, or personal and even intimate confidences, are reached.

But in literary forms, fiction, drama, lyric and epic and all the rest, the imaginative and poetic power of linguistic form comes into play. The normal symbolism of language is intensified when Aeschylus speaks of the 'unnumbered smile of ocean,' or Catullus of the 'laughter of the waves,' and Tennyson renders Catullus in English as 'the Lydian laughter of the Garda Lake below.' The 'sliding' brook or the 'breaking' waves say nothing about the movement of molecules in parabolas and the other phenomena of tides and rapids comprised in hydrodynamics, the statements of which constitute a less obvious kind of poetics.

A meteorologist makes observations recording the coincidence of a column of mercury with certain marks on a scale, and combines these with his analysis of previous experiences of drifting clouds, torrential rain, high temperature and high humidity, low barometric pressure, a dark and overcast sky, the fugitive conduct of birds and beasts. But it is not these events, merely as signs, but the utterance 'cyclonic disturbance', like the more specialized meteorological map with its graphs, isobars and isotherms, that is peculiarly human, verifiable, connectible and communicable. Wise men take equal delight in the creative intelligence of scientist and of poet. What the one means and symbolizes in his idealist map, the other also means and symbolizes in his idealist words:

MIRANDA: If by your art . . . you have
Put the wild waters in this roar, allay them.
The sky, it seems, would pour down stinking pitch
But that the sea, mounting to the welkin's cheek,
Dashes the fire out.   (Act I, Scene 2)

ARIEL: Jove's lightnings, the precursors
O' the dreadful thunderclaps, more momentary
And sight-outrunning were not. The fire and cracks
Of sulphurous roaring the most mighty Neptune
Seem to besiege, and make his bold waves tremble—-
                                        (Act I, Scene 2)

PROSPERO: I have bedimmed
The noontide sun, called forth the mutinous winds,
And 'twixt the green sea and the azured vault

Set roaring war. To the dread rattling thunder
Have I given fire, and rifted Jove's stout oak
With his own bolt. The strong based promontory
Have I made shake, and by the spurs plucked up
The pine and cedar. Graves at my command
Have waked their sleepers, oped, and let 'em forth . . .
                                     (Act V, Scene 1)

There is a strong infusion of magic and superstition in these lines that does not show in meteorology, but there is a hint that it was present formerly in the Caribbean word *huracan* (Shakespeare's *hurricano*, modern *hurricane*, French *ouragan*), literally 'the devil,' and a vestige lingers in the relatively prosaic 'hurricane of popular fury' or '*ouragan politique*'.

Neither philosopher nor poet nor scientist dispenses with constructs. Nature is seen as the structure of events in mutual relations and the poet, philosopher, and scientist offer each his own view of the same universe, expressed in his own symbolism. The lines

To think that two and two make four
And neither five nor three

do not say more than the arithmetician who sets one object of a kind against another of the same kind and calls these 'two', and then another 'two' and calls these 'four'; the poet does say more when he continues

The heart of man has long been sore
And long 'tis like to be.

He also lacks the courage of the arithmetician if he thinks of himself as

a stranger and afraid
In a world I never made.

Language is not representative, however, but pro-presentative and mis-representative simultaneously or by turns. Hence the paradox that poetry, which does not claim to be informative, shares certain qualities of dynamic and emotive discourse with advertising and propaganda, which do make such a claim; or that scientific discourse, which does not seek the aesthetic quality, may yet attain it, but by virtue of content more than of form. The hypothetic components of the sciences, built upon

systems of postulates by means of theorems developed with
logical rigor and verified by constant and repeated observations,
are not initiated without the illumination of intuition, that is
far from being the exclusive prerogative of 'literature' or mysticism that it is often claimed to be. Greek tragedy was held
in its own age to purify the emotions; this function seems to
have passed now to a different form of symbolism, music—say
the Saint Matthew Passion of Bach. But Dante, like Lucretius
before him, combined a scientific statement of the structure of
the universe current in his time with an aesthetic form of great
power. Will there come a modern Dante able to solve a similar
problem in the symbolism of our time, and of equal import?
The modern philosopher, we are told, will not say 'I was seated
at my table' but something like this:

> 'One of a certain string of events causally connected in
> that sort of way which makes a whole series into what is
> called a "person" has a certain "spatial-temporal" relation
> to one of another string of events casually connected with
> each other in a different way and having a spatial-temporal
> configuration of the sort denoted by the word "table".'

It would seem that we need a new language almost, certainly
a new grammatical category, not of spatial relationships solely
(as in the cases of nouns), or of temporal (as in the tenses of
verbs), but of space-time. Hardy's 'Drinking Song'

> And now comes Einstein with a notion—
> That there's no time, no space, no motion,

does not even attempt it; and Hart Crane's lines

> O Choir, translating time
> Into what multitudinous Verb the suns
> And synergy of waters ever fuse, recast
> In myriad syllables . . . pervasive Paradigm

seem to have been a mere accident. An epic of the modern
world might be written by a poet able to comprehend the significance of pure scientific achievement. But his grasp of science
will form his language, not his language dictate his science.

A composite work such as the Bible includes all kinds of discourse—it is referential in the historical and anthropological
books (Exodus, Chronicles, Kings, the first, second and third

Gospels, Acts); dynamic and emotive in much of the Prophets, Proverbs, the fourth Gospel, and parts of the other three (e.g. the Sermon on the Mount), the Epistles; aesthetic in books like the Song of Solomon and in many of the Psalms, though these are also emotive. 'Let your communication be Yea, yea; Nay, nay' is a Biblical formulation of the rule of binary opposition in linguistic analysis.

Scientific discourse has no monopoly of the meanings of truth. There are experiences which we cannot yet justify scientifically, and the poetic approach of a disciplined imagination may be the only valid approach. The scientific mode of communication is unattainable, or at least not adaptable. But imaginative treatment need not be devoid of significance, and it need not be delusive.

There is one variety of everyday discourse that presents peculiarities all its own—the newspaper headline, and closely related to it, advertising phraseology. These are distinguished, at least in modern English, by a compactness that yet manages to escape vagueness or ambiguity. It tends to encourage quasi-compounds as substitutes for traditional sentence types, e.g. 'non-stop throughway buses', 'better than leather miracle covering', 'Italian assassin bomb plot disaster'. Readers are seldom at a loss, there is no call for explanatory glosses of the kind that lead to a loss of confidence in language, to the destruction of the message, or to the substitution of some other device (e.g. a photograph or cartoon). In fact the device of the sentence-word or phrase-word is one that has often become standardized in many languages. Sanskrit, by just this means, puts into words logical propositions which in English are better expressed by symbolic logic. There is, therefore, no necessary lack of logical distinction, or of conflict, between the denotatory and connotatory senses of words, either of which is supposed to endanger language. The principle of binary choices (in meaning) comes to the rescue.

Literary discourse suggests writing; but much writing is not 'literature', and not all literature is written. Nor are the symbolism of writing and speaking the same. However, any symbolism exists in a hierarchy, in which derivative symbols are substituted, in ascending series, for protocol symbols. From the linguistic point of view, literature is a special type of language, and a piece of literature—all the way from the briefest, say an epigram consisting of a single couplet, to a work of many books, like an epic, or a history—is a linguistic act. This fact is what gives it reality, as part of our environment, of the world outside us. What then characterizes literature, from this point of view? Whatever is recognized as literature, is distinguished by certain peculiarities of structure and form. These may consist in features of rhythm, rhyme, assonance, alliteration, vocabulary and order, symmetry, and unity, such as are not usually observed in non-literary linguistic acts. Some may appear only in the written symbolism, for example 'eye-rhymes' or the devices of printing of some modern poetry—the length of line, unconventional spelling, absence of all punctuation, or even of upper-case print (capital letters), unusual combinations of word or phrase none of which would be noticed by the ear alone:

> next to of course god america i
> love you land of the pilgrims and so forth oh
> say can you see by the dawn's early my
> country 'tis of centuries come and go
> and are no more what of it we should worry
> in every language even deaf and dumb

and the rest of it; or

>   let joy size
> At God knows when to God knows what; whose smile
> 's not wrung, see you; unforeseen times rather—as skies
> Betweenpie mountains—lights a lovely mile.

In general the eye has become accustomed to demand a more distinctive symbolism of written than the ear of spoken unit (for example *rite, wright, right, write*). Moreover, all of these features are conditioned by the structure of the language in which a piece of literature is composed. Rhyme is impossible in Japanese poetry since the variety of sounds permitted at the end of a word is so small that rhyme appears in any utterance, even the most prosaic, of more than two or three words. The English liturgy of the Book of Common Prayer makes use of synonyms, e.g. 'acknowledge and confess', 'sins and wickednesses'. Welsh and Hebrew poetry have arrangements of linguistic features as intricate as those of a Greek pindaric ode; and this last employs elaborate metrical patterns possible only in a language where variety in the duration of syllables is a means of contrast. Chinese uses difference of pitch to distinguish meanings of homonyms and accordingly its poetry can employ arrangements of pitch as a pattern. Discontinuous morphomes (bon*orum* domin*orum*) are inevitable in Latin, concordance in inflexion being pervaded by them; accordingly these repeated endings lend themselves both to a sort of echo or rhyme, internal to the phrase, and also to a symmetrical distribution throughout a sentence. Inflexion also permits an arrangement of words such as 'Lo, the last age of Cumae's seer has come,' Vergil's

ultima	*Cumaei*	*venit-iam*	*carminis*	*aetas*
adj.	adj.	vb.	noun	noun

the so-called 'golden' line. Another, and illogical, arrangement of the order of words, possible to writers in an inflected language, and almost foreign to English idiom, arises when any one part of a sentence happens to consist of two words or phrases connected by a co-ordinating conjunction, or by the repetition of an emphatic word. There is an artificial distribution of the members of the co-ordinate phrase $(x + y)$ among the rest of the sentence $(C + D)$, so that we have, as it were, $xC + yD$ instead of $(x + y)$, $(C + D)$. Thus 'Now 'tis time to call for horse and chariot'

$$nunc\ tempus\ equos\ nunc\ poscere\ currus$$
$$C \quad\quad x \quad + \quad D \quad\quad y$$

stands for

$$nunc\ equos\ et\ currus\ tempus\ est\ poscere.$$
$$x \ + \ y, \quad C \ + \ D$$

Alliteration, prominent in English style, when it coincides with recurrent stressed initial syllables, is avoided in French which does not use stress for contrasted meanings, any more than English uses pitch. Thus the discrete units of speech—phonemes, stress, pitch, morphomes, words—are perceived as a continuum, just as the discrete portions of photographic film projected in rapid succession on a screen give the impression of successive but continuous action. But the arrangement must be systematic and orderly for the sake of the meaning, the continuity of the pro-presentation. In literature the order manifests highly elaborated features, for example symmetry, as compared with conversational discourse. But an analysis of the non-literary discourse of a treatise, for example on economics, reveals certain semantic units such as 'capital', 'capitalism'; 'socialism'; 'social structure' which recur in arrangements that are by no means disorderly or haphazard. Further study of literary forms, especially by statistical methods, promises to reveal comparable structural patterning in the identification of semantic entities, and so provide a better definition of meaning.

Statistical investigation has shown that the appearance of the epithet *pius* applied to Aeneas by Vergil in circumstances which modern readers find revolting, as at the moment of his desertion of Dido—'Can you bear this?' exclaimed Charles James Fox as he read '*At sum pius Aeneas*'—is determined not only by the metrical structure of the line (it is matched by '*at pater Aeneas*' elsewhere), or by the habit of using stock epithets, established already in Homer and copied by Ennius, but most of all by the sequence of words by which it is surrounded: Diana or Juno or some other supernatural being or occasion is in the contextual environment, and this gives *pius* its content; the word is relatively frequent in Ovid and Seneca, but not in Lucretius or Tibullus, or even Livy. It begins to rise again in the later historian Tacitus. But everywhere it is determined by the permitted sequence and arrangement of the units of utterance within which it occurs. Even in the professional nonsense of Lewis Carroll or Edward Lear and their imitators, the words they used were not in their dictionary and usually have never appeared again, but might well have been 'good' English words. There is nothing in the structure of *scroobious* that is forbidden by the patterning of English words. If a poet works with rhyme, the limitations of the language will repeatedly produce the same rhymed pair of words —both John Masefield and John Davidson have rhymed lines ending in . . . *fire* . . . *liar*. It is not, however, as 'patterns of pure sound' that words 'stimulate human response.' This assertion is commonplace, but baseless. The response (i.e. the meaning) is related to the sequences of the sounds in a purely conventional way, and neither *fire* nor *liar* has the least effect upon those who do not know English; or, if as in German *klein* 'small' and Greek *klein*(os) 'famous', the same written symbols occur in two different languages, the response in each case will again be very different. It is the purest coincidence that French *feu* (from Latin *focus* 'hearth') and German *Feuer* (cognate with Greek πῦρ 'fire'), or Latin *deus* and Greek θεός, which are not cognate, 'mean' the same things.

Since the orders of arrangement in prose and in verse are different, a peculiar effect is produced in poetry by the use of prose order. A favourite example is Macbeth's soliloquy on hearing that Lady Macbeth is dead, beginning (three instead of five stresses):

> She should have died hereafter

and, after a regular iambic pentameter:

> To-morrow and to-morrow and to-morrow.

Or in the line (T. S. Eliot)

> Pray for us now and at the hour of our birth

it is the reversed order of *at our birth* and *now*, or the use of *birth* instead of *death* that reveals the unusual character—almost artificiality—of the utterance. Literary discourse is said to be 'creative', in contrast with the reproductive or imitative character of conversational, day-to-day language; its peculiar variations and selections are realized in contrast with popular usage. The very term *belles-lettres* implies an element of beauty. This invokes aesthetics, and is achieved by the principle of selection. As in music, there is a kind of controlled grouping in the form of the highly elaborate acts of language which constitute literary discourse. The normal balance between form and content may be disturbed, at the expense of content, to such a degree that the reader is baffled. In extreme cases, interpretation is defeated; the writer has failed altogether—he has produced only a negative response.

The vocabulary of informative discourse reflects for the most part the contemporary environment—social, scientific, economic, religious and the rest; that of literary discourse draws heavily on a traditional environment, or on remnants of it, and may appeal even to an alien environment.

Much has been made of the fact that some words seem to appear once and once only. If this happens merely in a given author and given piece of writing, but is not otherwise peculiar to him or his writing, then it is of no great consequence—statistically it is on the same footing as a word that exists in the language but happens not to have been used at all in a given piece or writer. It is also on the same footing as a word that occurs only twice or three times, or with extreme rarity. Often such words are unusually long and have a relatively high and complex content of meaning, in contrast with short, frequent, but well-nigh dispensable words (such as *a*, *the*). An invented word, like Lear's *scroobious*, says little or nothing: it also provokes only the response of bafflement, or even a completely negative response. In this sense the 'once only' word to which the commentators call attention is of little importance. But the jawbreakers of Aristophanes and Plautus are comic; structurally they are long compounds that take the place of a phrase or a whole sentence. The use of archaisms or neologisms, of dialect or foreign words, indicates a selective process which emphasizes form more than the comparatively mechanical and automatic vocabulary of the non-literary discourse.

Of 'figures of rhetoric' metaphor and metonomy are constantly active in normal linguistic processes; they are normal, almost technical, devices. Any piece of writing may introduce new instances, and some of these pass into current usage. Once more the form, not the content, is more highly motivated than in conversational discourse, which gives only subconscious obedience to form. As for the theme itself, both a Shakespearean tragedy, for example, and a treatise on relativity, have to do with man's realization of himself in some part of the world in which he lives.

Aesthetic discourse also calls for consideration on a strict linguistic basis. One critic, starting from the linguistic symbol, the components of which he designates

$$E_s \longrightarrow E_f \overset{\longrightarrow}{\underset{\longleftarrow}{\rule{2em}{0pt}}} C_f \longleftarrow C_s$$

(here E means expression; C content; f formal or structural; and s the substance of the expression or content), maintains that there is an interdependence between E and C (marked by the double arrows), in contrast with the simple relation between E_s, E_f and C_f, C_s. But *horse* and *courser* and *nag*, though in a sense synonyms (they all mean the same hairy quadruped) would not be completely represented by this diagram. There are to be considered the differences of connotation (*c*) and denotation (*d*), and it is with connotation that aesthetic discourse is concerned:

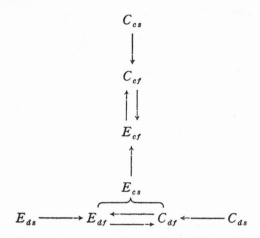

$$C_{cs}$$
$$\downarrow$$
$$C_{cf}$$
$$E_{cf}$$
$$E_{cs}$$
$$E_{ds} \longrightarrow E_{df} \rightleftarrows C_{df} \longleftarrow C_{ds}$$

and the result of its intervention gives a different picture of the relationship from the diagram of simple linguistic symbols. The reaction, even without a conscious dwelling on interpretation, is now much more complex. A *brothel* is a *house;* yes, but . . . The herb *ruta graveolens* is indeed bitter to the taste; its botanical name (Greek ῥυτή) comes from the same Indo-European root (*sur-, sru-*; note that *sr-* becomes ῥ- in Greek) as English 'sour'. The accident that English has *rue* and *ruth* 'grieve, grief' (Old English *hrēow*, Greek κρου- 'beat, strike' from a totally different root has added to the force of 'bitter rue' as a stock literary figure, as in *Richard II* (III, iv, 104-6):

> here in this place
> I'll set a bank of rue, sour herb of grace,
> Rue, even for ruth . . .

But Housman writes of 'sinner's rue,' the symbol of sorrow and repentance:

> Blue at my breast I fastened
> The flower of sinner's rue.

> It seemed a herb of healing
> A balsam and a sign . . .

In another poem he has *rue* 'sorrow, grief' no doubt—

> With rue my heart is laden
> For golden friends I had.

but there is just a hint of the flower:

> The rose-lipt girls are sleeping
> In fields where roses fade.

In such expressions 'feedback' satisfies the most exacting aesthetic taste. There is none of the primary equivocation and hedging that weakens the cumbrous allusions of non-literary discourse, in particular of the so-called 'learned' variety. An otherwise useful but misconceived figure of speech then ceases to function—for example, a simile that seeks to compare things which have no similarities may truthfully be described as nonfunctioning. Metaphor calls for intimate knowledge of the language that uses it (even though some metaphors are widespread, e.g. 'to under-stand' a compound of 'stand' with reference to mental attitude is found in many totally unrelated languages) and sometimes of extralinguistic environment. In Christian Latin, to repeat (deliberately) an example used already, *refrigerium* (used of the life after death) is a 'place of refreshment' from the heat of mortal strife; more extreme, in Burmese a lover tells his lass that she 'makes him feel cool', i.e. happy, a pleasant change from the devastating heat of the Burmese climate. The Burmese expression is not merely a matter of the thermometer, the Christian Latin not of the thermometer at all; but either may be interpreted in terms of goal-directed activity.

These are not poetic in the technical sense. In fact prose constantly shows features which are commonly believed to be peculiar to poetry. Every language has features of rhythm, governed by the sequence of emphasis, stress, pitch, quantity, and breath groups. These are inherent in the structure of the language and are concerned with conveying and distinguishing meanings, exactly like the sequences of phonemes, morphomes, or words. Accordingly they present themselves in prose as well as in verse. In Latin prose, above all of the orators, special attention was given to the cadence of the sentence; Greek discourages a sequence of more than four short syllables within a single word or phrase. Dickens, especially when he is senti-

mental, writes almost in blank verse; parts of Demosthenes
go almost as readily, but less abundantly, into iambic trimeters.
It is no exaggeration to speak of rhythmic prose; and again the
selection or rejection of any given unit of utterance, on the
ground of its rhythmic quality, may be regarded as a matter of
binary choice. We may suppose, but cannot prove, that there
is some cerebral process which exercises control over these
choices, to each of which the content is a matching accompani-
ment. Whether slow and deliberate, or rapid and spontaneous,
there are always the two factors of (1) the choice or rejection
of units of speech and (2) the organization of them. This
dicotomy is deep-seated: it is between utterance and language,
message and code, a sequence of events and a system of relations,
an activity and an institution, a chain of symbolic units and a
complex of habits. Not so much meaning, as poetic or aesthetic
quality, depend on and emerge from the rise and fall of these
two factors, choice and order, amalgamated in the flow of discourse. Form does not give content, but content is contained
in form. To abandon form is to become incoherent, like the
congenital idiot who has never learned form, or like the aphasiac
and demented who have forgotten it. Confusion and super-
imposition of incongruent forms is destructive of content (witness *Finnegans Wake*); and extreme elaboration of form, as in
some modern English poetry, hampers realization of content.
What gives a piece of writing or of speaking its character, is
the demand which it makes in 'decoding.' Continuity derives
from the sequence of discrete nervous impulses; if the discrete
elements in the sequence are disjointed, pro-presentation is
inadequate, and response poor and low; but the same result
follows from exaggerated novelty, the coding of which does
violence to the established pattern without corresponding gain
in pro-presentation. Structure is deterministic, value inheres
in it, and without it content evaporates. Poor 'orchestration'
gives poor results in language as in music.

It has been maintained that the meaning is given by the
sound. But an astute critic has remarked that 'murdering of
innumerable beeves' (Ransom) differs from Tennyson's line
'murmuring of innumerable bees' only by two phonemes. Those
two, the alternation of *d : m*, and of *v : zero*, disrupt an order
otherwise identical. No one can hear a buzzing hive in the

bawling stockyards. The physical characteristics of an utterance may indeed be reproduced by a spectrogram (see the illustration at the back of this book), a photograph, so to speak, of the acoustic features of an utterance. While it shows distinct patterning, it also shows how highly conventionalized is the link between the meaning and the sound.

'Poetic' devices appear to be at least as old as our most ancient linguistic records. There are features of verse common to the Rig Veda and Homer that suggest an original Indo-European metrical system. Arrangements of words in epic like Vergil's

Erebumque chaosque	*tergeminamque Hecaten*

(note the repeated -*que* 'and') are doubtless imitated from Homer, but may also be found both in Greek epic, and in Sanskrit and Germanic, where there is no question of mutual influence. Ancient liturgies, composed in prose, show marked rhythmical features in the structure and combination of phrases; so also do verses that were sung at harvest and vintage festivals, or intended to avert the evil eye at weddings or military triumphs, impromptu drama connected with the worship of agricultural deities, charms and prayers, large bodies of legal and priestly literature—all these are characterized by the obvious exercise of selection in their linguistic units. In a word, 'poetic' discourse organizes more selectively the resources of order and form in the interests of 'style' and 'value'. Its effect may be so marked as to enable a careful observer to identify an author as clearly as if the piece had his name attached.

The notion, therefore, that literary style reflects the psychology of an author is not well founded. It is only in cases of marked mental derangement that the deviation from normal mentality has a 'co-ordinate linguistic deviation from normal linguistic usage,' and this chiefly in the direction of incoherent jargon, an abandonment, not an elaboration, of linguistic order. Symbolism is not private once it is enunciated; what is designated as 'private symbolism' in modern poetry is largely in the nature of an aberration that manifests itself in perceptual confusion, e.g. of colour and sound.

The grammatical category of person pro-presents relative

position on the stage of life. Hence lyric poems again and again start with the first person of authorship; dialogue and drama need at least the second as well, and do better with all three. But fiction and narrative are largely composed in the third person, unless direct quotation or autobiography is included. The lecture or homily makes considerable use of the second person. Authorship is apt to project itself upon a screen and then stand back to admire the result. This leads to the plural of authorship, the editorial 'we'. These are trivial observations; but they illustrate, in a small way, how form may be coordinated with content.

Too much aesthetic merit should not be attributed to language, which primarily serves the ends of communication, not of aesthetics. The same world of experience may be at once subject matter for the scientist and for the poet or playwright. It is above all the form, the syntactic dimension, of language that distinguishes the poet's and the scientist's treatment of the same raw material. They see the same data differently, but we should never know it, if their insight remained unexpressed, a private affair. It becomes public in what they have to say; and what they have to say has ultimately the same content. Many varieties of discourse are to be found in conversational language; but the poet, the scientist, the preacher, the technician, and the rest, develop each one that form of discourse which serves best whatever it is that he has to communicate. Hence, the same item of experience may be known in two or more different ways—one aesthetic and intuitive, the other theoretic and axiomatic-logistic.

The finest achievements in both of these kinds of knowing and expression show a high power of creative imagination— of a Newton or a Shakespeare. Science, like poetry, religion, or the arts, is a symbolic form, each using its peculiar form of discourse. If such discourse attempts to transcend language as such, it still must be approached through language, commonly the mother tongue.

The poetry of mysticism claims to deal with the ineffable. This is a contradiction in terms. What is ineffable cannot, by definition, be said. Contrariwise, what can be known can be expressed. The reason why mysticism finds expression chiefly in terms of human passion seems to be just this, that mystical 'experience' is essentially a private affair, but that utterance demands that it be made public. The inconsistency is irreconcilable. There is, therefore, a risk that the form will be assimilated to analogy and allegory of any desired degree. Otherwise the demand made by derivative or associative content refines the form out of existence. Scientific language is occasionally not free from this risk; but the inadequacy is more easily detected, and scientists far less tolerant of 'meaningless' utterance.

It is useful to distinguish between *speech*, the gross physical performance of talking (including its written substitute) without reference to meaning; LANGUAGE in the abstract (in French *le langage*) as a total reserve of discourse from which concrete utterance (*la parole*) emerges in sequence, and *a* (particular) *language* (*la langue*)—English or French and the rest. Now, there is neither poetic, scientific, aesthetic speech nor poetic, scientific, aesthetic LANGUAGE as such, but all of these in a given *language*. Any particular *language*, together with its underlying LANGUAGE, is a social construct, namely of the particular speech-community which uses that particular code, of which an utterance is an individual rendering. There is, therefore, no poetic or scientific LANGUAGE at large; but there are poetic or scientific utterances in sequence, making up poetic or scientific discourse.

Scientific discourse tends to surmount LANGUAGE, so as to overcome the vernacular, and to become universal. But poetic discourse is highly peculiar to *a language*, so much so that translation is never more than an approximation. In poetic discourse there is a tendency toward individual dominance— in extreme cases verging upon unintelligibility. Everyday discourse shows both social and individual dominance, now the one now the other. The measure of poetic non-conformity of discourse reveals itself most clearly in the poet's verbal expression. This may be peculiar to a writer, or to a genre. For example the odes of Pindar all express in a peculiar way their writer; but the 'Homeric' language is that of a genre, the work of a literary corporation. It shows archaic and incoherent utterances combining distinctive patterns or codes, not always understood by the ancients; unusual phrase-constructs; and freely invented compounds, adapted to a tradition of oral composition. This accounts for an unusual catholicity of vocabulary, of morphological and syntactic choice, certain formulas in combination repeated over and over again at convenient metrical places in the line.

'Personal' poetry turns more upon differences of time and locale (contrast Racine with Victor Hugo), as well as author (compare Valéry with Claudel and Claudel with a surrealist, say Paul Eluard whose writing is unusually simple). Nevertheless, poetic discourse is the collective linguistic form of a gifted profession, it presents a stylistic and linguistic problem, not a critical one. Criticism has produced a discussion of poetry that amounts to little more than an exchange of opinion. The 'understanding' of minute dissection, as practised by critic and 'philologist' alike, is not sought either by the poet or by his audience.

A 'new' poetry comes hand in hand with new departures in a language, its total resources. The most recent English and American poetry partakes of the great changes taking place in the English language, which are part and parcel of the contemporary environment; the same is true of political propaganda, or of advertising copy. The same 'emotive' and 'dynamic' components pervade all three of them.

VII

THE STRUCTURE OF LANGUAGE

EVERYONE remembers the rhymes of a popular song in *South Pacific . . . dame, . . . same, . . . name, . . . frame;* or *. . . here . . . near; . . . other . . . brother*. These pairs of words are distinguished one from another by the contrast between *d:s:n: fr; h:n;0:br*. Similarly *ample:apple*, and so endlessly: we do not eat *bats* or *cats* or *rats*, but we do eat *fats*. The contrasts are just as clear in writing as in speaking. They show up in features of rhythm which accompany the sequence of linear phonemes, being supplementary to them; in fact if some other device is occasionally substituted for talking, as in the conventional and quasilinguistic whistling of a few communities, used as a simple means of communication across deep mountain gorges, a marked rhythmical contrast provides part of the 'mechanics' of the code.

Now it is not the minimal units, but their relations to one another, their mutual positions of occurrence, that perform the functions necessary to the working of the code. Two entities are said to be the 'same', so far as the system goes, if and only if they are characterized by the same relations, which is what gives them the 'same' values.

Awareness of linguistic events is in their associations by comparison or contrast. The most fundamental and thoroughly pervasive contrast is between order and disorder; this also is a question of association, of features of arrangement, and is a basic and indispensable principle in the description of any system. Human beings have developed a faculty of selection which depends on comparison (likeness, similarity, identity) and contrast (unlikeness, difference). In language, if anywhere in human conduct, these principles of contrast, of order, of choice and of regularity, are systematically integrated.*

* See Appendix 2

Definitions in linguistics seek to be operational, that is are given in terms of purely logical symbols. 'Operational' refers to something not entirely demonstrable, except in the terms of axioms and postulates already formulated intuitively, but clearly working within the context of the discipline. Operational definitions are those which provide a convenient and consistent treatment of a problem, given certain assumptions. It is this requirement of operational meaning which makes science 'scientific', i.e. productive of verifiable and repeatable results, logically connectible and communicable, provided that the conditions of investigation or experiment are not changed. The important thing is to be consistent in the method of applying the operations; then the resultant analysis is perfectly valid. This procedure is the keystone of the structural analysis of language. So too meaning is not directly sought, and would not be useful if it were, in the abstract; but contrastive function is sought. That is, a speech element x is either the same as, or not the same as, a speech element y—this is the only distinction necessary for performing logical operations on y, namely that the meaning of whatever is in question must be considered as relevant in terms of the functioning or operation both of the system and of the methodological scheme.

In order to find out whether a definition is admissible, it is necessary to find out with what set of linguistic rules it is connectible. Meaningful statements fall into two groups: (1) those expressing a state of fact which may be verified by experience; and (2) those which, independently of experience, are true or false by virtue of their logic.

But there is one other important factor. Every statement of a positive science refers to the actions of man, as observed by man himself. The linguist states his observations of the structure and use of spoken or written expressions which constitute one form of activity of large groups of human beings. Both the subject matter of study, and the statement of the results, are alike actions of men and also are about (linguistic) acts. False (i.e. contradictory or non-connectible) statements may be eliminated; the rest are all tautological. Tautological statements form the content of all axiomatically formulated sciences, which thus end in mathematics or at least in logic. In Hilbert's words 'everything that can be an object of scientific thought, as soon as it is ripe for the formulation of a theory, falls into the lap of axiomatic method, and thereby indirectly of mathematics.'

Linguistic phenomena are studied from two points of view, the historical and comparative; and the contemporary or descriptive. The descriptive or synchronic method rests upon a fiction, namely that theoretically language may be regarded as a status, a closed, metastable system. This fiction is operational; it gives consistent results, which in their turn fit coherently into historical or diachronic linguistics, and both into communication theory and, finally, into a basic philosophy of language.

The distinction between a language system and the utterances which constitute it is of first importance. Linguistics is a cognitive science—we are to discover, in each case, the inherent pattern of a language, not to impose an artificial, if elegant but predetermined, scheme (except perhaps as a tour de force), upon the crude data. Just as with other patterned natural or human development, so in every language there is a system, a pattern, a structure; it is the linguist's task to discover and to elucidate this pattern. The linguist is presented with speakers; from them he must elicit, clarify, and state the structure and the pattern of the language to which the utterances of its speakers belong. Without the pattern the language could not be; the language is the pattern and the pattern the language. Without system language could never have come into existence as a capacity for classifying and symbolizing experience; it would have remained for ever undifferentiated and chaotic.

Structural linguistics is content with the description of languages and language types. It explicitly and deliberately excludes the consideration of meaning, of the evolution of language, of the part language has played, for good and for evil, in human affairs, how it works, its virtues and its failings. It is barely interested in the social conformity of ordinary discourse, and not at all in the refinements, both individual and social, of linguistic non-conformity as it appears in scientific or poetic discourse.

Those who occupy themselves with structural linguistics are concerned to reduce the welter of data derived from discourse, the stream of speech, to neat, economical, and self-consistent statements of the system of sounds (phonology), of forms and words (morphology), and of the arrangements of order of the latter (syntax). Such systems are then compared with one another, and with systems of divergent types, such as pure logical systems, but this also is a task which structural linguists decline. It is all the more encouraging that initial steps toward the analysis of discourse as such (i.e. not as phonology, morphology and syntax) are being taken by a few devotees of symbolic logic.

Languages, after they have been analysed by this technique, may be classified as to structural type. That part of linguistics which has to do with descriptive or structural analysis, on a synchronic level, falls into four subdivisions pertaining to speech-sounds (phonematics), forms (morphomatics), arrangements of forms (syntactics), and meanings (lexicology). The underlying procedure is always contrast and comparison. This follows from the fact that we are dealing with systems of linguistic symbols and with the distribution of the symbols within each system. The system is a construct which formulates the mutual relations of the symbols—the acts of speech or utterances—that express states of awareness.

Considered objectively language is a series of physical events. Each complete utterance is initiated by the brain from a zero point—complete silence, there is a conversion of muscular into acoustic energy, articulatory and auditory control of the conversion, that produces a sequence of speech-sounds ranging through frequencies of about 100 to 8000 cycles per second (sound waves) and within a measurable duration, until silence is reached at the end of the utterance. Such a complete utterance is bounded by silence.

The total mass of material (speech) that might be subject to analysis is so large that it may correctly be considered limitless —all that has ever been said (or written) in all the languages of the world, or ever will be said or written. It matches the entire universe. Clearly such a bulk is unmanageable; no library in the world is big enough to hold it. Moreover, the differences between languages are such as to make impossible any attempt to control them simultaneously or comprehensively. In order to acquire some notion of LANGUAGE we take *languages* one by one. Here also the mass is usually too large to admit analytical operations on a practical or useful scale. Moreover to attempt to cope with the entire mass of (say) English or Chinese is unnecessary. Representative samples of a single status are sufficient—the rest is merely repetitive, for the same features that have been obtained by the analysis are found to occur over and over again. Instead of taking the language in its entirety, we may take a single book, or a longish treatise. In practice it is better to take specimens of various kinds, from different sources. A few thousand non-minimum utterances cover a good deal of the linguistic usage. If it turns out not to be an adequate sample, so that some matters are left obscure, it is always possible to go back and increase the amount of sample. The sample is then progressively broken down, if it has not been obtained in the first instance as short but not minimum units. We start with the bounded units marked off by silence. These are observed to be made up of other units, each of which within the pattern of the language has a recognizable beginning and end. There is a point at which a permitted sequence or arrangement of phonemes comes to a stop, and a new one begins.

The physical events of a language, when they are communicable (i.e. intelligible), are not random, but succeed each other in a sequence characteristic of that language and within strictly delimited possibilities—the permitted pattern of the language; anything else would be 'nonsense' in that language. Not even all possible sequences are admitted. This is true whether the symbols are speech-sounds (phonemes), or graphic surrogates ('letters'); and also true whether the units are minimal, or the larger segments, free-standing and meaningful, commonly called words, which may be defined as cohesive groups of phonemes (or graphemes) with strong internal statistical influences or probabilities. Writing is just as valid a system of expression as talking. Moreover, once the process has been initiated, the probabilities depend step by step each on the preceding events, until silence is reached once more—that very determinacy, which not only provides for communication and meaning, but which linguistic analysis takes for granted, and demonstrates by its very success.

These bounded segments, such as words and forms, are lexical and grammatical units. They are, so to speak, linear compounds of phonemes, just as a larger utterance (a phrase or sentence) is a linear combination of morphomes and words. A minimal form might be thought of as a molecule of LANGUAGE, and this in its turn as capable of being broken up into phonemes (atoms of LANGUAGE), each with several distinctive features into which it may be split.

The effective use of a language depends upon the parcelling out of its units; their orders of arrangement give the system of the language. We may take a bounded utterance, a sentence or phrase, or even a word, without destroying or breaking up the system, but a phoneme is ineffective, except in the rare cases in which a word is also a phoneme (e.g. English *a*, whether stressed or unstressed). Morphomes also may be words, and then are called free, as distinguished from those which appear only as parts of words (e.g. English *-ly* in adverbs). In effective communication there occur in sequence successive units, spoken or written, which are accompanied by corresponding 'responses' or meanings, and which have mutual systematic relations.

Descriptive method studies the ways in which the smaller bounded units (forms and words) are related to one another in the larger bounded units (the sentence), and also the functions performed by the phonemes within forms and words. In the process grammatical features of morphology and syntax are also uncovered. But it is misleading to attempt to classify these features until the forms have been isolated, described, and classified; and reduced to their constituent phonemes, which also must be isolated, described, and classified.

It is commonly found that recurring units are not identical. This is obviously the case with larger units—not only a book or a lecture is not the same as another book or lecture, except when copies are made, but one sentence is not the same as another sentence; if it were, nothing new or different would ever be said. But even phonemes are not phonetically identical (aspirated *t* in tin, unaspirated in *stop*); or morphomes and words (*man: men*), and certainly not their relations (*of the book, from a book, he is writing a book, he is writing for a book, a new book has come, go and get the book*). Nor are referends identical: a disgruntled private and an infatuated girl may describe a lieutenant in the same words 'I do love that fellow!' with totally different responses; 'I have some pumpkins' is either a certain number of pumpkins or very superior pumpkins, 'bats in the belfry', 'I dare say' (venture to say, or perhaps), 'the quick and the dead' (at a busy crossing or in biblical usage), all illustrate the point. But linguistically the overall status of the expressions is always 'the same'. This fiction is necessary for linguistic analysis, and harmless. So in speech-sounds: we say we talk alike, but paradoxically enough we cannot. Forms too when compared may be only partially alike, as French *port, porte, apporter;* Latin *uinco* 'I conquer', *uici* 'I have conquered'; French *cheval* 'horse' but (plural) *chevaux* 'horses'; or the partial agreement may be of other kinds, as Latin bon*i* numm*i*, bon*a* femin*a* (analysis isolates the identities *-i, -a, bon-, femin-, numm-*), French *il viendra demain, je viendrai demain* (*-dra* and *-drai* go with *demain,* but *-dra* also with *il, -drai* with *je*). As for the phonemes, in contrasts such as *pin:bin, din:tin,* we evidently distinguish *p:b, t:d* and similarly *a:e:i:u* in *pan:pen:pin:pun*) by segmentation, but ignore the phonetic differences that can be shown to exist between the *d* in *din* and that in e.g. *medal,* while recognizing a contrast between *t:d* in *metal and medal* despite phonetic approximation. In other words, in analytical procedures, we begin with the assumption that in a given language at a given point of time, the over-all status of that language can be discovered and described on any degree of detail. Equilibrium is assumed, the language is regarded as being in a stable, or at least metastable, condition. Otherwise description would be impossible.

According to one well-argued theory, language is not only a form of order, namely in the physical events of which it is constituted, but also the form by which content of experience and of ideas—both amorphous or disorderly in themselves—are made to correspond with one another, namely as expression or overt rendering. Just as a *phoneme* is the smallest unit of structural analysis, being a bundle of *distinctive* features, so a term is required for the smallest unit of *significance;* for this the term *glosseme* (also Greek, like phoneme) has been introduced. This is not the same as meaning; it is not meaning, but the ways in which languages handle meaning, that is at issue. Accordingly, a theory of the *system* (the pattern of mutual relationships of linguistic elements); of the *norm* (i.e. a set of rules based on the system and describing the limits of variation for each element); and of *usage* (a set of rules based on the norm and describing the limit of variation tolerated in a given speech-community at a given time)—this comprehensive theory is designated *glossematics*. It is necessary to take *practice*, i.e. utterances of individual speakers (or writers) as the crude data; and practice includes style. Here new, as distinguished from traditional and established variation (*seethe: sodden*) finds an entry (Hopkins' 'the just man justices'); but selection, which is controlled and limited by the demands of intelligibility, prevents variation from running riot, and historically plays an important role in governing practice, and therefore, that is through practice, in determining usage, norm, and pattern. It is once more the paradox that we do not and cannot, but yet must, talk 'alike'.

Where there are abundant materials (not solely the great literatures of the world, from Chinese to Icelandic, but also non-literary records, from Eskimo to Maori), there is also a tradition of interpretation which leaves no doubt about primary segmentation into repetitive like utterances. The shift from practice to usage, from individual rendering to norm, may often be observed, caught in the very act, when, for example, a peculiarity of usage (or style) passes into a rule of syntax, like the newspaper headline 'What do you mean responsibility' (in Plato τί ποτε λέγεις τὴν δικαιοσύνην 'What do you mean justice'). In other words, certain pre-glossematic operations have been performed before the linguist sets to work, either to describe a status (Old English, modern English; Classical Latin, Vulgar Latin, French), or to trace the historical connexions of one status (or even language) with another or others, or to compare these with one another. In such a situation it is advantageous to begin by reducing discourse to the segments existing in epilegmata (utterances) and their syntagmata (relations), unless this has been done already by dictionary and grammar, which thus constitute repertoria of source material. For some languages we find already provided a further valuable, if not necessary, aid—namely a reverse index, in which the words are arranged alphabetically backwards. In the case of a scantily recorded, long-extinct dialect this step is carried out *pari passu* with segmentation, being repeatedly revised as repeated inspection and observation teach the linguist to recognize fully the bounded units—in fact some forms of ancient writings provide interpuncts that correspond to the little patch of white paper that modern handwriting, typewriting, or printing leaves between such units. Engravers or writers of the documents had already recognized and isolated the words. But this is by no means always the case—words may be no more marked in writing than in the stream of speech itself, except perhaps by the spoken phrasing, which is now conventionally marked in many languages by marks of punctuation in print or writing, and these marks are by themselves quite inadequate.

Next these units are reduced to smaller segments—morphomes (minimum forms) whether formative elements (suffixes, prefixes, infixes, and the like) or words. This is done by making the cuts in accordance with likenesses (comparison) and contrasts (opposition) or substitutions (e.g. the pair *men:man* behaves like *boys:boy*, or *feet:foot* in the whole sentence). The words may be full words or 'empty' words (i.e. word modifiers, as in Chinese), or sentence modifiers (like Greek particles). This identification of glossemes and morphomes is morphology, which calls for the setting up of grammatical categories (like number, gender, tense, mood, voice), parts of speech (nouns, adjectives, verbs and the rest), and, wherever suitable, into characteristic patterned samples (paradigms—declensions and conjugations). In this way the system and norm are established, and individual usage, wherever it deviates, separated and distinguished; and even characteristics of style enumerated. Features of meaning, in operational terms (i.e. by tests of communicabilty and connectibility), and as determined by permitted sequences (this is a statistical matter) are also identified.

But the glossemes and morphomes are composed of phonemes. In glossematics these are reached next, by the same procedures of segmentation, comparison and contrast, and their distinctive features may be further discovered, as well as their contextual variants (allophones, e.g. non-distinctive aspiration or non-aspiration), and features of transition or juncture as one passes the bounds between words. From these the phonematic inventory is constructed.

In this way the structure of a language is completely analysed and described, all the way from phoneme to syntax and style. But the description is of a status which is subject to momentary if minute variation. This fiction of status ceases to be a fiction only when we describe a 'dead' language. Its form of order is completely stable; just as dead men are never disorderly, so the linguistic behaviour of the dead may be reduced to perfect order.

Before writing became a commonplace accomplishment travellers who stayed long enough in a foreign community learned to speak its language by listening, observing, and imitating. The method is still in use, but mechanical recording is both a convenient short cut, and far more accurate. The enormous widening of the Western scholar's linguistic horizon, since the middle of the fifteenth century, consequent upon the activities of Christian missionaries, of traders and voyagers, and more recently of anthropologists and linguists, is chiefly responsible for the modern technique of analysis.

But an unrecorded language which can hardly be said to be already well known to a linguist, i.e. known in approximately the way in which it is known to a native speaker, offers peculiar difficulties. In such a case it has been found advantageous to reach its phonemes independently and to begin analysis and description by discovering the phonemes first, so as to make a phonematic transcription of samples, before proceeding to extract forms or to formulate a grammar. There is also the theoretical consideration that the segments tabulated and compared in grammatical analysis are not really or necessarily distinctive, but are actually significant forms. Unless these are phonematically recorded, analysis may be erroneous, and—in the long run—seriously confused.

There is a remarkable congruity in verbal and written pro-presentation. In both it is necessary to distinguish between imitation and symbolism. The former is neither true writing nor true speaking, but mere pictography or mimicry, for it is not conventionalized or fully standardized. An important principle of inner form characterizes writing as well as language. Writing develops from one inner structural stage to another—from pictography through syllabary (which uses a grapheme for each syllable) to alphabet. These steps are necessary on the principle of linguistic economy or mechanics. Instead of devising a separate symbol with which to present every single item of significance, and every single detail of the mutual relations of these items one to another, all this can be accomplished with the help of fewer than thirty alphabetic symbols and their multitude of arrangements and rearrangements, of permutations and combinations. The really decisive step, from ideograms, which can be understood but not read aloud by a foreign speaker, i.e. do not give the utterances, to syllabary or alphabet, was taken when someone became aware that a picture, whether stylized or not, not only has a significance, but also stands for the sequence of sounds that symbolize that concept. We thus get, as it were, a symbol of a symbol, or symbolism twice removed. To utter the word *house* (or *maison*, or *casa*, or *domus*) is, so to speak, to make a conventionalized noise corresponding to the concept 'house'; but to *write* the word house, is a manual 'gesture' of the spoken or facial 'gesture'. There is a cerebral coding and matching process of the visual symbols, as well as of the audible, both with one another and with the significance implied.

Nevertheless, when language is taken in the mass, there is a fairly close one-to-one correspondence of the spoken and the written form, even though sound is the physical medium of the one, and light of the other. The set of spoken elements is the 'same', in terms of operations and objects, as the set of written elements—and may be identical, if the system of writing is sufficiently precise. In any event, it is necessary to reduce the spoken system to a graphic system before any consistent and thoroughgoing analytical operations can be performed upon it —other than intuitions or mere first impressions.

The basic phenomenon in writing and speaking, as in semantics and in many non-linguistic human activities, is man's capacity to classify numerous single items as members of a much smaller number of species. This labour of classifying and sorting is a device of economy; it crystallizes relevant features and abstracts them from a mass of non-discriminatory individual details. In other words it is a means of bringing order into disordered, or at least disconnected, observations and experiences. Even a phoneme brings together a variety of features into a single unit.

Writing has become secondary to talking, dependent upon it, although at first independent. It is not the only kind of secondary symbolism—telephony (electrical impulses), Morse code, spectrograms (photographs of sound), magnetic tape and plastic disks—these are all systems that have their own techniques of expression. When they are substituted for linguistic symbolism there is an exact correspondence at each step in the sequence. The spectrograph, which uses magnetic tape and sensitized paper, is a good example of this; in fact it reveals features of utterance that otherwise would have been only conjectured or even unsuspected.

We start from a sufficiently large sample of a language, about two thousand representative phrases of ordinary discourse, and extract the system from these; not from the minimum elements and then weave these into a pattern. This sample may be a tape recording or disk, or a written transcription, as nearly phonematic as is possible at this stage of the analysis. In either case it is possible to isolate bounded segments with a well-defined beginning and end that occur in identical, or nearly identical shape, e.g. in English:

> giveme*thebook*
> Hereis*abook*
> Isthis*thebook*whichyoumean?
> Thisisagood*book*
> *The*new*book*ishere

and so on. It is found, on observation, or it may be already known, that such a segment (*book*) always evokes the same response in the hearer, and is so intended by the speaker. Such a repetitive segment of utterance, with its corresponding response, is known as a form. If it is not capable of analysis into other smaller such segments it is called a *morphome*. But *books* or *bookish* (compare *boy:boys:boyish*, or *man:men:mannish*) are so analysable into *book*, *-s*, and *-ish*, so that now we have the morphomes *-s* and *-ish* (as well as *book*). Moreover, we note not only *book*, but other forms which evoke, and are so intended, a different response, e.g. *cook*, *hook*, *look*, *nook*, *rook*, *took*, and further that these differ from *book* in one and only one constituent element, the initial *b*, *c*, *h* etc., while the others *-oo-* and *-k* remain the same. Yet we may find in similar contrast *book* and *back*, *back* and *lack*, *book* and *boot*, *boot* and *bat*, *bat* and *rat*, *cat*, *fat*, and so on.

These bounded segments correspond roughly to the units isolated by lexicography. In terms of speech-sounds, they are the actually occurring sequences permitted by the pattern of the language, each of which reaches its end before the next sequence begins. Their total number may be very large—the contents of the lexicon and grammar, which imply that the preliminary or pre-glossematic procedures have already been performed. The theoretical assertion that such a procedure may be dispensed with, that there are no necessary grammatical prerequisites to phonematic analysis, is belied in actual practice.

But if we start absolutely from scratch, merely with the crude data mechanically recorded from the conversational exchanges of native speakers, these are first of all phonetically transcribed—as they 'sound'. To do this presupposes a training in practical phonetics, a good 'ear', and the ability to put down accurately what is heard, in a phonetic alphabet, which has one letter, and one only, for each 'sound'. The first segmentation is carried out here, into recurring features, same or partly same, that are observed in the sequences, e.g. *the ship's in:give me a pin* where the repeated *in* is noted, even though it will not turn out to be identical in the end. The investigator has recognized a vowel sound which he writes *i* and a following consonant which he writes *n*, and so on with the rest of his samples. It commonly happens that many of these segments will be found ultimately to be items that will go into the grammar or lexicon, e.g. *in* and after further investigation *pin*. This step may be completed with sufficient accuracy. The next step is to segment the forms into phonemes by inspection (for example *i, n, p* emerge from the pairs *pin:bin, nip:nib, pin:pan, bin:ban,* and *nap:nab*), a procedure justified by practice and also theoretically, as by means of spectrographic analysis, which confirms visually the aural intuition. Then the segments are justified by a process of substitution in sets of minimal pairs, e.g. *life: rife*. If these are found to be contrasted with one another (that is, not completely identical), then the segmentation is valid; if not, it is necessary to go back to the data and repeat the procedure, until valid segmentation is reached, the whole process being a matter of continual feedback. The purpose is to ascertain the minimal bundles of features of speech, and the regular distribution of them in relation to one another; for even in phonematic analysis tentative morphomes are being approximated, and the postulated morphomes will be verified by the phonological investigation. The elements, both phonemes and morphomes, are purely logical symbols for the performance of logical operations. The advantage of establishing phonemes early is that their total number in any language is small—it rarely exceeds sixty and is usually between thirty and forty, seldom as low as twenty or less, whereas the number of morphomes, though finite, is large enough to be embarrassing, and so to make the analysis difficult and uncertain, unless the language is already well known. The number of words, and the number of their actual arrangements, is larger still, though also not infinite.

In phonematic analysis all phonetic differences are divided into distinctive and non-distinctive differences, e.g. in *pin : spin* the aspirated *p* is not distinctive (it is the *s*- which distinguishes), though it is phonetically different in *pin* (being aspirated *p'*) and *spin* (*p* being non-aspirated), whereas in Greek φ (aspirated *p*) and π (non-aspirated *p*) were distinctive, e.g. . . . πῶς . . . 'anyhow'; . . . φῶς . . . 'man', and in English the distinction *p* (unvoiced) and *b* (voiced) as in *pin : bin* is distinctive, as can be discovered by the response of the native speaker of English, who will accept *pin* in *pin* and in *spin* as identical, but not *pin* and *bin*. Hence English *p* is a different phoneme from *b*, and Greek π (p) from φ (p'). For reaching such distinctions it is necessary to know at least that responses are different, and advantageous to know how they differ.

The same technique is carried out for all positions, initial, medial, and final, in the compared or contrasted bounded units; hence the usefulness of alphabetization both from the beginning and the end of the bounded units. At the same time we can see whether the occurrence of any particular initial is limited by the following sounds. Whenever it is possible to set up contrasts between pairs (as in the stock English list *pin : fin*, sin, *tin*; *pin : 0in*; *pin : man*, sun, hen; pin : pig, pi*ll*, pi*t;* pin : pat, pu*sh*, peg, pin : pen, pan, pun; *pin : dig, fish, will*), the distinctive phonemes emerge (in these few contrasts alone we find not only *p* and *n* but also *f*, *s*, *t*, zero, *m*, *h*, *g*, *l*, *t*, *sh*, *d*, and not only *i*, but also *a*, *u*, *e*), and the total inventory of English phonemes would be quickly reached, the point at which further investigation would bring no more results. Alternants such as aspiration and non-aspiration are (in English) merely positional or contextual variants, sometimes known as allophones. There may be, in certain positions, free alternation between the positional variants, sometimes the one, sometimes the other, in successive forms of the same word, without any contrast in meaning. The principle involved is that two or more sounds so occur among the forms of a language that none of them occurs in exactly the same position as any of the others, all the sounds in question being phonetically similar, since they share a feature absent from all other sounds, i.e. they are positional variants. This important principle, known as complementary distribution, guarantees against error in listing the phonemes of a language; it is the cornerstone of structural phonology. Thus there may be a large number of varieties of *t* in English, but (except in the case of free variation finally) no position is occupied by more than one variety of *t*, phonetically a voiceless alveolar plosive, a single phoneme with complimentary distribution (contextual variants).

It is necessary to show also what clusters of consonants the pattern of a language admits. For example English has initial *tr-* (*trend*), *thr-* (*through*), *dr-* (*drain*), but not, as might have been expected (since *r* often is in contrast with *l*, e.g. *rife, life*) *tl-*, *thl-*, or *dl-*. And so with all permitted groupings of phonemes into structural sets, determined by their occurrence in particular combinations and positions. The structural sets may, however, overlap, or there may not be complete parallelism in contrasted pairs. English has *pl-*, *cl-*, *pr-*, *cr-*, and it has *qu-* (i.e. *c + w-*) but not *pw-*. In general terms this means that no language actually shows all potential combinations and permutations of its phonemes; if it did the total number of words, assuming that none contained more than five phonemes, which is a low estimate, would be unnecessarily, even impossibly, large. Some of the 'nonsense' words in Lewis Carroll and his imitators satisfy structural requirements, but they simply do not occur elsewhere and evoke no response. There is, therefore, a somewhat low degree of efficiency in the use of the structural resources of a language, imposed by the requirements of comprehension and communication. In German, actual words of not more than four phonemes, arranged in five characteristic patterns, namely CVC, VCVC, CVCV, CVCC, CCVC (here C means consonant, V means vowel) amount to only 5·4 per cent actual efficiency, in Czech only 3·1 per cent, of the possible words that might have been constructed within the permissible sequences of those two languages.*

Since the phonemes discussed so far occur in simple linear sequence, they are known as segmental and are written to show only such distinctions. But a few phonemes occur simultaneously with others, as in vowel stress (*cóntract* and *contráct*), quantity (*bat: bad; can: calm*), intonation (e.g. contrast between assertion, exclamation, interrogation), and these are known as supra-segmental. Pitch is prominent in classical Greek, as ἄγων 'leading', ἀγών 'a contest', πείθω 'I persuade', πειθώ 'persuasion', ὦμος 'shoulder', ὠμός 'raw', θέων 'running', θεῶν 'of gods', and many others. Quantity is prominent in Latin: *mălus, măla, mălum* 'bad', *mālus* (fem.) 'apple tree', *mālus* (masc.) 'mast (of a ship)', *mālum* (neut.) 'apple' (*māla* pl. 'apples', but *mala* fem. sing. 'jaw').

It is necessary also sometimes to take account of the fact that in English stress sets in simultaneously with the first segmental phoneme of an initial syllable after a pause, and falls off slowly with a final syllable before a pause; and that such contrasts of transition or 'juncture' (as they are sometimes known) may occur internally with phonematic value in some utterances, e.g. *an aim* ('open juncture') but *a name* ('close juncture'), *a nice house:an icehouse, night rate:nitrate*. This peculiarity has played a part historically, as in *nap, napkin* but *apron, newt* (older *eft*), *nickname* (older *ekename*), for different practice may be standardized. On the stage an actor may be heard saying *a nuglier dwarf*, instead of *an uglier dwarf* ('than you couldn't be seen anywhere for a penny').

Experimental methods with instruments of recent invention are now employed to establish the minimum possible phonetic features and their maximum possible length, after which these are grouped together as a distinctive phonematic segment, since the successive or simultaneous elements which constitute it need no longer be kept separate. Moreover the segmentation may also be confirmed experimentally by means of the spectrograph or visible speech recorder.†

The phonematic principle was developed between the years 1925 and 1950. Hints of it are found as early as Sanskrit

* See Appendix 2   † See Appendix 3

grammarians, and the ancient atomists, Democritus and Lucretius; a thirteenth-century Icelandic grammar, and an eighteenth century French grammar, show some awareness of it. Two Swiss scholars, and a Polish, published ground-breaking monographs on the subject between 1875 and 1925. Since then progress has been rapid.

But the most spectacular advance was made, under the impact of war, during the last decade. For some time telephone engineers had been interested in devising machines that would give them a better understanding of the nature of speech-sounds as transmitted over telephone wires or by radio. They also hoped to perfect a device by which the deaf might be able to receive messages. In fact, as far back as 1867 Alexander Melville Bell had asked the question how speech might be rendered visible more efficiently than by conventional spelling. Gradually there grew up a study of phonetics which attempted to describe, in articulatory or physiological terms, the formation of speech-sounds from the larynx out through the mouth and nose, to specify the place and manner of articulation, and more recently ('motor phonetics') to include physiological activity at a lower level (bodily) than that of the larynx (e.g. intercostal muscles), so far as it also is concerned in speech, presumably in relation to supra-segmental phonemes. Early phoneticians used an artificial palate covered with chalk, and inserted it in the mouth in order to register roughly the position of the tongue in the production of a certain sound. Then there was invented the kymograph, in which impulses transmitted through a tube attached to the mouth and nose were traced by a needle on a piece of smoked paper attached to a slowly revolving drum. These tracings indicated nasalization, voicing, closure and release and some other phenomena such as aspiration, assimilation and duration, but not frequencies of wave lengths or distinctions of fundamental and component pitch. A throat-note recorder was a more recent device, that, with some improvements proved useful for transmitting speech among the crew of bombing planes above the noise of flight and battle. Still during the 1930's experiments had been made by taking moving X-ray pictures, accompanied by a sound-track, which showed the movements of the vocal organs during speech with a clarity that had not been attained before, and in fact revealed the articulatory movements in such a state of flux that it was difficult if not impossible to equate a particular configuration with a particular phoneme except in the crudest manner. Two conclusions follow: (1) the importance of transition-markers; and (2) that the status of minimal speech elements is only relative and more important for establishing the over-all functional pattern of a language structure than for the analysis itself.

Meanwhile the perfection of the cathode-ray tube had led to the invention of the oscillograph which pictures on a fluorescent screen the electrical frequencies corresponding to the wave lengths of a brief segment of utterance (e.g. a single vowel phoneme), but only as unanalysed complex waves. Moreover the picture is impermanent and vanishes so soon as the electrical current is shut off. A new impulse came in the first half of the last decade, with the need for breaking enemy codes. Even normal language is itself a code, and a message, to be intelligible, must always be coded, no matter how little or how far the code may diverge from standard language. Any code can be broken, the key discovered, provided that specimens of it of some length can be obtained in a form that admits of prolonged study. The spectrograph (or visible speech recorder) was perfected in response to this need, and in its turn has deepened knowledge of the acoustic properties of speech-sounds that are important for an understanding of their auditory perception. Recording on disks, or on tape, had already been highly developed, but the play-back still gave only a fleeting reproduction in sound, not a permanent picture or 'photograph' of the sound.

The spectrograph is a combination of magnetic tape and frequency record, with an analysis into the component frequencies of complex waves, preserved as a permanent picture. It makes a Fourier analysis of a complex wave automatically and presents it to the eye in a form comparable to that in which, or so it is assumed, the sound wave is presented to the ear— and by either or both to the brain. A deaf person can be taught to read what has only been said, once he has learned to interpret by eye such a complete and objective record of exactly what impinges on the ear of those who hear. Spectrographs in current use in speech laboratories will analyse in five minutes an utterance lasting 2·4 seconds in duration and ranging from zero to 8000 cycles per second. The analysis is performed by a battery of filters (i.e. tiny radio tubes attuned to successive frequencies). The permanent record is obtained by making an analysis of the complex waves of each speech-sound from a recording on magnetic tape and transferring it through a phosphor or light-bearing needle to sensitive paper mounted on a revolving drum, the needle advancing at a fixed number of cycles per second. With a large number of such needles evenly spaced the length of time for making the spectrogram can be greatly reduced. It is also possible to build at greater expense a spectrograph which will analyse almost instantaneously continuous utterances of longer duration than the 2·4 seconds to which standard laboratory machines are at present restricted.

A specimen spectrogram inserted with Appendix 3 is an analysis, virtually a photograph, of the words:

'Much have I travelled in the realms of gold'

with the vertical scale in frequencies (cycles per second) and the horizontal in milliseconds (thousandths of a second), and a phonetic transcription above the normal spelling. Variations in blackness represent variations in intensity.

VIII

THE ANALYSIS OF LANGUAGE

THE sensation of sound is produced by rapid fluctuations in the pressure of the atmosphere on the tympanum of the ear. If the fluctuations are irregular, that is non-periodic, we get the sensation of noise; if cyclic, regular, and in a sufficiently rapid periodic wave, as in speech, a musical sensation with features of pitch, which depends on the number of cycles passed through by the fluctuations of the pressure per unit of time; of loudness, which depends on amplitude, i.e. the amount, of the fluctuations in each cycle; and quality, which depends on the form or nature of the fluctuations in each cycle. Telephony regularly reproduces these three characteristics of speech; the strength of its electric current varies every instant directly as the pressure excited by the sounds uttered by a speaker. Radio makes use of the Marconi tube as an electric wave detector and various means of transmitting, and reproducing on a diaphragm, the original sound waves (pressure on the atmosphere); television and radar the principles of the oscillograph, combined with accurate selectivity in accepting or rejecting, as points of light or darkness, a multitude of units in such a way as to present on the screen at the end of the tube a pattern or picture which represents the original scene.

Within the cochlea of the inner ear there is what acts like a battery of filters—presumably the large number of nerve fibres, which analyse the frequencies, i.e. in cycles per second, within a range of zero to about 3500 or 4000 per second. (It is known that sound can be received also by the tips of the fingers, or through the soles of the feet.) The oscillations of a complex wave are translated into nerve-impulses which are carried to the brain to be identified with existing patterns; or, in the first steps of learning to talk, actually to establish patterns, neural schemata as they have been called, in the cortex of the brain. These were believed to be the abiding results of repeated stimuli upon the irritable tissue of the brain. More recently the greater importance of processes of guiding and switching various impulses along networks of paths and transitions than of mere excitation-patterns has come to be recognized. Be that as it may, in a spectrogram the oscillations (i.e. wave frequency) are recorded side by side from the bottom of the paper upwards, as both the filter tuning and the stylus shift together over the frequency-range and appear as a smear on the sensitive paper, grouped toegther in such a way as to give characteristic shapes for the speech-sounds, clusters, sequences in the syllable, word, or phrase. Before a stopped sound is a blank space known as a 'gap'(e.g. t in *much* [mʌtʃ] and in *travelled*, in the spectrogram), then follows a burst or release of the breath pressure that has been built up, producing a narrow and abrupt 'spike'; if the plosive is voiced, there is a bar on the base line (e.g. *d* in *travelled*, *gold*). For fricative phonemes (e.g. *ch*, *th*, š in *much* [mʌtʃ], *the* [ðə], *realms* [relmz]), we see irregular vertical striations called fill (wider than spike), accompanied as before by a bar if the fricative is voiced (ð, ʒ, but not ʃ). Vowels show a series of horizontal resonance regions or bars, from one to four and known by some 'formants,' which correspond to the concentrations of frequencies, e.g. *e* in *realms* [relmz]; in *I* [ai̯] the bars curve in passing from *a* to *i̯* in the pronunciations of *I*. As the voice falls at the end of the utterance (*gold*) the vertical striation become more widely separated from one another. Consonant spectra are not so easily characterized.

This account, intended to make intelligible what follows next, is by no means a complete description of the spectrogram. Transitions between sounds occupy about the same duration as in a steady position for a single sound, precisely as X-ray films had already indicated, and this fact helps to explain the historical phenomena of assimilation and dissimilation of sounds, which had been hitherto largely theoretical. There is a remarkable convergence of descriptive or structural and historical linguistics here and at many other points as well as with traditional phonetics. A vocal resonance chart based on spectrographic analysis is practically identical with the classical diagram of tongue-position (front:back; high:low), which X-ray had also shown to be approximately correct; and, as we shall see in due course, statistical investigations also converge in some matters of theory. Bar 2, numbered from the base line upwards, is usually significant, since it may be shifted, but its relation to bars 1 and 3 is important. The position of bar 2 is called the 'hub', patent or disguised when a sound is uttered in isolation; it connects different points in combinations of different sounds, especially vowels, and therefore is used for plotting positions. Different speakers of a dialect or language have approximately the same 'hubs' for the same sounds, a fact which reveals the general uniformity of verbal behaviour that has been learned as a social and psychological pattern of linguistic structure: each phoneme is relatively fixed, and may be recognized because the several utterances of it are consistantly similar. Hence the definition of a phoneme as a class of non-contrastive and phonetically similar sounds, or as a concurrent or simultaneous bundle of features. Thus the hubs of *k* (*c*) in *key:cat:cup:cool* are slightly variable, but the *k*-sounds make only one phoneme.

There is less difference in spectrograms of foreign languages than might have been expected. The reason is that the differences are not so much in the basic elements, the products of the same human anatomical apparatus, as in the way in which these function or are used; that is to say, in the structure of each language. Yet there are clear details, e.g. in the Spanish *r*, in the rare voiced sounds of Ojibway and the rapid shift of its resonance patterns (as contrasted with German or Irish or Arabic). English, Danish, German, Icelandic, and Swedish are all about the same; French (with Lithuanian-Yiddish) is quite 'extended'.

But there is the very greatest contrast with undifferentiated and repeated non-linguistic sound, such as music or crying, or with non-human sound, barking, mewing, and the 'song' of birds—animals do *not* talk. Electroencephalograms, which show the variation in brain potentials, can be spread out as spectrograms and so can electrocardiograms; but as yet no technique has been devised for the comparison or matching of electroencephalograms and speech-spectrograms. If ever this can be done, it may point to an answer to the old poser of whether 'thought' is sub-vocal language. In the meantime we have controlled experimental methods of getting at a far better acousto-phonetic description of speech than had been possible before, whether or not visual 'telephony' is ever reached.

If two phonemes of a language approach one another acoustically, then the listeners make an adjustment. For if they do not, the phonemes will ultimately combine, like Indo-European *ə* and *a*, which coincided everywhere as *a* except in Indo-Iranian. There are, to be sure, very great discrepancies among individuals. If auditory perception is poor, learning to talk becomes a slow process. Ready adaptation to a given speaker's peculiarities is the last thing acquired by children, about the age to 12 to 14, when linguistic habits are becoming fixed. An adult has usually overlearned his native pattern—which is the chief reason why it is hard to acquire new, i.e. foreign, patterns after adolescence.

Spectrograms show that in speaking there is a finite number of innervations per second from the brain to activate the vocal organs. Similarly the ear and brain discriminate in interpreting the continuum of speech that is received. This is transmitted as a succession of impulses, rather like bullets fired from a machine gun, the nervous activity pausing after each for recovery from fatigue. But it must not be supposed that the minimum differentiation of phonemes is what the brain interprets in terms of meaning. The economy of the brain seems to be concerned rather with the larger bounded units commonly known as words. The sequence of phonemes necessarily implies contradictory innervations coming one after another—e.g. both to advance and to raise the tongue simultaneously. Normally a speaker shows no effect of strain in such a case, though it has been suggested that this does happen to stutterers. Stuttering can be produced in normal speakers by making them listen to a delayed play-back of their own utterances, thus disturbing the normal timing of the innervations.

Further, a spectrogram reveals contrasts that are not all of them readily observed in articulatory or auditory terms. The contrast of voice *p:b* or of openness *a:e* is simple and obvious. But there are others more subtle, among them the frequency (cycles per second) and the amplitude of sound waves in time (i.e. continuous sequence). For example, when frequency is plotted against amplitude, it is possible to observe in the diagram a contrast between a centripetal and a centrifugal clustering tendency of the resonance regions (bars) of a sound. Thus in the received pronunciation of English, the vowels *o, a, e* (*pot, pat, pet*) show the centripetal tendency and are therefore described as 'compact', whereas *u, ə,* and *i* (*put, putt, pit*), with the centrifugal tendency, are described as 'diffuse', and we have a contrast between compact and diffuse. Others are between grave and acute, concerned with a contrast between clustering in low frequencies (grave) or high (acute), e.g. English *o, a, u,* are grave, *e* and *i* acute; or between tense and lax, which refers to energy of articulation, measured by comparing the greater or smaller sum of deviations of the frequencies against the mean points of 500, 1500, 2500 cycles per second, set up as a standard from an arbitrary neutral position. When this is done with two vowels that are opposed to one another in respect of this particular feature (e.g. French *ɑ* in *pâte, a* in *patte*), there is always a significant departure from the mean. In consonants a similar contrast appears in the duration of the auditory period (e.g. *f* tense, *v* lax), or in the intensity (i.e. strength of explosion, e.g. *p* tense, *b* lax). Even the obvious distinction between vocalic (vowels) and non-vocalic (consonants), or its correlate consonantal and non-consonantal, may be regarded in precisely the same way, as a matter of yes-or-no situations, i.e. binary choices. The essential principle is that of selection, the selection being governed by the pattern, or coding rules, of a given language in a given status, for instance contemporary standard English.

Now the appearance of several of the contrasting features, which may be called allophone markers, in a speech-sound, taken concurrently, characterize that speech-sound, and the whole bundle of them constitutes a phoneme, precisely as determined (but less trenchantly) by the procedures of substitution (or commutation), distribution, and free variation already described—the convergence of the two techniques of segmentation and spectrography is noteworthy. Thus English *o* is vocalic, non-consonantal, compact, grave and flat; *ə* is diffuse, acute, and plain; *p* is non-vocalic, consonantal, diffuse, grave, oral (contrasted with nasal), tense, and interrupted; *v* is lax and continuant (contrasted with interrupted).

Evidently the spectrograph makes available for inspection and study (*a*) the organization of speech-sounds into distinctive features, or clusters of distinctive features, and (b) the correlation of these acoustic facts, as a system of relationships, with the potentialities of perception, distinction, and classification which are found consistently within the human ear, nervous system, and especially the brain—all of which is important for language. The nerve responses are related to sound waves by a logarithmic function; by building this function into the spectrograph, the output of which is discrete and measurable, we approximate (visually) the nerve response itself (auditory). Augmented by the use of a play-back technique, with certain additions or subtractions, the spectrograms tell us precisely which features of a speech-sound or a sequence of speech-sounds are important in the perception of that sound or sounds. Thus binary features are isolated, and an objective account may be given of each speech-sound instead of merely impressionistic descriptions. The more recent development of communication theory turns overwhelmingly on a binary system of digital coding. Here again is a convergence, and agreement, of disciplines that is a strong guarantee of their scientific validity.

In every language certain features are reduced to contextual variants (e.g. the phonetic distinction between the *k* of *key* and the *k* of *cool* in English), so that the distinction may be said to involve a certain degree of redundancy—it adds nothing new. But this is nevertheless a matter of the greatest importance. For when phonemes are broken down into their inherent distinctive features, that is into the ultimate discrete signals, the number of such contrastive distinctions is still smaller than the number even of phonemes, and hence these clues are readily perceived. It is as if the atom of speech, the phoneme, had been split into its constituents. Redundancy, therefore, makes language more trustworthy and less subject to distortion; by reducing the number of discriminations to be made, we reduce the effort of choice, and thus verbal behaviour becomes an economical and satisfactory form of communication.

The underlying intuition, the long-standing impression, that there is something about sound waves which enables the hearer and speaker alike to distinguish very similar sounds, e.g. between palatalized and non-palatalized consonants, has been put upon a scientific basis by the spectrograph, which enables us to see how energy distributions enter into frequency components of the sound waves and how these differ from one another for separate phonemes as bundles of distinctive features on a basis of binary choices. This is the greatest contribution so far, of mechanical equipment to linguistic theory.

Analysis usually calls for synthesis. Just as a chemist attempts to reproduce synthetically a compound that he has succeeded in analysing, so communication experts have constructed a speech synthesizer or artificial talker, which enables them to investigate the responses of listeners to predetermined and accurately fabricated frequency distributions, and especially to ascertain what variant sounds 'sound like' in differing phonetic environments. One such device is an electrical analogue of the human vocal tract, which seeks to approximate the corresponding positions of speech-sounds.

The mechanism of speech may be regarded as a variable acoustic circuit, excited by appropriate periodic sources. Hence a synthesizer, capable of producing speech-sounds, singly or in succession to form whole words and sentences, seeks to incorporate variable elements electrically excited. Its fundamental components are four simple tuned circuits, each corresponding to one of the resonance regions. The resonant frequencies are varied over the normal ranges of resonances in speech-sounds. By proper adjustment and periodic pulsation, a synthetic speech-sound is heard from the loud-speaker, and the sound changes in obedience to readjustment of the resonances. A prearranged sequence of sounds is coded on teletype tape and this is fed through a machine for operating relay switching circuits. The whole device has some obvious (and alarming) potentialities.

What this valuable and now very successful but highly complicated machine does is, quite simply, to convert the patterns of a spectrogram, or hand-painted strips of film, back into speech. The principle is electro-optical, that is the visual patterns are converted back into electrical frequencies and these reproduced through a speaker. One conclusion appears to be that movements of the lips and jaws are less important than those of the tongue. These and like machines have converted so-called 'laboratory phonetics' into a more truly experimental science. The problems of analysis into discrete units have been more precisely posed and resolved, and physical correlates found for phonemes and their allophones (contextual variants), for the nature of syllabicity, and above all for the differences which are 'felt' to exist between different languages. The syllable now appears clearly as a group of speech-sounds with a vowel or vocalic element at its peak or centre. Not only are the experimental operations performed automatically with both accuracy and speed; it is now possible to carry out a controlled manipulation of different acoustic stimuli and of their effects on perception—to determine, in short, just which components of a speech-wave the ear uses as cues and which are essentially non-distinctive and therefore contribute little or nothing to understanding.

The identification and distribution of such small units as phonemes is only part of the story. Language is not perceived in these small units, which by themselves convey no meaning at all. It is with larger units that content begins to emerge. These larger units evidently imply a sequence of phonemes. The question has been raised recently whether the order is reversible. It has not been shown so far that the probabilities which appear in direct order must also be reversible. Usually speech played in reverse is as unrecognizable as music played backwards. But this does not mean that if the probability is zero that in English *th-* will be followed by *l-*, then the probability is also zero that *l-* will be followed by *th-*. English words may end in *-lth*, for example *wealth, health*. The last word written backward is *thlaeh*, in which final *-h* is also abnormal. But *-h* was possible in Old English (e.g. *troh* 'trough'), and *thl-* did exist in pre-dialectal Germanic, becoming *fl-* in Western Germanic (O.E. *flèon* 'flee', Gothic *thliuhan*). There is no human impossibility in the use of the pattern—it simply does not occur in modern English.

It has, however, been known to happen that in cryptography a code may have been read correctly but in reverse order—when this is rectified, the decipherment is seen to have been accomplished. If consonants occur in both final and initial positions, it is not usual to find complete agreement in the intervening phonemes—as *pit: tip, pot: top, put: tup, tick: kit, dog: god*, except in simple three-phoneme groups such as these. The situation seems to be accidental and exceptional. But an initial sequence (CV-) may be reversed exactly (-VC) in the final position, e.g. *coop*:*took*, *pot*:*cop*, p*it*:*ti*ck, p*ut*:*took*, *cop*:*lock*, *bu*d: *tub*, *dig*:*bid*, *bud*:*dug*, *dig*:*give*. In *bib*, *cease* complete reversal makes no difference—the word reads the same both ways. Other examples are *some*:*fuss*, *goose*:*soon*, t*ough*:*fu*ss, *thi*n:p*ith*, *thumb*:bis*muth*, *shu*n:*rush*, *chee*se:*each*, *jui*ce:*huge*, and the like. The limitations on such events are very wide. Word games, ciphers, acrostics, riddles, anagrams, crossword puzzles, 'magic squares', disguised prayers and the like, common in all known languages, all make use of these properties of words.

But when we come to larger clusters of consonants, longer sequences of phonemes, and when we also deal with words of more than one syllable, the limitations become progressively severer. Thus a reverse order may be possible only in initial and final position: *play*:*help*. The clusters *sp*, *st*, *sk* occur unchanged both initially and finally. But these are simple situations. With a highly inflected language like Russian or Latin, and with polysyllabic words, reverse order, though statistically predictable, is unrecognizable, and contrary to the linguistic convention. In English, out of a theoretically possible 11,000 initial three-member consonantal clusters at the beginning of a syllable, only about 40 occur. Of 576 possible combinations of two consonants, only 137 are utilized by the language.

Modern English has no initial clusters of four consonants, finally they are rare and do not occur outside grammatical endings such as *mpst* in *glimpsed* (past), or *ksps*, in *sixths* (plural). Even final clusters of three consonantal members are all formed by adding *s*, *z*, *t*, *d* to possible two-member clusters, that is the usual grammatical endings, which in English are now very few in number. Moreover *s*:*z* and *t*:*d* are positional variants, some finals (e.g. *sh*, *ch*) cannot have *s* or *z* added without the intervention of a vowel (*wash*:*washes*, *church*:*churches*), so that the structural type is very restricted in extent. There are only nine possible three-member clusters initially, and these are formed of *s* followed by possible two-member clusters. Such low efficiency of use must be the effect of restrictions imposed by intelligibility.

The view is gaining ground that rigorous phonematic segmentation has a certain artificiality about it, to which actual perception has nothing corresponding. Articulatory movements are seen to be in rapid transition. The theory of allophones has long pointed the way to such contextual markers among phonemes, and their presence is now suspected among forms and words and arrangements of words.

It seems not impossible that overlap in features belonging to different segments does occur almost as if it were itself a separate element. A mere fraction of the stream of speech is enough every now and then to identify the continuum—since the limitations on what may occur are severe and constantly operative. The contextual rules of exclusion and admission are coded in our memories, as a result of lifelong habit, which behaves like a statistical analysis, and allophones are so to speak statistical averages.

Finally, observe that consonants may be classified according to various degrees of constriction of the vocal tract into three groups. These are written C^1, C^2, C^3; it has been maintained that in a syllable the extreme limit of which is $CCC + V + CCC$, there is in English a normal arrangement in consonant clusters classified thus: $C^1C^2C^3VC^3C^2C^1$ (e.g. *pride* $C^1C^2VC^3C^1$). This indicates that consonantal clusters are highly ordered, and limited in number precisely for this reason.

Just as a phoneme is divisible not into other phonemes, but only into distinctive features, so a morphome is a minimum form, not capable of being analysed into smaller forms, but only into phonemes. But it has a meaning, which a phoneme has not. The morphomes of a language are strictly conditioned by the permissible patterns of that language. Their number is finite, though much larger than that of their constituent phonemes and allophones. Some morphomes occur only as parts of words, e.g. English -*ing* in *loving*, or -*nt*- in Latin *amant-is* (gen. sing.) 'lover, loving,' and these are known as formants. English -*er* in *lover* also occurs independently *err*, but *hammer* and *spider* do not show it. Each language must be described in its own terms. Formants may be repeated or discontinuous in an inflected language, e.g. *feminarum bonarum* 'of good women', a redundancy which English has long since abandoned, but which was necessary to the Indo-European structural type.

To identify the constituents of a formative or syntactic group of words in the continuum of speech is the problem of decoding the molecules and atoms of morphological and syntactic constructs, i.e. permissible orders of arrangements of morphomes, of forms, and of words.

The status of such linguistic elements depends broadly upon their position in relation to all other elements in an utterance. This may be marked, as in English, by the simple order of morphomes in sequence; or, also in English, by other characteristics such as stress, pitch, and juncture; or, in other languages, the status may go unmarked by any of these, as in the syntactic elements of a highly inflected language like Latin, of which a long utterance, a whole period for example, will not be readily understood by a modern reader unless he is familiar with its particular system. The principle of identification turns once more, therefore, upon substitution.

But when it is decided that, for example, *oldwomanish* or *oldmaidish* functions as a unit, the ultimate components (morphomes) of each are discovered by making cuts into two and only two constituents in such a way as to accord with the responses of the language, that is *oldmaid* and *ish*, not *old* and *maidish*, since either of these is a grammatical equivalent; for we must know not only the sequence, but also the ordering of the morphomes. So *ungentlemanly* is analysed *un* and *gentlemanly*, not *ungentleman* and *ly*; but *gentlemanly* is *gentleman* and *ly*, not *gentle* and *manly*, for either of these might be substituted for the whole: He is *gentle*, He is *manly*, He is (*un*)-*gentlemanly*, so far as grammatical function goes.

A similar procedure is used when the frame of reference is an entire phrase. Thus in *He's an elevator operator* we segment at *He's* and at *an*, leaving *elevator operator* as a unit $(A + B)$, but in *He's a big-time operator* the corresponding part of the utterance is analysed as $(a + a^1) + B$. Occasionally the users of a language perform such operations themselves, as when in English we speak of 'the teens'; and so in French or German an analysis is performed automatically by the insertion of words between *ne . . . pas* or *wenn . . . gleich*, both of which are functionally units as much as English *not* (no . . . whit) and *although* (all . . . though). The line of demarcation between morphology and syntax may thus seem fugitive; but in practice a line must be drawn, since otherwise a total unit to be described may become so unwieldy as to be statistically unsatisfactory. Substitution also guarantees the validity of analysis: in $x + $ '*-ly*', x is filled by so many possible alternatives, whether the resultant pattern matches *kindly* (adj.) or *slowly* (adv.), that we do not hesitate to isolate *-ly* as we might in *kindly* as a grammatical substitute for *kind*. But if *-ly* adds nothing (i.e. it is 100 per cent determined), it may disappear, and we commonly read and hear 'go slow', not 'slowly'. Similarly substitution (and agreement) in *man:he:woman:she* identifies these four morphome-words; or *much beer:many beers* gives the morphome *-s* (occurrence in number). Newly discovered inscriptions in ancient languages do not always mark divisions between bounded units (words), and almost never mark morphomes. The writer of this book has several times had to interpret such inscriptions, and even large numbers of them, in dialects of which there existed neither dictionary, grammar, nor commentary. But the analysis proceeded surely, and interpretation followed easily.

We distinguish, as examples, a few characteristic processes in English: (1) compounding, which, as in all languages, is subject to patterned limitations (thus *untruthful*, but *unful(l)* 'empty' does not occur); the following are typical: *upstart*, *sunup*, *he-goat*, *bindweed* (adjective plus noun), *greyhound* (hybrid binominal 'dog-dog'), *chimneysweep* (noun plus verb), *breakfast* (verb plus noun), *hide-and-seek*, *son-in-law*. (2) From these examples of stem + stem, distinguish stem compounded with a bound form, which may be prefix, suffix or infix. Patterns differ enormously from one language to another. Turkish permits only suffixes; Bantu favours prefixes; infixes are common in early Indo-European languages (the *n* in *stand:stood* is a relic of an infix), and such patterns are clearly revealed by analysis as part of the essential structure of the language. Mere indiscriminate addition of a random character does not occur.

A morphome may be no more than a single phoneme, e.g. the final *-s* of English verbs (*he hits*) and nouns in the plural (*books*), or the indefinite article *a*. In order to mark the contrast between the presence and absence of a linguistic element, linguists have invented the device of a 'zero element' (marked 0), thus *he cut*-0 (past tense):*he cut-s*, or *sheep*0 (plural):*sheep* (singular).

Reduplication means repetition of a form, or part of it. It is a characteristic formative device in many early Indo-European languages—the classical Latin *spopondi*, the perfect of *spondeo* 'promise', has plagued many a schoolboy by its reduplication and consequent loss of internal -s- by dissimilation, but late Latin also used *spondidi* with internal reduplication. If an entire word is repeated, like English *dilly-dally*, the existence of the simple form *dally* (but not **dilly*) identifies the underlying form.

In some situations totally different words are used within the system. There is usually a historical explanation for any given example of this phenomenon, known as 'suppletion', e.g. *I go:I went* (Gothic *gang:iddja*, French *je vais:je suis allé: j'irai*, Greek ἔρχομαι present: ἦλθον past: εἶμι future—all meaning 'go'), or *good:better:best, bad:worse:worst* (not yet the schoolboy's *dead*), like Latin *bonus:melior:optimus* and *malus :peior:pessimus*, instead of the 'regular' *true:er:-est* of English or *-ior:-issimus* of Latin comparative and superlative degrees of adjectives. Such complete alternation in a system is a serious modification of the predominant pattern. Less violent disturbances appear in alternations such as *sing:sang:sung*, or *house:to house*, or *safe:save;* or in *ox:oxen, child:children* compared with the usual -s.

Contextual variants also pop up under conditions of morphomatic pattern—like *spo-pondi* above from *spo-spondi*. These contextual variants may become part and parcel of the established pattern, such as German or Turkish, or Mongolian vowel assimilation, or the palatalization of consonants in Russian. Loss of stress in compound English words is a variety of dissimilation e.g. *góld* and *físh*, but *góldfish, mán* and *kínd*, but *mankínd*. The conditions are complex and unsystematized except in pairs such as *cóntract:contráct*, where it is not a question of dissimilation, but of inherited distinctions of stress-pattern, which in this case combine phonematic distinction with morphomatic function. The differentiation of stress in *exécutor* and *execúter* is accompanied by an alternation in the consonant written *x*, viz [gz]:[ks], also an inherited pattern.*

Constituents, especially when in English they are also free forms, regularly imply syntactic functions, e.g. *redcoat* (possessive, the man who has a red coat), *thoroughbred* (adverb plus participle, 'thoroughly bred', i.e. true to line), *cutthroat* (verb

* See Appendix 4

plus object), *bittersweet* ('bitter and yet sweet', i.e. a conjunction
is implied).

Forms are normally associated with a certain function or
functions. Thus in English *man* has the function of actor
('The man bit the dog') or goal ('The dog bit the man'; so
'to the man') or predication ('That is the man'), and the like;
others the function of state ('to be') or of activity ('to enter').
In modern English, older distinctions of form such as Old
English *lufian* 'to love' but *lufu* 'love' have long since been lost;
and now we are able to say 'we cannot stomach' something or
other, and speak of 'a write-up', but in context the different
functions of such forms as *love, stomach, write* and their corresponding meanings, are as clear as ever.

In the permissive orders of arrangements, therefore, each
function may be performed only by certain forms, or by their
substitutes. When all such forms are assembled they make up
a form-class, with its corresponding class-meaning, e.g. English
master, Latin *dominus* and *dominum* etc., *mistress, domina* and
dominam etc., *he* and *him*, Latin *is* and *eum*, *masters* (*domini*),
mistresses (*dominae*), *I*, and *we* (*ego, nos*), *thee* and *you* (*te* and
uos). By combining the meanings of the function and of the
class in each case we discover grammatical categories such as
number (one or more than one), gender (masculine or feminine)
and case (nominative or accusative, corresponding to what was
above called 'actor' and 'goal'). The difference between *is*
and *dominus*, or *eam* and *dominam*, or in English between *he*
and *John* or *her* and *Mary* (say *John loves Mary, he loves Mary,
John loves her*), is simply that the referend of *is, he* etc. is not
disclosed in that particular utterance in which it occurs. Difficulty arises only when there is a sum of categories in a unit
of form, a state of affairs characteristic of inflected languages
such as Latin where in *dominum* the final syllable *-um* belongs
to all three categories of number, gender, and case. It is by
means of contrast (*dominus, domini, domina, dominae*) and of
substitution (*eum:is, eam, ea*) that these facts could be recovered if all the Latin dictionaries and grammars were lost,
or if Latin were a newly discovered language.

It must not be supposed that these grammatical categories
are somehow the counterparts of reality. The concepts are not
truly general beyond certain groups of languages. Grammatical

terminology has been hampered more than helped by its own unsuccessful realism, and it is impossible to give a universal definition of such terms as mood, voice, subjunctive, passive and the rest. In those situations in which a form-class, that is all the forms having the same function or functions, is made up entirely of words, then we have a word-class (e.g. all the nouns, all the adverbs and so on). Such classes of words constitute the several parts of speech of that language.

Morphological analysis is a dangerous tool that sometimes leads to specious but invalid distinctions, as if for example from *pilgrimage:image* a cut were made at *pilgr,* or from *boiling, boy* and *prince* and *princeling,* we should conclude that a morphome *-ling* occurs in *boiling,* or similarly if we should attempt from *boil* and *boiler* to analyse *spider* or *hammer* into *spid-, ham-* and *-er.* Every language has forms whose constituent units overlap, as in *-ling* and *-ing,* but the criteria of substitution and meaning eliminate gross mistakes. So with *first-nighter: fortnight, residential roofer:industrial roofer, Neapolis* (accusative *Neopolim):Neapolitanus* and Greek Νεάπολις: Νεαπολίτης ('Neopolitan') but νέα πόλις 'new city' (accusative νέαν πόλιν), like Latin *iusiurandum* (gen. *iuris iurandi,* abl. *iure iurando): iuris prudentia* (acc. *iuris prudentiam, prudentiam iuris*); English has no *greenhouse: *greenerhouse* or **very greenhouse,* which prevents faulty analysis in the same way. The whole procedure, in morphology as in phonology, may be reduced, in simple terms, to the recognition and classification of same (or similar) and different (or dissimilar) word patterns in a language, with a view to discovering and describing that pattern.

In English it is possible to make a distinction between derivational and relational morphological constructs. Thus a complex form such as *oldwomanish* grammatically might replace any adjective that is unanalysable into morphomes (*young, old, stale, poor, good, bad*) and is said to be derivative by comparison with such simple forms; but a Latin complex form *gradūs,* unlike the complex form *gradŭs,* may not replace a simple form (e.g. *lac* n. sing.) and therefore is said to be relational (gen. sing.)—the relation involves grammatical, as distinguished from lexical, meaning. Thus the adjective *manly* is a derivational, the participle *playing* a relational, form.

Evidently the unit of analysis 'morphome' is a logical or

operational term. No definition of it is desirable or necessary beyond this, though several such have been offered. Selection, and the changes rung upon it, gives a language its character. The initial consonant mutations of Welsh, for example, are in point:

> *i'w tad* 'to his father'
> *i'w thad* 'to her father'
> *i'w dad* 'to their father'

where the alternation *t:þ:d* (radical, spirant, and soft 'mutations') was determined historically by the variant forms of the possessive adjective, that is by the presence of sounds long since vanished; but it is now a matter of decision or selection concerned with variant patterns, not of any morphomes that could be recognized as possessive or as adjectives or pronouns. Irish shows the same syntactical peculiarity, which is characteristic of the Keltic languages, thus *bo* 'cow', but *an vo* 'the cow', *ar mo* 'our cow'. If English has but one 'case' form, used indifferently in all positions of nouns and adjectives, with a few alternants in the pronouns (*I:me*), but Finnish has thirteen; and if English has no true grammatical gender at all (i.e. agreement of endings in the adjective and noun) but Bantu twenty 'gender' classes of nouns (i.e. formal distinctions), Chinese no declension, conjugation, or gender—these also are matters of selection and of consistent application of whatever method has been selected. Languages vary enormously in this respect, in syntax as in all other features. Cree is reported to make nice distinctions of identity of persons or objects by grammatical devices, so that 'he took his hat' has four different varieties of expression depending on whose hat was taken (*A* . . . *A*'s . . ., *A* . . . *B*'s . . ., *B* . . . *A*'s . . ., or *B took B's hat*).

The object in syntax is still to discover the relations between the parts of the expression. A useful scheme is as follows: (*a*) a relation of interdependence, e.g. in an inflected language of the Indo-European type, the morphome of case and the morphome of number, for the one never occurs without the other; (*b*) determination (or unilateral dependence), where one morphome presupposes the other, but not vice versa, e.g. in Latin the preposition *sine* 'without' will be followed by the ablative case, but an ablative is not necessarily preceded by the preposition *sine*; and (*c*) constellation for a looser dependence, in which one item neither excludes nor presupposes another, e.g. Latin accusative and plural number. Of these three relations (*a*) is a function between two constants, (*b*) between a constant and a variable, (*c*) between two variables.

In making an analysis of a text we move to less and less general units, compiling an inventory of those elements which have the same relations, that is can fill the same 'position' in the stream of speech, and between which there is in each case a particular function. The number of elements decreases at each stage from sentences to morphomes, consistently with all procedures of linguistic analysis. But it must be confessed that little progress has been made in the development of the technique of contrasts and comparisons in syntax. Most of the observed units are more easily dealt with either as formal (i.e. morphological) or as stylistic.

The selection of this or that item of vocabulary may be determined by two parallel traditions, as in modern Greek which has for example, both *spiti* (from Latin *hospitium*) and *ikos* (from classical Greek οῖκος), and both meaning 'house', or *khrónos* and *étos* 'year' in the standard spoken and learned usage respectively. Far more promising is the analysis of discourse. In extended discourse we come every now and again to a break in the utterance. This is not a matter of exhaustion, of the physical inability to continue without stopping to take a breath, or of expressing logical predication, or 'complete thoughts'. It is that every language has its own constructs (i.e. repetitive patterns of order) of free-standing, bounded units (words). Those which occur again and again, as on greeting cards, invitations, messages of congratulation or condolence, may be dispatched at very low cost by telegraph, precisely because their pattern is standard. Each sentence is bounded, i.e. it is not part of a larger independent argument. The best definition of a sentence is precisely this, that it is a maximum syntactic construct; or, as an Arab grammarian is said to have put it, a sentence is that after which silence seems best. But there is no limit to a new start. Sentence follows sentence until the speaker or writer chooses to stop. Analysis of what he has said or written extends over the whole, not merely over a single sentence.

Even superficial observation soon reveals certain 'waves' of utterance in identical or similar environments, particularly if a rhythm is repeated in short stretches as in most forms of composition known as 'verse'. Verse turns to continue the rhythm, prose goes straight on with a rhythmical pattern that is less repetitious, more variable, and saved from being completely irregular only by the over-all linguistic pattern. But rhythm apart, it is found that certain strings, e.g. in a recent treatise on economics the string *free enterprise or a controlled economy*, recur in syntactical environments which vary hardly at all in pattern. The author's statements are highly determined, and this would doubtless still be true if his political views were the opposite from what they are. The content varies from one speaker to another, or from one group of speakers to another, but the form is something that is imposed by linguistic structure. Total differentiation of structure rapidly exceeds the limits of intelligibility, and suggests dementia; most systems place a high premium upon a near approach to identity of structure in the interests of communication, but allowance is made, within limits, for increasing structural and functional differentiation in inverse proportion to frequency of usage. A work entitled 'Structural Methods' (in linguistics, and perhaps in any subject matter whatever) is found to consist of excruciating repetition of pattern while enumerating variant detail. Sentences regularly fall into equivalent segments that recur in the same environment, and sets of like segments are limited in number, though the actual segments themselves, if listed separately and counted, would be numerous enough. There is rigorous selection and high determinacy in the pattern of each set, ample variation in the individual units or segments, but not in their types. Certain elements occur regularly in association with others, e.g. transformation of tense in reported as compared with quoted discourse in English, transformation of mood in Greek or Latin in the same grammatical situation, but subjunctive mood only in Latin, in Greek either subjunctive or optative in accordance with the syntactical patterns of that language. The pattern is a matter of historical evolution, that is selected, and it can be traced easily enough. But indiscriminate mixture of tenses or of moods, as the case may be, is rare or non-existant, and editors tend to remove it by 'emendation'. Differentiation of high frequency is a contradiction in terms. Subdivision of

sentences, grouping of words into phrases, grammatical transformations, are all conditioned, therefore, by the pattern of a
particular linguistic status. From the largest practicable units,
i.e. periodic sentences, down to the smallest, such as phrases
consisting of not more than two words, the fundamental process
of analysis is that of segmentation into two and only two units,
then of each of these into two more, and so on, until no further
division is possible; and all on the principle of 'same' or 'different' in the total syntactic constructs*) of the language. For
the speaker and listener alike the coding process is the same—
a building up of utterances, in accordance with the permitted
pattern, and by a principle of binary choices at each step. In
the theory of analysis substitution or commutation are labor-
iously applied; the speaker and listener perform identical operations automatically and unconsciously. The only thing likely
to be overlooked is that the fiction zero (*nil*) is a useful device of
analysis. (See Appendix 5.)

The upshot is that language, notwithstanding all the refinements of analysis, remains a continuum. Phoneme merges into
morphome and morphome into construct, construct into discourse. The continuum extends from speaker to hearer and
thence to the entire speech-community. But the community has
its historical descent linguistically and is itself normally a linguistic ancestor. It is not to be assumed that the language
makes the culture. An entire speech-community working for
generations is needed to make the language as a self-perpetuating system, capable of a status between complete rigidity and
complete fluidity, that dynamic equilibrium on which human
development depends.

Our lines of cleavage are set up for purely analytical and
descriptive convenience, not because they correspond to events,
for they do not. It is not possible for linguists to hand over
phonetics to physics, and meaning to sociology, as some have
proposed, without making structural linguistics utterly sterile,
a risk of which this subject is already in great danger. A linguist's description of a language is of little help in learning
the language; recently published structural accounts of European languages rebut any disclaimers to this judgement.

* A syntactic construct is a construct of words; a construct is a recurring
'same' of order.

Word games like Scrabble, crossword puzzles, alphabet-ciphers, several of which were invented by Lewis Carroll ('Word-Links' 1878, 'The Alphabet-Cipher' 1868 [?], 'Doublets' 1879, 'Mischmasch' 1882 among others) are all based, as was pointed out before, upon a rough-and-ready observation of the facts that linguistic analysis formulates precisely. In modern English only a small percentage (about 7 per cent) of words in use are grammatical markers (the article, prepositions, auxiliaries; words like 'every, all, any'), but their frequency of occurrence varies considerably between standard and popular usage. The latter fails to make good use of the resources of the language, and therefore falls back upon words such as 'and', which it employs nearly twice as often as good standard usage; or 'so', which it uses six times as often. The remaining 93 per cent are nouns, adjectives, verbs and adverbs. There are striking structural ties among these, not very numerous, but far reaching in their applications, pairs such as:

arrival — arrive	big — bigness
deformity — deform	wide — width
óbject — objéct	
mother — she	boy — boys
father — he	man — men
book — it	boy knows — boys know
friend — befriend	dirty — dirt
joy — enjoy	manly — man
strife — strive	bookish — book
dignity — dignify	famous — fame
dogma — dogmatic	confident, confidant — confide
phoneme — phonematic	creative — create
peace — peaceful	loathsome — loathe
faith — faithless	
true — untrue	séparate — separáte
true — false	big — bigger, biggest
more, most beautiful	good — better, best
broad — abroad	fetch — bring
ground — aground	sea — seaward

* These details have been worked out most clearly by C. C. Fries *Structure of English* (New York, 1952), to which I am indebted for the above examples.

and finally a few tied pairs such as *bang shut, blow open, loom large*. Structural observations such as these have proved quite helpful to adult learners of English, and even to native speakers whose acquaintance with their mother tongue is limited and substandard. Contradictory systems at any level may occur among bilingual speakers. An extreme situation exists when a dialect or language is about to become extinct. For example, in the first century of the present era Gaulish was being replaced by Latin and apparently it was possible to say either *equos* or *epos* 'horse', either **srudis* or *frudis* for 'river'.

System underlies linguistic process, but it has its own limiting conditions; the system provides the mechanics. What we all know instinctively of our mother tongue may, therefore, be stated systematically.*

A logical system of grammar which will fit any pattern, ancient or modern, is forecast, and should furnish the proof that linguistic change consists in stabilizing the relations between the members of the system, a theory so far held only empirically. The rules of this logic will put every unit into an appropriate class. In inflected languages the number of options may be large, but none will be impossible. In its descriptive statements, whether Vergil's 'First let me rage out this rage of mine!'

hunc sine me furere ante furorem

is grammatically construed or not, is a matter that will be disregarded, though there are two possible classifications for each of six words, a large total possible misordering; and likewise in French *deux cents* and *cent deux*, whether or not the order is considered significant. Those who wish to know these things will need also to take account of meanings. Even if most of Vergil's contemporaries did not hesitate to regard the words just quoted as a sentence, surely there would be such hesitation over 'Man knew that John was poor a Paul', but not over 'John knew that Paul was a poor man', notwithstanding logical acceptability of either, for *John*, *Paul*, *man* are variables. Nevertheless a promising quasi-arithmetic notation has been proposed in which this particular difficulty of syntactic description has been solved, and others like it. Eventually, no

* See Appendix 6

doubt, special statements will give place to a theory of syntax which will become part of a general theory of language. For language is a constant of human life, like breathing or the beating of the heart, independent of an alleged external reality, and independent of its own fluctuations and variations.

IX

THE NEURAL BASIS OF LANGUAGE

NOTHING is more discriminating than language, which makes its choices almost automatically at every step from phoneme to morphome, more deliberately from word to sentence to paragraph to finished book. But discrimination plays a part in the cultivation of every human activity, through observation, classification, imagination, social and other forms of organization, constructive thought and scientific progress. In what does this power of discrimination and especially linguistic discrimination consist? It is above all a form of consciousness, that awareness of self and environment which is the very stuff of language. Other animals appear to have consciousness, as well as man, and perhaps plants (if not sticks and stones, the ice and snow, the hills and dales that rejoice and clap their hands); but among these their brains are so developed as to leave some forms even of animate creation able to communicate only in such a way that we do not perceive the full details of their communication with one another. More is known about the communication of insects (especially of ants and bees), and of fish; and there is no doubt that vertebrates in general are not greatly different from man. The technique of electroencephalography indicates that in sleep the ryhthm of the alpha waves in the brain becomes long and slow. It is suggested, on the basis of experimentation with animals, that in sleep stimuli from the outside world are hardly reaching the brain and that reverberating circuits from the thalamus at the base of the brain to the cerebral cortex (see the accompanying diagram) are in abeyance, with the result that the discriminating awareness of waking hours is greatly reduced. In particular, the sensation of sight is suspended and those of hearing and smell reduced; there is a general unawareness of the stimuli which provoke speech

149

until the sleeper is aroused. Talking in your sleep is abnormal and not completely successful. One of the foremost authorities

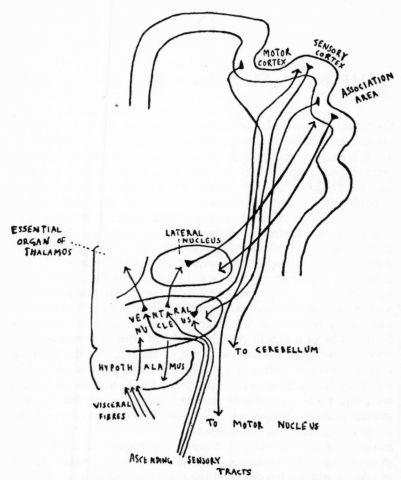

Diagram of Thalamic, Hypothalamic, and Cortical
Connexions of the Human Brain
(after Campion and Elliot-Smith)

describes consciousness as a 'function of nervous tissue in action' and believes that it will sooner or later be described in terms of electronic activity.

What we know is common property which has been perceived, observed, collected, and classified by millions of sets of senses and nervous systems and handed down through thousands of years, generation after generation, increasing in volume by fresh additions step by step. Such an accumulation of experience is peculiar to the human race—each generation of which need not start exactly where every previous generation started, but does learn, slow as it is in learning what to discard and what to adopt from its new adventures, especially when those new adventures come fast upon one another in bewildering shock, as during the exciting epoch in which we live. But the accumulated bulk, such as it is, would have been impossible without some means of fashioning, exchanging and transmitting information. That means is language. It is chiefly, if not entirely, due to the perfection of this instrument that man has taken his present place in the animal kingdom. Animals have a restricted power of transmitting and calling up impressions of limited kinds, but this is distinguished from speech by the total absence or undeveloped character of differentiation, pattern and convention, by which meaning is attached to spoken or written symbols. But how? It is this element of symbolism and convention that effects the enormous increase in the power of arriving at and transmitting intelligence. But how? No wonder if this tremendous achievement, for good and evil, has been repeatedly ascribed the world over to superhuman intervention; even if we were to imagine such a beginning, there still would be grave difficulty in accounting completely for the development and transmission of languages as solely a matter of stimulus and response, once the procedure had been given. A modern story of Babel is not enough.

Everything man knows has come to him from outside during his whole existence through the medium of the familiar five senses of touch, smell, vision, hearing, and taste, which link us to the external world. To these it would appear that a sixth sense should be added, the sense of equilibrium, which not only gives us a confident feeling of partaking effectively in the outside world, like the other five, but contributes to an internal regulatory or discriminatory power. The capacity for selection, for making binary choices, for adhering to a pattern while at the same time manipulating its infinite possibilities of individual fluctuating fabric, clearly enters at some point in human evolution.

When a person speaks he uses, besides his lungs, to provide a current of breath and voice, his tongue and his teeth and his lips, among other organs. These are intimately concerned with the sense of taste, and were so long before the human brain had reached that stage in its evolution at which a tentative link between sound and significance was formed, or could be repeated again and again independently of a fresh confrontation with the identical external situation. Again the sense of hearing plays its part, for the deaf are at great disability when it comes to learning to talk. It is now thought that the hairs in the inner ear may well function to serve as something rather like minute antennae in picking up the vibrations of impinging sound waves which are then carried along nerve fibres to the brain. The most recent theory of hearing accords well with what we know of the mathematical properties of linguistic structure.

But we use also our noses for talking (nasalization), and not merely to smell something to talk about: certain phonemes depend on passing through the nasal as much as through the buccal cavity. Smelling is a complicated process involving nose and brain, and discrimination once more is concerned with patterns or recognizable configurations and linkages in the neurons of the brain. Physically the sense of smell has been ascribed to controls exercised by the inhibition of certain enzymes contained in the olfactory organs. Here again is system, a system causally linked to discriminatory nerve signals so that complex odours are perceived and distinguished. Be that as it may, and although indeed we no longer smell our way through the world, the highly organized power of olfactory perception and discrimination implied is entirely in accord with cerebral activity not in principle different, or at the cortical level dissociated, from what is believed basically to underly the processes that go on in subvocal speech.

When you read or write you use the sense of vision in a discriminatory way, and at the same time the muscular activity of the hand, which plays an overwhelmingly large part in the sense of touch. Touch also is highly discriminatory, and perceptive of a great variety of qualities that can hardly be appreciated effectively or 'manipulated' without linguistic labels.

One grapheme is distinguished from another, even more obviously than one phoneme from another, and a whole string of them in a patterned sequence is grasped and understood by eye in this way. The blind are especially skilful in tactile discriminatory power, and the deaf too can feel, and in a way 'hear', what you say with the help of unusually sensitive fingers. Ability to comprehend qualities of depth, i.e. three-dimensional vision, is a property peculiar to the human eye; experiments are being made in newly hatched chicks, fitted with spectacles, that promise new discoveries about the ability of organisms, through their nervous systems, to see objects and determine whether they are near or far. These experiments may teach us whether this capacity is innate or not, and how it functions. Already it appears that the mechanism of vision is quite comparable to that of hearing in the way in which both of these senses discriminate, as they transmit, impulse by impulse, the stimuli that are interpreted as hearing and sight respectively. A linguist approaches these matters with hesitation. But he interprets spectrograms in a similar manner, and feels encouraged to believe that units comparable to words, and strings of such units, are credible segments of information that are being fed in succession into the network of nerves in the human organism and returned again, while we act successively and indifferently as speakers and hearers, readers and writers. So far as spoken words and sentences are involved, there is also under close automatic control and measurement, by the organism, the mechanism of respiration, between the patterns of which, and those of spoken language, there may turn out to be a relation not so remote or unsystematic as superficial inspection might indicate. The whole is co-ordinated and controlled by elaborate selective and discriminatory functions that we must believe were built up, presumably by trial and error, through the long ages of human evolution and are now inherited at birth ready for individual development in infancy and childhood. At all events, all this is a physiological and neurological matter, not something transcendental or totally inaccessible.

Talking is a skill acquired with no small difficulty, perhaps the hardest thing a human being ever accomplishes, from the moment of birth to the day of his death. It is an activity, like all others, controlled by the brain, a capacity that evolved step

by step with the evolution and development of the human
brain as well as of the human larynx and total anatomical
structure of man's mouth, of his vision and his peculiar powers
of perceiving and appreciating the infinitely varied properties
of nature that lie around him, and of making abstractions from
these events and from their features; it is a means of classifying,
designating, recalling and pro-presenting them to himself and
to his fellows. The peculiar disposition of the human brain
lies behind all this. The problem of how and why we talk at
all is a neurological one (and psychological, in regard chiefly
to some of the upsets that interfere with an established ability
to talk), a problem to be resolved and understood through the
workings of our complex nervous systems, the linkage of our
vocal organs, our sensory organs and muscular activity into
one complex, highly co-ordinated whole which accommodates
itself to our past and present experiences and their consequences. If one were completely informed of all these factors
in a given person at a given moment, it would be possible to
predict whether he would say anything at all, and what he
would say.

Clinical evidence is abundant to prove that damage to the
brain brings with it damage to the capacity for and control of
language. Thus lesions along the nerve trunks entering the base
of the brain, or of nuclei in the hindbrain, may paralyse, if
only temporarily, muscles of the lips, larynx, and tongue which
are innervated from this source, and, if the paralysis is limited
to one side of the face, produce a blurred enunciation, if on both
sides of the face complete inability to articulate. Disturbances
of the functioning of the same organs may also be produced
by lesions at a somewhat higher level, including that of the
lower brain (cerebellum). These are (1) disturbances of articulation and (2) poor or disordered co-ordination of the vocal
organs, which shows up as lack of rhythm, monotonous, ex-
plosive, singsong, and staccato speech, not, however, in these
cases accompanied by paralysis.

But when the levels of the brain cortex are affected, and
especially the association, sensory, and motor areas (see the
accompanying diagram), and when vision and hearing are also
involved, there is a loss or impairment of recognition—in the
broadest terms of 'knowing'—and of that power of symbolism

which makes possible linguistic meaning by means of convention as a tie between spoken units (in their proper sequences)
and referends (i.e. that which they symbolize). Recent observations made on the human cortex during operations undertaken
to alleviate or cure specific conditions have made it possible to
ascertain with some precision just what areas of the cortex
are involved in certain disabilities of speech, such as failure to
recognize spoken words or their meanings, or to recall them and

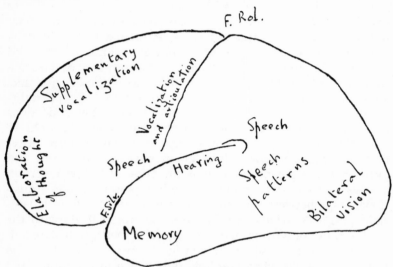

Diagram showing principal cortical areas
(after Penfield)

so express them. Or there may be a visual instead of an auditory
lack of recognition. One form of incapacity is the sheer inability
to 'remember' just how to make the vocal organs work, even
though the subject may know perfectly what he wants to say;
another to understand written or printed words. This latter is
a serious disability, because language is normally acquired and
perfected and used through a constant co-ordination of vision,
hearing, and speaking in association with objects, symbols, and
meanings, so that without co-ordination the names of things
are lost. Some subjects lose the power to put sentences together
and hence to utter any complex notion. Temporary derange-
ments of the brain caused by poisoning, alcohol, or extreme

fatigue are apt to show concomitant disorders of language, which disappear when the causes are removed.

It is well known that the specialization of the *right* hand over the left is accompanied by dominance of the *left* hemisphere of the brain over the right; and this, the more usual state of affairs, is believed, on good evidence, to be a product of the evolutionary steps which led at once to the peculiarities of human binocular vision and of symbolic capacity as it manifests itself in language and the arts. Inheritance obviously plays a major role not only in this more usual organization, but also in the percentage of cases, estimated to be about 25 per cent, where the specialization and dominance are reversed or but incompletely established. It is, however, at large, a right-handed world in which we live, with implements like scissors, golf clubs and suchlike built for use by the right-handed, and insistence on writing and reading linguistic signs in one way and one only—left to right, top to bottom, right to left, as the case may be. Exceptions, as in some ancient documents in which alternate lines go in opposite directions, and even have the posture as well as direction of letters reversed, are few and far between and probably represent a brief transitional stage between an older right-to-left and the later left-to-right practices, which certainly has something to do with the kind and use of writing materials as well as with right-handedness: it is easier to see what you have already done if you go from left to right when you hold only a pen in the right hand than when you hold a chisel in the left as well as a hammer in the right, and there is some danger of smearing the ink in the former case unless you do go left to right.

But if the neural activity is not definitely established in favour of one or the other practice, then there is hesitation over words of more than one syllable and reversal of those orders of phonemes that can be reversed and still give a word in the language concerned like *pot:top*. If the reversal is only partially possible, as in *bud:tub* it becomes even more obvious that something is wrong, and it is now so good as certain, from the evidence of electroencephalograms made of stammerers and normal speakers, that the stammerer's trouble arises in the first place from confusion of direction in phonematic and graphematic order both, the neural impulses being themselves contradictory when there is pronounced lack of cerebral dominance. The controlling statistical averages, and their necessary leadership in routing innervations, are disturbed and confused, or lack a sure capacity to perform their 'switching' operations. This is probably the fundamental reason why orders of arrangement in language are not reversible except in a small minority of short words, and not at all in whole sentences.

As time goes by the difficulty may become aggravated through the psychoneurotic condition it has itself helped to create. If the subject can be trained to fix his 'directions' in a chosen hemisphere, there is some prospect that use and habit will become stable and permanent, and the trouble alleviated or even removed, especially if emotional strain can be avoided. An ability so complex as the power of language, so definitely co-ordinated with a variety of other and equally complex functions, is easily upset and may become for a time altogether inhibited. Insufficient attention has been paid so far to the imperative need of equilibrium for its effective functioning. In the disorder known as Ménière's disease, in which the sense of equilibrium, without which everyday life cannot be carried on with success or even comfort, is impaired, there is damage to the inner ear, where the sense of equilibrium is located. Hearing and talking go together, and impairment or poor functioning of hearing cannot but affect an activity which is known to be subject to a statistical regularity, and to have equilibrium of pattern and order. Speech activity and speech disorders, in their simplest aspect, are cerebral activity and cerebral disorders. A highly abstract concept, even if it can be 'realized' (which is doubtful) without speech, certainly cannot be communicated without its corresponding linguistic symbol. Habits of responding verbally have wrought over long thousands of years a total transformation in the relation between perception and conceptualization which is hardly to be understood or explained except in terms of the organization of the human nervous system and, above all, of the human brain for the purposes of speech.

Language is a signalling system made up of ordered successions of noises, tones, transitions, pauses and other features; it is now an articulated (i.e. jointed) phonation, though originally simple and reflex, that has become, under the influence

of social organization, relatively independent of the precise
conditions of utterance, that is it can be and constantly is
abstracted from time, place and circumstance, shows a high
degree both of differentiation (e.g. in phonemes, morphomes,
words and their combinations), and of conventionalization—
'meaning' is not a natural, but a learned and acquired manifestation. This is so in everyday discourse as well as in the
imaginative or constructive pro-presentation of poetry, fiction,
law, religion, and science; it is what makes even deliberate
lying and misrepresentation possible, to the extent that it is
hard to see how pro-presentation would be possible without
these 'distortions' of language. The one is a concomitant of the
other, misrepresentation the price we pay for pro-representation
and for the very possibility of taking new steps instead of
being imprisoned at the far end of a 'dead-end' street where
everything might be 'just so', but would stay 'just so' to all
eternity. Even scientific advance is often made through error,
and truth wrested from mistake.

But modern methods of mass communication have greatly
magnified the dangers inherent in conscious and deliberate
misrepresentation. The voice from afar, over radio or television, has a mystic and even magic quality which the half-
educated seem unable to resist. It may any day be impossible
to challenge a voice that will sound familiar and authentic,
but will for all that be only synthetic, and will proceed from
unverified and unverifiable sources, at the very moment of
uttering instructions or commands that normally ought not to
be disobeyed. Here is a new peril in winged-words, swift as
light, and hitting their mark with a vengeance. Language has
always functioned in the dark of night as well as in the daylight,
but here is a new kind of darkness.

Pro-presentation is the most striking feature of all in language. By this term is meant the displacement or detachment of
language from external circumstances or experience. One may
know, through linguistic symbolism, what a 'house of ill-fame'
or a 'brothel' is without ever having been in there, just as a
man may know what the ocean is and have spent every moment
of his life in Nebraska or Kansas, or a rhinoceros or giraffe
without having seen either one; I may be in my garden planting
tulips and talking about the nature of God, or about immortal-

ity. There is no necessary connexion between what I am doing and why I speak or what I am saying: a self-starting or trigger mechanism will set me off altogether independently of where or with whom I may be. Moreover I must talk in the conventions of some particular *language*. A dog, a highly domesticated animal accustomed to living with man, that yet has acquired habits of conduct nothing like so complex or integrated as those of a young child, does not usually bark without something to bark about; and wild animals are even much more discreet about making a noise. Besides, a dog does not bark in English in the United States and in French in France, German in Germany. There is no such convention about the noises he makes, very little differentiation among them as compared with the phonematic distinctions in language, and even those of a vague character devoid of any true pro-presentation. He whimpers if hurt, but he does not name his hurt, or talk about his surgical operations. In fact he understands and commands his world far more by smell and hearing than either by vision or by barking. The features that mark true linguistic communication simply are not there.

In time, as well as in space, language spans great distances. Your morning paper, or a public lecture, will present to you excavations carried on in Egypt or Mesopotamia and a reconstruction of life as it was lived five thousand years ago, five thousand miles away. Or instead you will read a verbal anticipation of events to come, a five-year or seven-year plan, or a scheme for flight to the moon. Neither Ulysses' dog nor Darwin's performed such feats of prediction, or of recall of the past, as these linguistic acts imply. At the same time language is liberating in another sense, both for the individual, upon whom it confers an individuality and power of self-expression and even, if he should be so gifted, of the expression of his own new thoughts or discovery or invention; and also for society as a whole, to which it gives the medium for making plans of new and long-range developments. A township that proposes to build a new road could not organize its plans and blueprints, let its contract or engage its engineer with his crew of men, without language. The only restriction imposed is that the language must function within its own orderliness and its own pattern. Otherwise social organization would be so restricted as to be totally different in character from what we know, and individuals would get their food, clothing, and shelter, if at all, in a very difficult way and in very meagre supply.

Thus language is substituted for a direct perceptual context of wider extent, of the whole horizon and of everything within it, of continents and oceans. The vital force is vocal symbolism, the semantic aspect of speech, whether informative or dynamic, affective or emotive; the capacity for understanding the deepest meanings of words and, comprehensively, of whole theories. This present discussion is part of it, and all the arguments of politicians and the logicians, the artistry of mathematicians and poets, the brilliant expositions of scientists. True intellection rests upon the richness and instantaneousness of waking consciousness, that unites into one controlled linguistic entity the mechanism of lungs and lips and ears and brain in active communication between man and man, a record and successful recombination of experience of, and intuition into, those things that need to be expressed and understood. Language is the vehicle of law, education, philosophy, the sciences, government, of all our human affairs and our conduct of them; the great peril is that these, or any of them, degenerate into a rigidly fixed set of mere speech-habits.

A moment's consideration will show how deepseated is the element of convention. There is nothing in the mere phonematic sequences *horse, cheval, Pferd, equus,* or *misatim* that they should all mean the same object; that is something which the speakers of English, French, German, Latin, or Cree are respectively agreed upon as a matter of habit and convention. The real problem is how they come by such a habit. This is not a matter merely of linguistic history: *equus, ἵππος, aśva-, aspa-, aihwa, ech, eb(-ol), eoh, ἴκκος, yuk, ecco,* and *eppo,* to name no others, can all be shown to have come by regular processes of development from a postulated **ek̂u̯o-s* 'horse'. The problem is how did convention arise at all, even in the most limited sort of way, in the first place? And how were the utterance and its referend, once established, kept in association? The subsequent development of hosts of new meanings of a symbol and loss of old ones, new utterances, new referends, new conventions would seem to have been a relatively easy matter once the first step had been taken. This is not idle curiosity or speculation. It is the question of how man, though he be as frail as dust, has become the lord of creation; and, more important, of how he may so order his ways as to make them pleasing at least in his own sight and that of his fellow man, if not of God. The linguistic symbol is a power in its own right. Without it each man jack of us would still be less than a Robinson Crusoe before he met Man Friday. As things now are he can react to his own subvocal stimuli through a chain of cerebral events, do something about a problem more than merely shout or utter a cry; he can even exhibit originality; and he can associate steadily with his fellows and yet not lose his own individuality. Hardly less remarkable is the way in which language comes in an unpremeditated flow, word after word, and sentence after sentence, and normally in obedience to the established types of phonemes, morphomes, words, and sentence structure, in perfectly articulated phonation or in its graphic (i.e. written) surrogates. Memory covers many different things, but language is one of them, perhaps the most important of all. Recent study of memory reveals here also cerebral activity, with a neural basis.

This study of memory defines it as 'the modification of behaviour by experience', a definition more than broad enough to cover linguistic behaviour, and especially the flow of speech which comprehends both contemporary alternations and re-groupings, of sounds, morphomes, and words, and historic lingu-istic changes, that is changes in a system which itself partici-pates both in producing the changes and in regulating the product. Memory is a condition of intelligent behaviour in the present as well as the more or less simple recall of the remote and intervening past and the anticipation of the future. It operates through the linguistic categories of tense, aspect and spatial relations, or their equivalents. It shows a curious selecti-vity of its own, which infers the capacity to record, to re-member, to recognize, and to put to use whatever 'impact' an event or events have left behind them, events linguistic or non-linguistic, even as small and brief as a phoneme or group of phonemes regarded as units of 'information' occupying but a fraction of a second, and yet accumulated, as it were, in vast numbers, estimated to be far larger than the total number of nerve cells in the brain. There are also to be considered the

facts of latent and activated memory, and of partial or complete 'erasure', of forgetting. Moreover memory traces may be
modified, as in the apperceptive processes of language learning,
in which first impressions are augmented and corrected by
subsequent knowledge; memory is both constructive and associative, the latter over long lapses of time. I never pass a
brewery without remembering the smell of my grandmother's
stone-flagged kitchen on brewing day, a place which I have
not visited for half a century, and that despite the fact I have
forgotten much that happened there, and practically all that
ever was said there.

There is a mathematical theory of the behaviour of nerve
networks that promises well to account for memory as the
result of the effects produced by cerebral activity upon neurons,
and which is compatible with a current theory of language as
statistically regulated. There is also valid evidence for the cerebral localization of specific kinds of memory—visual, aural,
vocal—which are not without bearing on memory for language.
In any event it is a tenable hypothesis that memories are no
more static than language itself, but plastic under the influence
of the passage of neural impulses, and especially may be
established at synapses, the gaps between the ends of nerve
fibres over which the impulses leap, thus creating patterned
pathways which might well be accomodated to the manifold
permutations and combinations of linguistic units, and to the
changes which occur in the uses to which these are put, the
additions and losses to which they are subject. The analogy
of electron beams scanning the face of a television camera tube
has been invoked; in fact the electrical activity of the brain
of living animals has been picked up experimentally as visible
light and shade, leading to the discovery, in the living brain,
of travelling forms, shapes, or figures, corresponding to stimuli
entering the brain through the sensory organs. The apparatus
devised for these experiments functions like a crude television
set, turning electrical brain waves into visible light and shade.
There is something like a rough and ready parallel with communication theory: responses to sound, for example, look in
these pictures like twin peaks that become a single peak as
they travel rapidly over part of the brain. Spontaneous figures
also appear, just as language is a self-starting activity which

triggers itself; these are regarded as parts of still larger figures which arise and expand and then fade away, like a spoken sentence. They have been observed in those parts of the cortex associated with the function of language, notably the visual and sensory-motor areas. Glow lamps connected with amplifiers, and electrodes placed on the brain of an animal are used in these experiments; one may think of a fluctuating pattern of lights in a large city going on and off, as the cerebral impulses travel over the networks of nerves in response to stimuli which evoke or are evoked by an experience, such linguistic experience being either vocal and external or subvocal and internal.

Mention should be made of new mnemonic contrivances, small flat ferro-electric crystals, which are capable of retaining a large number of binary units of information and which, it is suggested, may be put to use in decreasing the size of telephone switching systems or of contrivances requiring electronic storage of information, such as the machines now employed for mathematical calculations, or machines which are already being foretold that will perform translation mechanically. The binary code for feeding information to these crystals is in the form of infinitesimal positive and negative electric charges, and it is not astonishing to hear that words and sentences also can be memorized by them, for the principle of binary, yes-or-no, choices in language behaviour is now something more than merely an attractive theory of language structure that owes everything to current information theory.

We have said that there is a paradox in language: it is daily both an age-long tradition and a new starting point, both stable and variable; its meanings are in part what you bring to it. It functions effectively through the alternation of input and output, but it behaves in the individual also as if it had an internal circulatory system of its own. Actually there have been dissected out fibres that circulate neural impulses between the cortex of the brain and the thalamus (a mass of nervous matter at the threshold of each cerebral hemisphere), through which ascending and descending nerve fibres pass. Sensory impressions, including those of language itself, spoken or written, are transmitted through the thalamus to the motor and association areas of the cortex, and the impulses which activate the vocal organs in speech, or the hand and fingers in writing, are returned from the cortex through the thalamus. They may, so to speak, be short-circuited in reverie or subvocal speech. If they are not activated or not fully activated, whether internally or not, things remain subconscious, or on the fringe of attention, on the tip of the tongue and escape us; brought into the focus of attention, they become articulate, activated, clothed in words and are recalled to consciousness in verbal symbols. Beliefs, conviction, abstraction—concepts like the famous triad of the good, the true, the beautiful—seem to be built up in this way, symbolically linked in discourse and conversation with their corresponding referends, and developed throughout life, to and beyond physical maturity. This implies an intimate correlation of the appropriate areas of the cortex with various skills such as reading and writing, listening and talking. It appears not to be a question of 'mental images', or even of engrammatic patterns or traces, but rather of neural impulses travelling along networks of paths and switching points that correspond to the statistical properties of language itself. The nerve cells of the brain 'fire'—or fail to 'fire'—impulses which by their very activity both build up and modify structural patterns for subsequent use, a dynamic process which nevertheless operates over enduring but 'plastic' structural traces, reinforced by repeated stimuli and impulses. There is, admittedly, much that is bold in this hypothesis, but it is highly plausible in the light of structural linguistics, and even more of mathematical and statistical theories of language.

The statistical or 'probabilistic' hypothesis satisfies the requirement that the brain has been capable of growing this way, as a self-organizing construct in which linguistic elements function deterministically even though the detailed interconnexions do not. It must have the capacity to direct its own performance in accordance with its own success or failure, by trial and error, in accordance with the relative probabilities of language patterns, that are not hard and fast but, within limits and especially with the passage of time, variable. Every time the 'trigger' mechanism is 'fired' successfully it modifies itself. The theory is that the network, by means of the activities that play over it, signals automatically to itself in such a way as to remake the probability statistics of its recurrent patterns. This is not unlike the structure of *language*, its hierarchy of abstractions and their outward symbolic manifestation. Science and philosophy thus become, as it were, a continual correction of language, keeping it 'up-to-date'; but language itself is continually subject to change in all its features, meaning included. It is not reproduced from generation to generation, but only imitated. Over long periods of time the accumulated effect is obvious—President Eisenhower does not talk a bit like King Alfred, though he may appear to talk exactly like his father, grandfather, or great-grandfather. The linguistic term is no more static than the network of neurons and their synapses; even scientific discourse, much as it would like to be able to do so, does not presuppose complete stability in language. Every year yields, if not of new structure, a harvest of new words, some of which survive and pass into wide usage.

Linguistic units, whether regarded as the stimuli (to the listener), or the product of the cerebral activity (in the speaker) are capable of extremely complicated, but not random, groupings; of variable grammatical configurations or lexical symbolization; and, as centuries go by, of thoroughgoing repatterning.*

Infants are born literally just that—speechless, not able to speak. A child is ready to learn to speak only when the cerebral cortex begins to function. The necessary mechanisms are preformed at birth, but they have not yet become, so to speak, organized: no pattern has been built into them, and learning to speak (for a child) is actually learning part of the child's environment, of the world and of life about him, not as an end in itself but as a means to accomplishing many specific ends.

Neurons are all-or-nothing 'firing' devices, which either transmit an impulse or are completely inactive. The brain's orders come chiefly from the outside world through sensory organs, being transformed into electrical pulses of particular identifying ranges—in the case of sounds from 10 to 400 pulses per second. The neurons perform their computations on such a basis, but in the binary system (which uses the digits 1 or zero, like 'yes' or 'no'); and they constitute a network comparable say to those of intersecting streets by which we can locate addresses in a strange city. Coded positions are located by a process similar to that of mathematical integration, automatically and at high speed. Every linguistic form has its position. But linguistic

* See Appendix 7

processes involve far more complex circuits than those of simple reflexes, and in particular involve the discrimination of differences and extraction of similarities. For such a purpose the neurons are arranged in loops around which signals circulate and may be 'remembered', firing one another in succession around the loop back to the first cell where the cycle is started anew on its next round.

Now the most primitive of human creatures had evolved a crude but effective manual skill, dependent upon a delicately adjusted stereoscopic vision—the power of focusing the eyes on one place, which uses just the kind of cerebral activity we have been describing. Such a skill, and others like it, and eventually any form of higher experience, could only have been imparted to the members of a community, and especially to the dependent young, with the help of a close correlation of nervous and muscular control through the organs of hearing and utterance, however rudimentary the tie between symbol and referend, or however simple and concrete the latter. But even the most restricted kind of speech of this sort reinforces the procedure or pattern in which other forms may be substituted for a particular utterance; and, by repetition, also reinforces itself once it has become conventionalized and detached from the event—as is the case of an infant learning to talk. It is the direct outcome of an emergent and evolving human organism.

Upright posture had a profound effect upon the vocal apparatus in such a matter as getting the tongue away from the larynx, which is important for the production of human differentiated speech-sounds; and upon the possibility of encouraging single-handedness. Perhaps the use of the right hand was favoured at first by mere accident, and then widely copied by imitation; but specialization, say in holding an object in the left hand while fashioning it with the right, would have the consequence of setting up dominance of the left hemisphere. Again binocular vision is possible only with a brain structure such as man has, in which the 'neopallium', a small region over the lower brain, has grown into the entire cortex of the greatly enlarged human brain. The visual, motor, association and other areas together, bringing in increased and more acute experiences, seem to have encouraged the evolution of a necessary means of communicating the rudimentary discrimination made by mankind in his new three-dimensional observations, observations of qualities such as shape, size, form, texture (now that his hands also were liberated), distance and relative position that can hardly be conceived as capable of being dealt with effectively, 'handled' so to speak, at this stage otherwise than by overt, detached, expression, in short by symbolization in sound, the physical mechanism for which was at the same time becoming available. The co-ordination of visual and aural impressions with motor control of mouth, tongue and lips, all linked by circulatory neural impulses through the thalamus, puts to use the seeing eye, the accommodating tongue and latitudinarian ear—which is what they still are, all at the service of the understanding mind and active fingers, bringing also the hand under the control of the eye in ever more skilful drawing that culminates in pictographs and ideograms, and at last in true syllabic and alphabetic writing. The development of the human brain is the outcome of perfecting this co-operation of hand and eye, of ear and tongue: we end by talking our way through life. The refinement of our intellectual discrimination still has a long way to go, but it has come a tremendous distance already from the relatively simple association of tactile impulses from the lips and tongue—those speech organs again—with olfactory and gustatory impressions, giving rise for example to vague but remembered notions of how something smells if it is to be safe and satisfying to eat, or of where water is to be found. This was done in the tiny area of the neopallium as a receptor for impulses of taste and smell; and thence has evolved the cortex in all the vertebrate animals. There was thus already the power to control the lips and tongue; the development of the association area seems to have come next. The limbs, tails, horns and mouths of modern animals, like their legs and feet, have been adapted to the performance of relatively few specific acts. The human mouth, tongue, teeth, lips and throat are in a different category, being more generalized—they are used not solely for seeing, holding, tearing and devouring food, but also for producing differentiated speech sounds and for their combinations into symbolic vocables.

It is not necessary to travel to Europe, where a language map resembles a patchwork quilt, to be aware of differences of language types—German and Hungarian, Basque and Spanish.

Even within the United States the contrast between English and Paiute, for example, is startling enough. Usually an American need not trouble himself much about the strange contrasts of, say, Chinese or Korean habits of speech and his own. It is only since 1941 that events have compelled the attention of thousands of young American men toward such matters. If any of these have paused in the learning of Japanese or Tagalog or Malay or Russian or what not, long enough to reflect upon the structural differences of English and the Far Eastern or Southeast Pacific or Eastern European language, or whatever it was they were learning to talk, there was excited in them the same sort of wonder that gave rise to the legend of the Tower of Babel and similar stories in other traditions. It happens that the Hebrew fable is known best to most of us through our religious inheritance, but it is far from being unique.

But there is a far more striking structural feature common to all known languages, past and present. This is what I have called, since about 1941, *selective variation*. The gradual development of this theory has come about with the growth of two new approaches to linguistic study during the last quarter century. These are (1) structural analysis; and (2) statistical investigation, which has recently been carried further than before by telephone engineers, working with the sharp mathematical tools of classical probability and mechanical statistics. The theory of selective variation brings the knowledge obtained in these disciplines into harmony with descriptive, historical, and comparative linguistics, and at the same time provides a satisfactory account of the origin of linguistic types; perhaps even of the origin of language itself. Finally, we are now in a position to predict, given data over a sufficiently long period of time, the course which a language is following; and also to see that reverse predictions are possible. Indeed, there are some striking illustrations of such predictions that were subsequently confirmed by the discovery, in archaeological explorations, of languages, or of linguistic forms, long since extinct; that encourage the hope that we may apply the new theory to retrograde as well as to direct prediction with confidence.

Structural analysis teaches us that all language is selective; for if it were not so, no language could be intelligible. Of the sum total of possible human speech-sounds and their permutations and combinations, only a small submultiple appears in a given language, and even this does not exploit fully its potential range. If we were limited to the perpetual use of one sound only, that would be no better than an infant cry, or the bleating of a sheep; if we could freely utter a different one every time we opened our mouths, that would be the gibberish of the congenital idiot. Again in morphology, it is selection, and the changes rung upon it, that give a language its character. Mutation in the Keltic languages is now merely a matter of selection concerned with alternative meanings. Of the three structural types, isolating, agglutinating, and inflecting, and of their analytic, synthetic and polysynthetic subdivisions, any dialect or language selects, so to speak, certain features or procedures, and uses them consistently. This is assumed as an axiom, to be absolutely true, for descriptive purposes, by all students of language; even historically the axiom is suspended only in the sense that one congruous type may come historically to be displaced by a different—but, within itself, still congruous—type.

So too in syntax and in vocabulary, there is a selective limitation in any given language or dialect, accompanied by a corresponding diversity as compared with other languages or dialects. Without the former, that is with entire freedom of choice, no two people would have the habit of making the same decision or choice of saying any one thing more than once; without the latter, that is with no diversity, everybody would forever talk alike—but after the manner of poultry, not of human beings. In sounds, forms, structure, syntax, and vocabulary, that is to say in all its features, together with their corresponding meanings, every language is selective. Hence I conclude that language strives toward equilibrium, a conclusion confirmed by 'information theory', and by the mathematical theory of communication.

Historical linguistics teaches us that language is forever undergoing change. But the changes are regular. A phonematic substitution, that is the substitution, in a given language or dialect, of one phoneme or speech-sound for another, not being due to borrowing or to external influence, has no exceptions, provided that the statement of it is completely and accurately formulated.* Relative frequency plays a major role

* See Appendix 8

here, once a linguistic substitution is initiated. A pattern once
established, if historic change disturbs it—this is variation—
then selection sets to work toward, and eventually reaches a
new pattern. So that the variation is selective. This is true of
all languages that have been examined from the historical and
descriptive (i.e. structural) points of view.

Now come the communications engineers with their mathematical proof not merely of statistical regularity in language,
again striving toward equilibrium, but with evidence that the
probabilities of choice in the successive speech elements in
modern English and other languages, as well as in other 'continuous information sources that have been rendered discrete
by some quantizing process' obey a precise formula. In other
words, we have to deal with a situation in which there is a
tendency of the system 'to become more and more perfectly
shuffled', i.e. regular.

Language, the reader will recall, is a system of like or partly
like recurrent vocal features, together with their corresponding
meanings; it is also a systematic symbolism, which a logician
might like to replace by a still more rigorous symbolism; to a
mathematician it is a 'stochastic' process, i.e. it generates a
controlled sequence of symbols from a finite set. Selective
variation at once suggests an analogy with biological evolution.
This is rather superficial. Language is not an organism. But
it is a form of behaviour of the human organism; and it represents a form of adaptation of certain human organs to specific
ends. Languages yield under the pressure of external forces,
and either die out or are adapted to the new environment.
The fingers that reduce them to writing, as well as the vocal
organs that utter them, are products of evolution that unite
in man both the toolmaking and the talking beast.

The tales in which the birds and beasts talk to one another,
or to their mere distant human kindred, are charming, all the
way from the Sanskrit *Panchatantra* down to Uncle Remus
and Kipling's *Jungle Book*. But their conversation is not convincing; it is just too human. There are many tall tales, too,
to account for that major mundane mystery, how did talking
begin at all? Or to explain the diversity of tongues. Even
scholars from time to time have speculated on answers to these
standing riddles, usually only to be ridiculed for their pains.

It takes some courage to venture to be heard on this subject. It also requires some effort of imagination. But what we know now about the functioning of the brain and the patterning of language encourages a new attack upon this ancient problem, of a kind that need not presuppose supernatural intervention, or be mere guesswork.

The problem, then, is to show that linguistic structures, characterized by regularity of pattern by probabilities of choice, are adapted to word-coding with a minimum of effort. In the words of a young French mathematician, who has occupied himself with this question, it would appear that language is a message purposively 'produced in order to be decoded word-by-word in the easiest possible fashion', that it is 'built out of a sequence of words', the relative frequencies of occurrence of which are governed by 'a statistical distribution law'. From this point of view language is, objectively, a body of physically discrete events in the sequence of which relations of similarity occur in a statistically definable pattern. The physical units are matched to corresponding neural and cerebral events, i.e. responses, in a way that makes easy what is on the face of it a stupendous and incredibly astonishing feat of comprehension or symbolization. It would further appear that all this is possible only by the peculiar device of recombination and permutation of a small number of distinctive linguistic features (technically known as phonemes), which the human organism learns early in life to recognize and to reproduce. It must be supposed that human evolution included, with other things, the growth of the power by which precisely this kind of selective process among vocal noises, and their recombination, was achieved; and that in turn the stability of the device, once accomplished, and also the equally important factor of convention, were preserved by a force within language itself, that guaranteed, as it still does, the equilibrium of pattern. Individual utterances are, as it were, decomposed by the human brain and 'averaged into all acts of speech of a single speaker, and then into all acts of all speakers', as Mandelbrot puts it. He continues: 'This averaging process is the one which leads to the formation of a common language as a tool'. In particular, it gives the elements out of which language is built. Thus language is a sequence of concrete entities. But, and this is the new and important discovery, if a statistical estimate is made of the probabilities of occurrence of the concrete elements, these turn out to be identical with the probabilities of words.

We have indeed still some questions to ask. How did the human brain and vocal mechanism develop in such a way as to make language not only possible but even indispensable? This was answered some twenty years or more ago by the eminent comparative anatomist Sir Grafton Elliot-Smith. The factors, whatever they were, that led to the evolution of man, led at the same time step by step to the evolution of language. Upright posture, the freeing of the hands and arms, getting the tongue away from the throat, the development of stereoscopic vision and the emergence of the entire frontal area of the brain, led to new powers of perception and these in their turn to an appreciation and designation (i.e. linguistic symbolization) of objects, events, and qualities in the external world—mass and velocity, space and time, form, colour, texture—which is a specifically human attainment. Many of these objective qualities and the subjective abstraction of them, not to mention such higher level abstractions as freedom, justice, liberty (and their opposites) cannot be symbolized, given a meaning that is, without the help of language.

But it still requires an effort of imagination to see how the element of convention arose. Once it was established the rest is easy. Let us imagine, then, a class of subhuman animals using, as animals do, noises produced in their throats as an emotional outlet in the presence of urgent need, say some sudden danger. One of them, A, sensing peril, emits such a cry; B, who is quick in the uptake, goes off with A to safety; but C is deaf and is lost; D takes the cry to mean all hands to battle stations, and he, too, is eliminated; E has a slow mind and never associates the cry with the danger. He likewise vanishes. Here is survival of the fittest at work. But the families and associates of A and B now have the opportunity to learn the cry and its meaning.

There would be a great deal of trial and error both here and at later stages of the newly evolving symbolism. For it is not until B and a and b and X and Y and Z can *repeat the same cry, and with the same meaning, in the dark, or when the danger is not there*, that the convention and the pro-presentative power of language are established. By degrees new items will be added to the 'vocabulary', and those who possess them will have an enormous advantage over the others of their class, and so live them down. Which is perhaps the reason why our non-human ancestors have not survived!

These first cries may have been imitated or not, or may have been so in some cases and not in others. But so long as they remained imitative, they were not symbolic or strictly linguistic. It is true, but this is a very different matter, that language once invented is handed down generation to generation by imitation, not by reproduction. Indeed, it is this very fact that leads to variation, which, beginning as free variation among individuals, tends in certain cases to become standardized, and so evolves into those historical changes which are seen, for example, in the relation of English to German and of both to Gothic, and of Gothic to Latin or Sanskrit, and so on back to a common source called 'Indo-European'. But the striking thing about historical variations is the regularity with which they are carried through. Any innovation, once it has been selected out of manifold possibilities, is made part of the system and the equilibrium of the system is thus restored; at the same time older features disappear completely.

It might be argued that any innovation may take place anywhere at any time. But until a change has been finally and completely adopted it is not part of the system; it cannot be said to have been systematized until it is already a *fait accompli*. In this sense we think of a language as a closed system; in fact no language could be structurally (i.e. grammatically) described if this were not so, for we should not know what changes would come to be accepted and what not, nor can we usually know this in much less than a hundred years after the event.

By the invention of the discrete entity, something like a word, and a number of such, and also by the far greater invention of the possibilities of combining these symbols to match 'ideas' (complexes of associated responses), by the grouping and regrouping of them, language was started on its never-to-be-finished journey. For this biologically unique instrument is capable of far greater refinement and more orderly application yet.

Mathematical formulae have been worked out by communication engineers which give, among other things, experimental and theoretical data on the statistics of words as well as of graphemes. The most exciting thing about one of these is that it corresponds to the famous second law of thermodynamics, which is concerned with entropy or increasing disorder. In the case of language it is a 'negative' entropy, and thus a measure of order. As Schroedinger says 'the device by which an organism maintains itself at a fairly high level of orderliness (equals a fairly low level of entropy) really consists in continually sucking orderliness from its environment'. Now language, we said, is not an organism, but it is an activity of organisms and it adapts itself, as they do, to the continually changing demands made upon it by its environment. Otherwise we could never say anything new. In one sense change in language is change in culture. Latin has become French and Italian and Spanish step by step with all the social, economic, political and other changes that have taken place during the past two thousand years. If the environment becomes too severe and so hinders adaptation altogether, then the language is said to die—like Etruscan in ancient, or Tasmanian in modern, times.

But whatever type and structure a language employs, like the inflexional of Latin or the 'analytical' of modern English, it carries out that structure and type consistently. It is thus that its status is established and maintained. Presumably—and the mathematical theory of communication points to the same conclusion—this has always been so, as a necessary condition of the very possibility and effectiveness of linguistic symbolism. Presumably also, therefore, the same feature was present, in a rudimentary way, already at the very birth of language. Out of a welter of possibilities, correspondingly vague in precision of significance, a few were selected for particular symbolism of a limited kind. In time their number was enlarged, new are still being added, others discarded. This same process of selection is inherent in all linguistic history; but it is combined, as we saw, with variation. If language could not change, it would be incapable of coping with new demands, new concepts, new discoveries, new inventions—more likely it would have served only to prevent them. The brutes start each generation where the preceding generation started, man nearer to where the previous generation stopped.

These two principles keep the instrument in order. It was selective variation that created and maintains the equilibrium. This puts the matter almost in Darwinian terms both as to the evolution and as to the subsequent development of language.

Thus the progressive freeing of utterances from dependence upon perceived conditions, of the sentence-word upon a total perceptual context, has been a selective procedure of taking and combining only a small part of available or possible methods of structure and expression, and of using these selected conventional, almost arbitrary, units consistently and coherently within a patterned framework, not merely monosyllables and not merely sentence-words, but both of these and of everything in between, and at the same time, and this is the important thing, selectively and consistently. 'Roots' (i.e. semantic entities) are combined and 'sentences' broken up—both methods have contributed something, but they need not have been mutually exclusive. Rather they were complementary. The processes of selection and variation 'dissolved' them both, in preparation for the fashioning of distinctive and consistent typological systems. The linguistic units, in their mutual relationships, and thus a language, form a self-perpetuating system, capable of a metastable condition of dynamic equilibrium upon which linguistic function and efficiency depend. The basis of the dynamic equilibrium is selective variation, not an uncertain drift. It is the whole speech-community working for generations that is needed to make the language, of which the individual gives only a rendering.

The date at which human speech began may have been a hundred thousand years ago, presumably among a group of already highly selected primates, whose genetic properties made this stupendous development possible and at once obtained thereby a tremendous advantage in social cohesion and material gain. They would learn to live, as generations passed, in the conscious planning of measured time; to extend their resources for mutual protection and sustenance, and for survival; and to evade hand-to-mouth solutions of the issues raised by their slowly expanding perceptions, by a deepening grasp and control of their environment, until a quickening mastery of language hastened new discoveries, simple inventions, an elimentary specialization of crafts, even the first stages of agriculture, and in the far distance still, the possibility of exchange and transport. There would be crossing at first between speakers and non-speakers, and the forms of speech would no doubt both become diversified by selective variation, and spread by geographical expansion, with new groups of speakers at distant places. In recent times genetic influences in language are no longer limited to the mere ability to speak; they determine instead the differences between average ability and all the intervening degrees between imbecility and genius pure and undefiled. In a sense every human being's character for speaking is genetically determined. But all accept the linguistic pattern as such, much as their use of it may vary. How far the diffusion of a language over large, genetically unrelated, groups can affect language structure, is a question that linguists refuse to consider seriously. So far no evidence has been adduced to support the view that such effects have taken place. Nor does language determine mating groups; if members of these happen to speak a common language, that is a fact which, so far as language goes, is only coincidental, not fundamental. The barriers which language sets up between nations and classes are neither high nor permanent. They are constantly being crossed and broken down. Geographical isolation is now ceasing to be the potent factor it used to be when communication was difficult and uncertain. At one point the influence of language has been and remains considerable, namely on the lips of individuals so greatly gifted by their inheritance that they tower head and shoulders above their fellows. These men, whether outstanding poets or discoverers or statesmen, scientists or scholars, have in language a most powerful instrument for guiding their own, and in gradually diminishing measure, succeeding generations. So, too, individual intelligence makes its mark significantly, manifests itself clearly, in language; and social coherence is both favoured by and favours a common language, all the way from family, tribe or herd, to clan, nation and federation, the end being not yet reached among possible if still unrealized large and not very numerous federated states.

The advantages of sound for use in a signalling system, such as the facts that sound carries well, will turn a corner, and be effective in the dark, or that a sound made by X produces similar sensations in X to the same sound made by Y, seem to have impressed themselves upon quite early forms of animal life. The depths of the sea, where life began, are not silent, or fish mute. Fish are now believed to use the sounds they make as a communication system of their own, if not exactly a language. The use of rhythmic dancing movements, evidently systematized, as well as of odours, by bees for similar and very highly organized purposes of communication, was discovered nearly twenty years ago; quite recently it has been suggested that bees use also a sort of tone language, of supersonic range. Some are inclined to see ritualistic movements here, prediction not report, and certainly it is never negative communication; but in any event there is something not unlike the definition we have already given of meaning, as goal-directed activity, that is carried out for a purpose still in the future and imagined by the performer, thereby implying memory. In a similar fashion, the 'conversation' that goes on in a session of rooks or other birds, say a flock of starlings, has been interpreted by careful observers as preparation for action. Perhaps the cries of our imaginary primitive speakers were imperative rather than indicative. To move from emotive utterance, concerned with future time, to descriptive, that relates to the present or past, was a feat of genius, and was necessary for true linguistic memory. Even in recorded languages, the distinction is not always clear. Old English has no future tense; Indo-European past tenses in general are old forms of other significance (momentary or perfective) that have been given a reference to past time with the help of an adverb, augment, reduplicative or other formative device; such common forms as present-perfects, or the use of the perfect for the instantaneous future, the late development of secondary tense forms, some with the help of auxiliaries, and the constant use of a single form with reference indifferently to past, present, or future at need—all this indicates how shadowy the line of demarcation may be. But with the recognition of time, dependent in part upon observing velocity, and of place, dependent upon mass or volume, would come the recognition of fixed and enduring objects to which identifying 'names' could be assigned.

A single sentence in language, as in music, is perceived not in real time, the few seconds that it occupies, but simultaneously, as a unit, just as the referend is not an item of 'reality' but both it and the symbol are a whole, each interwoven with the other: the very utterance and apprehension of the symbol disturb the nature of the referend.

Modern theory of neural circulation, as we have seen, thinks of the circuits as making and remaking themselves. This suggests the concept of purposive action, in a somewhat different sense from that in which the evolution of the human hand or eye may be so regarded. Like a torpedo which pursues a ship by 'listening' to the noise of its propeller, so negative feed-back returns some of the output of a nervous system as corrective input, until by eliminating error it achieves its goal. This also introduces the idea of purpose. In the same way historic changes in language occur almost as if the linguistic system had the purpose of reducing its own error to a minimum in obedience to its own principles of economy.

Very simple calculations can be made to show genetic relationships of languages, excluding both chance and mere onomatopoetic agreements, provided that the intermediate stages are known both chronologically and geographically. It is a matter of disentangling traces of cultural diffusion, archaic residue, and cumulative historical transformations. There seems to be a good prospect of calculating the rate of, and amount of resistance to, structural modifications, and especially of morphomatic decay, in which a constant K for the average rate of retention of basic 'root' morphomes per millennium is sought. But it must be admitted that some historically known time-depths between related dialects do not agree very well with the calculated estimates, granted that the vague theory of autonomous drift has at last been successfully repudiated. But there is no likelihood as yet of showing monogenesis, a single origin, of all the languages on earth, however plausible it may seem. If ever the anthropologists succeed in demonstrating a sole place of origin for man, then the monogenesis of language would follow, for notwithstanding some courageous attempts, language has never been demonstrated among the apes: speech is the prerogative of man alone.

Slow as the rhythm of linguistic development appears to contemporary observers, hardly noticeable except to those who deliberately give their attention to it, actually it is very rapid. Since the use of writing began, a few thousand years ago, many languages have disappeared, many new ones have arisen and even if these can be seen, as is often the case, to be descended from ancient languages, still the changes that have wrought these results have been both swift and thoroughgoing: Irish bears hardly any resemblance to Hindustani.

Linguistic adaptation is more like cultural or social adaptation than biological: it is part of large-scale anthroponomics. The date of the oldest known record of a language is no indication of the date of its origin; that can be known only if we have the records of its still older source, as for example Latin from which one may say the Romance languages were derived sometime during the Middle Ages. Or archaic features may be preserved in what looks like a haphazard fashion—Irish and Welsh have a middle or passive voice in -*r*, analogies to which are known also in Hittite, Phrygian, Tocharish, Latin, Osco-Umbrian, and a little more remotely comparable forms in Sanskrit. To account for this and many another such state of affairs, the theory of overlapping dialect-waves in the original locality of the Indo-European languages was proposed; but some of the facts may indicate nothing more than partial inheritance of a common feature, followed by independent parallel or divergent development. Only complete written records over a long but continuous stretch of time could be conclusive. The theory of selective variation, implying teleological adaptation and typological specialization, comes nearer to satisfying the several factors of the problem. Indo-European, then, does represent (p. 6) 'the age of declension', a suddenly widened understanding, which was making unprecedented efforts to cope with previously unrealized and very involved relationships, which its modern descendants now attack with simpler devices. Indo-European languages have, or until recently had, a complicated morphomatic structure with an abundance, and at the same time, remarkable clarity of formative elements, each with its quite definite grammatical and presumably semantic values. Since the formation of Indo-European, in the third millennium BC, a complicated grammar, built up no one knows how rapidly or how slowly, has nearly everywhere been transformed out of all possible direct recognition.

Life in general, as we have said, is disorderly. If mankind were one tenth as orderly in the rest of his conduct as he is

in his language, which is itself by no means a matter of perfect
order, this planet would begin to resemble a paradise. If the
theory of selective variation in language wins recognition it
will be chiefly due to the influence of statistical ideas. The
argument as advanced in principle is a statistical one, even
though a detailed statistical proof is not yet available. The
rise and growth of LANGUAGE seem destined to be brought
under the law of entropy, together with the world in which we
live, even life itself; and that law is the prototype of statistical
law governing just such unidirectional processes as linguistic
evolution.

X

LANGUAGE: SOCIETY, INDIVIDUAL, AND SYMBOL

OTHER disciplines as well as linguistics proper take an interest in language—psychology, anthropology, sociology among them —and we begin to hear of biolinguistic, psycholinguistic and ethnolinguistic studies. Philosophy has always been preoccupied with language; and modern science seeks to satisfy itself that it does escape from operating solely with verbal systems of logical constructs based on sets of postulates. More extensive still in popular appeal—indeed this attracts also the lunatic fringe—is a somewhat naive account of language that seeks to find in it at once both the source of all human error and also the promise of universal salvation.

A language is a conventionally transmitted and acquired system of symbols, and as such part of a civilization. But it is not the only subsystem of a total culture, a complete description of which would show precisely where and how connexions are made by each subsystem with the others. For our present purpose it will be enough to consider a few of the ultra-linguistic connexions which terminate in the linguistic system.

It is not a new observation that concerted action of the many springs from the power of command exercised by the few. Political giants contribute pragmatically to political theory and to its language, the more extensively the more successful they are. But so do the less powerful: *civil disobedience* comes from Thoreau as well as from Gandhi, *paternalism* is applied to industry as well as to states. Emotive and emotional force soon enter into words like *anarchism, Americanism, communism, minority rights, pink, red, scab, bias, prejudice* and many others. The segmented morphome *ocracy*, like *ology* or *ism*, is a mark of the times. Social and political evolution, as opposed to biological, both sustain and draw sustenance from language. Without it man is no better off than any other animal; in fact he is worse off, being defenceless. And those men whose use of language is so unintelligent as not to differ from a simple reciprocity of response to stimulus are not notably better off than animals that only resemble man. As an individual, man has no self-defence. The bond between individual and society is supplied by language. Interpersonal relations, dependent upon linguistic communication, have been woven into a fabric that holds together the other subsystems upon which survival and well-being of individual and society alike depended. Now international communications and relations seem likely to play a like role between total cultures, civilizations, and perhaps nations as the units, new facts of language being created to manifest new facts of politics. For example, an intelligent way out of the perils of power politics has become necessary for survival: if the risk of destruction has been created by the human mind, the human mind has only one other choice before it, to find a way of dealing with that particular risk. This is not beyond human intelligence. To believe so is to abdicate. Man has loosened tremendous energy by nuclear fission; now he must decide, and decide intelligently, what to do with this energy.

These ultra-linguistic aspects of language reflect the relations between individuals and groups of individuals. The relations arise from the coincidence or overlapping of their individual fields of action, combining the individual fields upon a common ground, namely a language. Languages have histories not only in the sense of historical grammar, but also in the history of the actions which are performed through the mediation of a language common to a plurality of agents. The separate energies of all the members who constitute a language-community are vital forces, the operation of which works out both their own history (as a group) and also the history of their common language. The forces can only be expressed in action, including linguistic action. Languages are thus institutions; the study of Western European institutions, for example, is among other things, the study of certain sets of speech-habits and of their referends. The linguistic institution is an index of an inner state, as well as of outer relations of its authors, to which their linguistic record is the first key. It is a set of relations that has existed among successive generations of a community of human beings, who have lived and acted within its evolving framework. In fact the framework changes so slowly in human terms that the description of it as a set of relations is justified. But slow as its changes are, it does change, as the result of creative personalities or minorities—the rest copy. The most powerful force by which a mass of mankind is set in motion towards an external goal is the universal and primitive kind of imitation which language both is and evokes. Without being a natural object in itself, language is still an energy of groups of living beings working through their institutions. Doubtless irrational as well as rational factors—hopes, fears, prejudices, and the like—are involved, both of individuals and of communities, and the psychologist and anthropologist are now attempting to examine and to understand, from their own standpoint, linguistic behaviour with the same detachment as a linguist does, or as they treat other human behaviour, and even with the same detachment as a biologist would regard his specimens.

Language is not solely a pattern of behaviour of a mere animal. Intelligence and reason, inspired by superior personalities, serve to leaven the whole lump. Archaism and futurism alike in language are attempts to thwart or hasten growth in the historical continuum of language.

Its property of quasi-self-propagation is highly deterministic; it also has the properties of mutation and recombination, the intrusions of uncertainty from the outside which interfere with its levels of organization. Selection exploits the results of intrusion and variation by means of adaptation, another order of determinacy. The consequence is an irreversibility of development, which overcomes the danger of unlimited diversification. The new emergent systems that arise after periods of turbulence are apt to be quite different from the anterior system; the structure of Italian and French or English is not at all congruent with the structure of Latin or of predialectal Germanic.

Whenever communication is not directly between one speaker and another, but passes through a chain of speakers, there is some risk of distortion and error before it reaches its destination. Each handling increases what has come recently to be called 'noise', i.e. anything which interferes with completely identical reproduction of the original message; the ratio between the message and 'noise' never improves in such cases and usually deteriorates. This is true, for example, of translation and of any transaction in which translation is necessary; then communication must be to some extent impaired. It is simply a fact of the transmission of information, whether the translation is done by machine or by man, and whether within the same culture (say from Italian into French) or not (say from Latin into French, or from Hopi into English).

The range of communication which members of a speech-community enjoy obviously must be extended when they are in contact with other speech-communities, unless the language barriers—which in the distant past usually are associated with natural physical barriers such as dense forests, high mountain ranges, broad oceans, deep rivers (except lengthwise) and the like—are hard to overcome. Celebrated examples are the ancient Greek dialects, and more recently New Guinea, and the Indian dialects of California. Even a prolonged suspension of the force of natural boundaries, as under the Roman Empire, when a centralized political power and the stable communications which it set up spread a common language, does not insure permanent results, for after the empire collapsed, a frontier such as the Pyrenees reasserted itself linguistically as well as geographically and politically. In the same way, economic advantage, or anything that may lead to it, for example trading or conquest, will widen the communication-range, as to the north of California, where Chinook jargon, virtually an auxiliary language based on an Indian dialect supplemented in part by English, in part by French, has served this function, just like pidgin Enlgish in China. In the Middle East the dragoman (which means 'interpreter') has always been a familiar figure. Evidently contact may be active despite differences of language; there is no necessary agreement between areas of culture and areas of language: the number of languages of the world and of cultures do not agree. Wherever language and culture overlap or intersect—a single culture being carried in several languages, or a single language spanning more than one culture— it becomes necessary to vary the code. Historically, at least over a long extent of time, slow changes in language, as we have seen, march with changes in culture. And if language is part of culture, then quick change from one dialect or language to another, even the most rapid back and forth change, may be regarded as such momentary transformations. Then it is the individual who is affected, not the group, and the question of personality-organization and culture comes up.

Some aspects of culture, notably cultural behaviour that is learned, passed down to later generations, and diffused beyond the area in which it originated, are commonly allied quite closely with differences of language. The line of cleavage between one language and another is still more sharply drawn by political than by cultural lines, with a limited number of bilingual speakers along the frontier; but most languages are ready to borrow cultural words rather freely. Culture and language alike are apt to be directed and controlled, the former notably so, by individuals who exercise authority or enjoy the proper prestige; language less so—in modern North America the language habits of the younger generation are not at all supervised at home, at least among English speakers; and not much in school, in contrast with the strict control exercised in, say, Iceland by parents and teachers alike. Finally, attempts to make a dying language run counter to the cultural direction, as in Ireland, give little evidence of success.

Doctrinal statements about language, when professedly intended to be statements about it as a variety of cultural behaviour, have not achieved any clear or convincing correlation between the two. Native speakers seem to be unaware of what is alleged to be an extremely close correlation; and if it exists, it escapes the outsider, the uninitiated, no less. Those chiefly concerned rarely are moved to make public statements of their own position, and when they do it is for theoretical or ideological reasons, as recently in Russia. Here the existence of class-languages, clear enough in English, is denied; language is held, like the intellectual atmosphere as a whole, to rest upon economic structure.

The matter deserves more than passing mention. The fact seems to be that a language is the expression of the attitude of a certain speech-community towards its culture, that is to say towards the sum total of conditions in which it lives, both natural and as transformed by human activity—a combination of external phenomena and of human responses to them, together with the unceasing interaction of the one upon the other and all its products, including man's sensations. We say that language mirrors the psyche, and it the culture, of a language-community. There are no metaphysical assumptions here. But the so-called 'metalinguistic' argument goes much too far. It would imply that modern technical discourse, which is part of our Western cultural inheritance, is merely a by-product of the economic conditions under which we live; not that modern science, and the tremendous feats of engineering and processing that have derived from it, and the contemporary economic structure, have sprung from an intellectual matrix. Why then did the West develop scientific methods just when it did? On the historical evidence alone, it was that very intellectual atmosphere of freedom, which conceived and brought forth both the French and the American revolutions, which also in due course, as a later offspring, gave us modern science. The same spirit has thriven exceedingly in manifold intellectual endeavours, if not in politics. Here is the ultimate source of the twentieth-century economic prosperity of the Western world. To suppress this spirit of adventure will be to fill our discourse with fearful restraints, tribal taboos, frustrate the individual mind, kill its genius, and stifle its utterance—you fail to conform at your peril, and then intelligence withers. A community does not rise above its leaders, any more than a stream above its source.

It can easily be shown, on purely linguistic evidence, that those linguistic features which underlie our modern Western civilization—concepts such as mass, force, energy, volume, time and space, gravity and so forth—have evolved from older stages of Indo-European languages which were not at all unlike those of many American Indian dialects, even in detail, in which modern scientific expressions could not have been formed. Aristotelian Greek could no more have formulated modern chemistry or physics than Arabic or Hopi; nor can modern English cope with some of the theory in articulate discourse, but only in formulae. We need our language renewed and remade at many points for this purpose.

The very notion that behaviour such as throwing a lighted match into an empty gasoline drum (and thus causing explosion and conflagration) was prompted just by the fact that the drum was called 'empty', or turning on fans to remove smoke from a burning textile factory just because fans are said to 'ventilate' (the idea being to remove smoke and enable operatives to reach the seat of the blaze, but in the end they succeeded only in burning the factory down), is extraordinarily naive, if not altogether false; even it were true, still there is nothing to prevent the English language from having stated the true state of affairs. It was merely individual lack of intelligence, ignorance and stupidity, stimulus-and-response behaviour, that caused these two celebrated catastrophes of the alleged influence of 'linguistic' behaviourism, for the insurance inspector's interrogation did indeed expose just such folly. The theory that linguistic behaviour controls non-linguistic behaviour in all its detail is erected on an unfounded assumption that is itself derived in the first place from an examination of language. Nothing is added to the hypothesis by referring back to the linguistic usage. And when appeal is made to languages of totally different cultures and structure, namely North American Indian, the supposed 'message' is so distorted by transmission as to be useless for the argument. Systematic variation in non-linguistic behaviour in response to identical linguistic stimuli, so far as it occurs, cannot be attributed to the linguistic system.

'Ideology' is the modern name for what the Greeks called *mythos*, and cultural anthropology misses the point so far as it interprets the word *myth* as implying symbolic interpretations solely of natural phenomena. In our own day, patterns of ideas, it need hardly be pointed out, are clothed in language as well as acted out in behaviour—take totalitarian and authoritarian dogma, whether of church or state. Myth (linguistic) and ritual (behaviour) depend on one another in an extremely intricate way. But there is at least one obvious analogy. The principle of determinate organization, to the exclusion of excessive disorder, which is characteristic of linguistic structure as well as of linguistic change, has a corresponding feature in patterned cultural behaviour which sometimes appears in a verbal pattern, as when we learn that over forty Navaho informants, all of them, described a piece of their witchcraft superstition not only in identical words, rendered in precisely the same way into English by as many as eight different interpreters, but at the same time asserted that they were telling something known to them not as a definite tradition, but as something learned casually. Apparently Navaho and Welsh have the same linguistic pattern in distinguishing, or rather failing to distinguish, in certain circumstances, as is true of Latin also (in reference to the sea) between *green* and *blue* as English defines these colour names, not because the speakers cannot see any difference, but because the *expression* of this particular differentiation is not part of their habit. Just so native speakers of a language that does not distinguish between initial *th-* and *s-* fail to accommodate themselves, in speaking English, to what is an essential phonematic distinction of English (as in *sat:that*, or *sin:thin, sick:thick*). There are other permissive variables in culture, as in language, but within the framework of the pattern. Anthropology, like linguistics, and the natural sciences, is concerned with discovering and describing uniform modes of relationships between human beings and things. Few tasks are more urgent, in lessening the scope of international antagonisms, and especially between those peoples who on the one hand share, in greater or less degree, the twentieth-century civilization of the west and those who, on the other, do not, or who are popularly said to have a 'primitive mentality', than to interpret cultures one to another in such a way as at least to prevent this device of partitioning mankind from becoming at the same time a justification for racial or social oppression. Be that as it may, the best means of studying 'primitive' modes of behaviour is through the study of 'primitive' languages, and especially of their structures. Much might be learned in this way of relationships between language and other aspects of culture. Genuinely 'primitive' language is altogether outside the scope of modern man's knowledge; it is lost in the remote past. But it is not to be doubted that patterns of culture, belief, ritual and the like, and patterns of language, are structured, both in form and in content. A language exists or existed only in the people who speak or spoke it, and for this reason, if it is completely recorded and perfectly understood, it has an absolutely complete referential apparatus of linguistic symbols for locating every referend known to these speakers.

A social structure may be compared with LANGUAGE as external or superior to the individual, whose several social performances, taken one by one, are comparable to his several linguistic performances; and the language of the community to the collective 'conscience', both being constrained by a pattern coextensive with the community. Thus a linguistic change goes through two acts: (1) in the individual rendering of the language, (2) in its spread through the entire community. The change, when it is completed, is a social norm; for linguistic usage is just as apt to approval or condemnation as other social usage, and the inner form of a language to the same workings of the social conscience—the term being used broadly —as other social acts. Phonematic, morphomatic, and syntactic structure are, so to speak, the social expression of phonemes, morphomes, and syntagmata. This is and must be so, since an infant learns his language in a social setting. Even the special 'languages' of certain trades and occupations are socially conditioned.*

The discovery of the importance of binary choices in linguistic structure has naturally led to the suggestion that cultural facts may be objectified in the same way. The possible alternatives, for example, in many social situations may be presented as 'yes or no' choices, precisely like the corresponding linguistic alternatives. It remains to be shown, however, that morphomes may be closely matched, one to one, with anthropological data, despite some optimistic claims. But the analogy between a mathematical description of the strategy of such a sophisticated psychological technique as bluffing at poker, and social manoeuvres, is not so far-fetched as it seems; and a theory which interprets social organization as a quasi-'mechanism' that guarantees the continued existence and operation of the group, in effect as a form of 'communication', may readily be compared with a linguistic system that passes through a transmission channel characterized by input-output and negative feedback.

The discontinuity of an infant's nervous system with that of its parents' means that in learning to talk it imitates, does not reproduce, what it hears. Given a group in which the social control over the utterances of, for example, a and o or t and d, is not strict, as in fact it is not in many parts of North America; or in which control is similarly lax in the use of traditional forms, arrangements, and meanings; and provided always that

* See Appendix 9

conditions of disequilibrium are present; then, the stage is set
for such deviations to become fixed in the habits of a growing
generation and to be handed on intensified to the next, so that
in a few generations the old way is completely abandoned. For
otherwise an excess of phonemes, morphomes, and arrangements
gives rise to chaos and destroys communication. Language
bridges the gaps between the generations, between social sub-
groups, and between individuals very effectively on the whole,
but anyone may note for himself doubts, inadequacies, and
occasional failures in communication. The complete carrying
out of a particular divergence—not more than one or two at
a time—is testimony to a therapeutic force, inherent in language,
designed to re-establish its own efficiency and equilibrium.
Social factors reinforce this power—family or community life,
which is unifying within its own circle, separative without; religious unification or cleavage as the case may be; trading centres
—anything which brings people together and keeps them in contact makes for uniformity in linguistic habits. Contrariwise,
whatever exercises a separative force encourages diversification.

Associative interference in language operates to restore an
impaired pattern, or impaired meaning. It is as if the circuits
had become crossed at some point in the neural paths, and the
pattern of *istarum* is followed in *dominarum*, and of both of
these in *dominorum* when *dominum* (gen. plu.) ceased to be a
distinctive form; or French *venu* replaces Latin *uentum* (from
uenio 'I come') which is in danger of confusion with 'wind' or
'twenty', *rendu* replaces *renditum* which is about to give *rente*,
and *rompu* replaces the *ruptum* (-*a*) that will become *route* (a road
broken out, *uia rupta*). Blendings like *brunch*, *globaloney* and
'slips of the tongue', lapses, or forgettings, mistakes in hearing
or reading, are individual deviations which sometimes come to
be accepted, if at all, within a restricted circle; only a few
spread throughout the entire speech-community. The normal
pattern is followed, even in words manufactured from strings
of single initials, like *Unesco*, *snafu*; or from pairs and short
groups of letters as in some trade names, e.g. of petroleum
products. Apart from these deliberate creations, however, such
departures from usage as lapses are produced by psychological
factors as well as linguistic. In extreme cases of psychological
disturbance, the linguistic disturbance also becomes extreme.

Simple blends and extensions are apt to occur between two words of similar rhythm and phonematic structure, as well as of associated meaning. Once *oversee* acquired the meaning 'cast the evil eye upon', *overlook* became infected with the same variation; time and space run into one another in words like *long*, colour and sound in *clear, bright, dull, deep* and above all in *chromatic*. Linguistic responses, such as the name of a colour to a given patch of actual colour vary considerably, even though the name may be better remembered than the colour-sensation.

There is some evidence to indicate that synesthesia such as associates the meanings of colour and sound under a single word may extend to smaller linguistic units. But it is debated how far this is normal at the phonematic level. Some individuals do most positively report that they associate certain vowels and consonants with certain colours, and similarly certain names of numbers, of the days of the week, of seasons and months, even inflexional units. Such 'colour-hearing' has been reported chiefly from young adults, and may be a recollection or prolongation of childish habits; it is generally assumed that an infantile 'picture' has been preserved in some few cases longer than in most persons—if indeed it ever existed in these others. As-sociation of colour with emotion—*green jealousy, blood-red* or simply *red anger*—is more commonplace; *light* may even be *dry*. These phenomena are frequent enough to show that here is a normal activity of language.

But it is an activity that passes almost at one step to abnormal usage; and this, in its extreme forms, to genuine deviations deep enough to impede communication or to stamp the speaker as himself abnormal. In schizophrenia language is profoundly disturbed, and any deep or prolonged emotional upset may manifest itself in the subject's abnormal use of language. It has been suggested that the elaborate system of symbolization in the terms of which human life is lived, to the extent that none but the simplest and most concrete verbal statements approach identification with 'reality', render mankind peculiarly vulnerable through that aspect of his being, the ability to speak, which is also one of his greatest glories. Another factor is perhaps the prolonged infancy and childhood of a human being, the very period when language is being learned being the same as that at which physical and psychological maturity are still far ahead of him, so that language is always ready to slip back into a childish or infantile regression.

A most important feature of aphasia is the stratification of grammatical categories, indeed of linguistic features as a whole, that is, the order in which they are lost. In a sense a baby is aphasic. Children do not invent their speech units anew, but copy as closely as they can, almost mechanically, what they hear. There is first a period of babbling in which an infant may produce all possible varieties of phonation, but by the time he is ready to say something, the number is greatly reduced. Certain phonemes have been selected from the overwhelmingly large possible variety, on the basis of adult speech, and these are ordered into the child's system of sounds—it is now an acquisition, an achievement of his own. In fact at this point entire phonematic substitutions are observable, subsequently erased, or most of them, by correction on the part of elders. Gradually the phonematic pattern is accommodated to that of standard usage.

Aphasia is a similar process in reverse. The linguistic system is, as it were, taken apart. Children first acquire a vowel a, then an occlusion at the front of the mouth, usually p, soon followed by a contrast $p:m$ (*pappa:mamma*), and then t (*:p*) and n (*m*) or d (as *tatta, dadda, nanna*). Now come i and u and e. From this point, no fixed sequence can be stated; but the contrast $u:i$ comes before that of $e:o$, and $i:e$ earlier than $u:o$. In aphasia there is some evidence to show that features last acquired are those which are first lost. This is demonstrable with longer units, whole words and phrases, as in senility, where not only are new acquisitions hard to come by, but there is marked weakening in the retention (feedback) of recent acquisitions. It is remarkable too that the phonemes first acquired in all observed languages (p, t, m, n and a, i, u or e) are the minimal equipment, and also those of most frequent occurrence, both singly and in combination. Rare phonemes like Czech r are learned last of all. Maximal contrast and differentiation is thus provided for.

In that variety of aphasia in which the names of things are lost, it is often found that the ability to identify colour-patches is also gone. This fact may have some bearing on the problem of synesthesia; but it has also been interpreted more broadly as loss of the ability to abstract a given attribute, and to categorize objects on the basis of this attribute alone. The subject's behaviour is too concrete, and verbalization, when it occurs at all, is regularly associated with particular and specialized environments, as in the case of a patient who named animals in the precise order in which she had seen them in the zoological gardens, as belonging to a concrete situation, not as the names of objects, and certainly not as a scientific classification. Comparisons have been made of the effect of aphasia on a writer, a musician, and a painter respectively. The writer and the musician are disabled, but the painter's work unaffected. Musical phrasing and patterning would appear to be analogous to linguistic, or at least controlled by neural and motor activity in a manner analogous one to another. In fact the study of language, whether normal or abnormal, derives greater cogency from broadly based studies of human behaviour as a whole than from limited attacks; especially it is the cognitive processes that are connected with the meanings of words that are cardinal, and meaning is unfortunately just that aspect of language which strict linguistics neglects. The agents that accomplish the task of language, that abstract characteristics from numberless and complex impressions, fix them, remember and recognize them, are first of all the units of significance, the symbols; and next the bonds between them.

Psychologists who have studied language so far have devoted their attention to the learning of language by infants, and to children's use of language; to the phenomena of verbal association; and to exploring the abnormal use of language. Verbal behaviour by normal adults is easily observed, but it is difficult to control or to generalize about. The language of a community as a whole is that of its normal, functioning members. Even though statements are made about it in such a way that they purport to describe verbal behaviour as a whole, they are actually based on separate instances of individual usage; evidence which is a catalogue of particulars, however, does not always yield broad generalizations, and except with regard to children's language, there is little to report. There is no indication whatever as yet that grammatical features, e.g. inflexional structure or a preference for the active construction, have psychological any more than cultural implications.

The development of random 'vocalization' of babies into command of a particular language has been shown to depend upon (1) a suitable neuro-muscular-motor system, which is a matter of inheritance; and (2) a particular environment—that is exposure to normal language, and preferably only one language; (3) rate of maturation. The subject must also be a human baby—others do not learn to talk, not even in the best of environments or with the best of training. Random 'phonemes', from which the repertoire appropriate to the particular environment (i.e. the language spoken in the baby's hearing) is selected, come long before words; words are perceived and, within limits —that is in a few, concrete, meanings, are understood before they are produced; they are few in number to the end of the first year, after which progress is made rapidly; naming-words come before attributives or verbs, prepositions and conjunctions and pronouns towards the age of two, and combinations in phrases or sentences later still. There is some disagreement about whether specific or general meanings are learned first; on the whole the evidence seems to indicate that early meanings are specific, but may be applied too generally. There is disagreement also about the order in which certain vowel and consonant sounds are produced. Again, on the whole, it appears that vowels are the earlier, but the evidence is divided as to which, and also as to which consonants. The view stated above has a good deal of supporting evidence, but contrary observations have been reported. It is clear, however, that a child is not only encouraged by other speakers around him, but also by himself—he early begins to hear his own voice and this reinforces his own efforts. If left entirely to himself, he would go on expanding his verbal behaviour, though the result would not accord with any standard language. Its development would be circular, continually turning in upon itself, and would not get very far, since language is a social undertaking. Under normal conditions, the utterances of children already show statistical distributions that accord with those of adult language, but over a much smaller range of vocabulary. Reduplication is characteristic of the first efforts to produce words, just as it is of babbling, but this almost infantile habit is soon abandoned. Vocabulary increases rapidly between the ages of two and six, but estimates of its size vary widely. Between the same ages the standard pronunciation is still to be acquired, and children's speech is not easy to make out by anyone not accustomed to the particular child, partly because structure also has still to be learned. To pass from whole phrases, virtually of one-word sentences, to a sentence of some complexity, with normal orders of arrangement, may take up to the tenth year. To a linguist the best way of accounting for the acquisition of grammatical features such. as noun-verb, active-passive (or middle), subject-object remains that of binary oppositions. This is not always a matter of form; but if it is not, it is usually a matter of order.

Since language is a systematic symbolism, the question must be asked, how is this systematic symbolism perceived? And to this question a psychological answer may legitimately be sought as well as a neurological one. A number of psychological factors are involved to which there are genuine linguistic correlates. Certain recognizable psychological types, under stress, do mirror themselves in characteristic verbal behaviour. The capacity for seeing things as patterns and through symbols is inborn in human beings, ready for organization under the impact of experience. The experience is presented in large groups of stimuli as verbal terms which lead to certain conclusions that in turn justify themselves by successful predictions which make possible a certain control of the environment—ask and ye shall receive: there is a generalized reinforcement through repeated and successful experience which gives a broad organizational control. Experiments with the substitution of equivalent stimuli, a distortion of assumed values by modifying the accepted pattern, show that for a given unit of perception a new value will often be accepted for the assumptive pattern without hesitation. In some such way, it is supposed, the manifold individual linguistic variations of response to a given situation are accommodated within the total linguistic pattern. Now speakers do control what they say by their own feeling for their own muscular activity, just as in reaching out the hand to pick up an object—a series of signals flows back through vision, touch, and the proprioceptive receptors to inform the central mechanism how far the hand is overshooting or undershooting. So speaking is movement, expressive movement. But obviously in speaking no shift can take place instantly from one articulatory position to another—speech is not in actual usage cut into sequent pieces, no matter how brief. Here also there is the problem of overshooting; the problem of contradictory innervations; and what is still more troublesome, of the identification of speech elements when we know that actually there is no identity that, for example, to return to the phoneme, the *p*'s in *play, cap, spin, peer, poor* are not the same; or the *a*'s in *gag* and *dad*, and so with other phonemes—the context varies the performance continuously and through all its length at every step, every day. Yet these contextual variants are recognized by all of us as the 'same', we treat them as identities. The criterion, it will be recalled, is complementary distribution —though the *a* of the context *g . . . g* occurs only there, and the *a* of context *d . . . d* occurs only there, they are allophones (contextual variants) of the same phoneme, statistical averages. They are established by distributional criteria, on an articulatory basis that is verified acoustically. Speech units are ordered on a basis of muscular rather than acoustic characteristics; and controlled (by the speaker) in the same way that he controls other activities such as playing the piano, by proprioceptive, kinesthetic feedback, confirmed by a 'calibration' of acoustic 'monitoring' exercised over both his own habits and the utterances of other people. On this view the phoneme, like other speech units, emerges as a highly abstract unit. Finally, in addition to the transformation of the signal into a form suitable for the nervous system, and to identification of the units, there is the comprehension of meaning which, from this point of view is defined as involving a neural form of cross-correlation.

The question is how do we recognize the configurations, segregate them against a background which is simultaneously perceived? The process is auditory and visual so far as language goes, partly tactile (in writing, using a typewriter, or in reading a Braille text). The following are some of the factors to be considered in looking at language as a systematic symbolism: (1) selection, by comparison and contrast, at each step from initiation to completion of the finished utterance, of the appropriate symbol from the totality of possible symbols of a hypothetical environment, namely linguistic; and, presumably, also at the origin of language, or in the course of its evolutionary development and modifications. (2) A tendency to complete and enclose the field, to fill out the pattern. (3) A faculty of grouping, of treating similar situations alike, in the same way; and (4) constancy in producing similar reactions to similar situations, to like stimuli. These two factors (3) and (4) are at the very foundation of the human ability to use organized sequences of sound as a means of communication at all, since language must be both *conventional*—which means that the same stimuli evoke the same response in different members of the group, that is, in the case of language the 'same' linguistic symbol evokes the 'same' linguistic response; and *metastable*, that is in equilibrium. This is the constancy of language, that it strives always to overcome the tendency to randomness (variation) which is inherent in the system; to keep its own elements in balance. In the hierarchy of senses, vision and hearing are supreme for this purpose, even though they are in a measure at cross purposes: for visual localization it is better to be deaf, and for acoustic to be blind. Notoriously the deaf and the blind develop the contrary sense more acutely than those who are neither deaf nor blind, granted that the blind do see through the language of those who are not blind, and the deaf hear through the digital communications ('talking on your fingers') of those who are not deaf. (5) Assimilation, that is of members of a group of symbols that tend to appear alike, is also of great importance for a systematic symbolism; it must be present in order that members of a class of speech-elements may be consistently identified as such, as members of that class and of no other. And finally (6) relevance must be raised to, and kept at, a maximum. This is the quest for 'meaning', the highest stage of organization of the system.

The very fact of linguistic symbolism, a tremendous simplification of the raw data of the universe, is the best testimony to the human necessity for classifying objects: it is not merely a matter of the existence of, but of the necessity for, a pattern, if the system is to work at all. Only so are objects manageable in terms of systematic perception, whether auditory (in talk) or visual (in writing)—the 'rules' of perception, and the characteristics of the system are the same for both. Domestic animals learn to respond to (but not to produce) some of the symbols, that is they recognize their systematic character—to deprive them of this by repeatedly confusing the symbols in a random manner, once the symbols have been acquired, is to induce a nervous breakdown. The symbols need not indeed be linguistic, though frequently they are, as in giving commands to a dog. But one may ring a bell instead of saying 'here's a bone'. In either case there is a symbol; and it is man-made.

Symbolic meaning is a correlation of (*a*) the datum or referend; (*b*) matching in the neural network; (*c*) the symbol, the order being reversed for the hearer—symbol, matching, referend. Or one referend may call up another, or a series of referends; this is pro-presentation. But there is properly no direct connexion between symbol and referend. It is the mistaken identification of these that is responsible for the worst abuse of language. Language gives us the power to arrange 'reality' into convenient and empirically successful categories, and thus 'manage' it; but it is also a cage that intervenes between human awareness and the flow of phenomena,* of the raw data. If the deliberate fault of postulating a direct connexion between symbol and referend is committed, or if this is done innocently by the unsophisticated, it gives rise to the dangerous illusion that by manipulating the symbols it is possible to manipulate the referends. Those who aver, erroneously, that language fashions our thought should face the question: what fashions language? Another danger is to exclude the referend. Here we have the vicious practice of verbalism, of moving repeatedly from symbol to cerebral construct and back again, of responding entirely to *one's own verbal response*. Vast amounts of pernicious nonsense are created by this kind of linguistic self-abuse, in extreme cases with pathological consequences, not only in individuals but in societies and nations, in politics and in religion, in pseudo-sciences of various kinds, in scientism and all sorts of cults—artistic, literary, aesthetic, fads and frauds of every kind, even some comparatively innocent goings on of nature lovers, college clubs, shop clubs, splinter religions, splinter parties, and so on. Quite opposed to such linguistic behaviour is intelligence. In fact this is where the behaviourism of psychological theory breaks down. When an 'intelligent' result appears, that is because a previous stimulus-and-response relation has been suspended or discarded. If this never happened language would be reduced to the permanent status of a liturgy or ritual.

* See further Appendix 10

XI

MATHEMATICS, STATISTICS, AND LINGUISTICS: THE MECHANICS OF LANGUAGE

A BETTER title for this chapter* would be *Glossodynamics*, or perhaps Glossostatics, that is the study of the forces that produce and regulate linguistic activity and equilibrium. The subject in its present form is new, and it has not been properly named. Part of it has come to be called 'Information' Theory, as understood by communications engineers, whose practice has suddenly been given a theoretical underpinning that is almost entirely mathematical and statistical. Language is not mathematics; nor is its communication all physics, or 'information' statistics. But it is possible, on the basis of the mathematical theory of communication to set up an 'informational' theory of the structure of language. 'Information', in the engineers' sense, is conformation more than information, since it deals with statistical regularity in the transmission of signals, the probability functions of which are usually derived from relative frequency. Amount of 'information' is more strictly a matter of selection; entropy a matter of uncertainty; and redundancy a matter of inefficiency.

'Communication' in the technical sense is transmission (of information); entropy a measure of disorder; and the amount of 'information' is a measure of the statistical rarity of a message. Logical symbolism seems to provide an appropriate method for furnishing a theory of meaning, at least until a statistical technique can be developed. To return to our examples of the thermometer and the conventional languages of the Burmese

---

* Some readers may prefer to take a short cut by omitting a few pages 204, 208, 209-10) of this chapter without seriously impairing the argument.

young man greeting the object of his affections, and of the early Christian hopeful of immortality, the efficiency of their respective languages, on the basis of the evidence of experience or belief, would be greatly reduced if they both were transplanted to Spitzbergen, for they would then be making inefficient statements, statistically indefensible in terms of prevalent temperatures, and indeterminate in the context in which they would be using 'cool' or *refrigerium*, about their respective interests.

There are certain obvious analogies between communication systems such as the telegraph, or systems using sound waves instead of graphemes, and human speech: the sender encodes a message by translating it into other signalling units, the message is carried over the channel, is received, decoded and reaches its destination. On the basis of these analogies, 'communication' theory is relevant to linguistics, to which, considered as a whole, it gives a mathematical foundation. The fact that the transmission may be electrical, instead of direct between speaker and hearer (sound waves) is immaterial, for with telegraph, telephone, or radio, the signals are always transformed back into the system of which they were parts before the transmission, and in the same orders and probabilities, so that the intervening transformations may be ignored. We are entitled, therefore, to be optimistic about the possibility of connecting 'communication' theory more closely with linguistic theory, and especially that part of it which is concerned with structure; in other words, it provides a useful model of certain aspects of language.

It is sometimes objected that there is no one-to-one correspondence of grapheme and phoneme, or that the graphemes show irregularities or inconsistencies of use. This is true; but there is consistency in the inconsistencies, and in sufficiently large samples the inconsistencies are levelled out. As the number of chances becomes larger and larger, the effects of each single event becomes less and less important and tend to cancel out; the final consequence approximates the average with great accuracy. It should also be observed once more that, in reference to statistics, frequency refers to frequency of occurrence, *not* to frequency of wave lengths as in spectrographic analysis. Statistics are based (like descriptive analysis) on the assumption that we have to deal with a linguistic status, in which there

is an interdependence of the particular linguistic elements that
are under study, in relation to one another. The evolution
and development of language, based on observed facts of historical languages, presumes also a functional classification of
the mutations that characterise the shift from one linguistic
status to another, but statistically only one status is considered
at a time.

Entropy is a function of the state of the system. The entropy
of a given status, for example of the graphemes, is proportional
to the logarithm of the probability of their occurrence, which
is determinable from the system of the particular language
concerned, and the glossodynamics of a stream of speech would
seek to describe or to predict changes of state. In an isolated
system, change of state increases the entropy or measure of
disorder.* If in any potential change of a system the condition
for the change is not satisfied, then the change cannot occur
and the system is in stable equilibrium; thus glossodynamics
aims at describing completely the behaviour of all imaginable
systems in equilibrium, when various factors such as pattern
and lexical content and the concentration of the various components are altered. The statistical problem is to determine
the distribution of the assembly of the several systematized
units over the status in which the assembly finds itself. This
mathematical problem has a general solution, which describes
the behaviour of language systems in equilibrium, in such a
way that their behaviour is known quantitatively when the
conditions of equilibrium such as phonematic or morphomatic
pattern or lexical content are altered. The equilibrium is metastable, that is it is stable compared with all other states differing
only infinitesimally from the given state; unstable equilibrium
is not realizable.

The theoretical formulation of linguistic equilibrium demands
the application of statistical theory and the calculus of probability. The number of systems is large and very few have been
described statistically;† even if those of practical importance
had each to be investigated in detail before anything certain

* This statement refers to physical entropy, not to the quantification of
'information' which (see pp. 211, 258) is referred to as negentropy.
   † A critical bibliography of statistical linguistics edited for the Permanent
International Committee of Linguists by the present writer, is now available
(1954).

could be said, there would be no prospect of reaching any conclusions on which a working hypothesis could be established.
But the mathematical theory provides a number of theoretical
propositions which simplify the problem: (1) turbulence occurs,
i.e. a succession of incompatible phases, rendering the system
temporarily unstable until recovery. This is extremely rapid

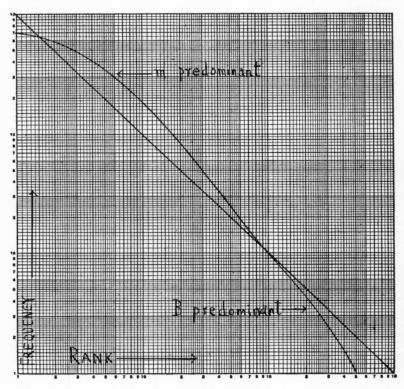

DISTRIBUTION OF FORMS

change, a sort of linguistic 'landslide', such as is observed historically, for example in the evolution of the Keltic languages,
or when one system impinges upon another as during the Germanic invasions which hastened the evolution of the dialect of
the Île-de-France. The resultant system was in each case quite
different from the previous one, pre-dialectal Keltic, or vulgar
Latin of Gallo-Roman. Obviously the event of such conditions

cannot be predicted; but changes once initiated can. In like manner astronomy predicts the return of a known comet on its path; but not the arrival of a new one.

(2) In each phase the number of undetermined variables is not arbitrary, i.e. determinacy is relatively high. Indeterminacy would be variation at every step of every utterance in every system, i.e. senseless disorder. This does not occur. Complete determinacy would end in a minimum of variables endlessly repeated. This also does not occur, but is prevented by selection, which in essence is reference, or the convention of symbol-referend, the elaborate relationship of the symbol not merely to what is symbolized, but also to each of the multitude of users of the symbol, and of the ordered symbols one to another. Prediction or extrapolation is made from the observation of successive phases over some hundreds of years, that is from established distributions of order; it is not the prediction of a new disturbance. But the theory of selective variation applies both to the maintenance and to the establishment of a system, both contemporaneously and historically. The rank-frequency distribution of morphomes, statistically determined, appears to tend dynamically toward a condition of equilibrium that may be represented graphically. This distribution is rationally ex-perienced in qualitative terms, quantitatively it is manifested in statistics, represented in graphs which until recently were believed to be linear (on a double-log scale), with a slope of minus one. Parameters have now been introduced that modify this linear distribution at each end.* A paraphrase of this curve is to say (a) that the statistical distribution which it depicts corresponds to the neurological coding of language, that is, the way in which the brain decodes what is heard and encodes what is said; and (b) that the distribution is produced by the operation of selective variation.

(3) The highest degree of precision in prediction is reached when prediction is based on quantitative analysis; results are limited in qualitative terms. It has been felt that the symbol-referend relationship makes a quantitative analysis impossible. It would appear, however, that such an analysis may be pos-sible in terms of the sequences that determine the occurrence of the symbol. For, in any prolonged piece of writing or dis-

* See the graph at p. 202

course, we find not only a sequence of certain morphomes and words in certain orders, but also some among these constituents which occur more than once, and some (for example articles, conjunctions, prepositions) of very high frequency, necessarily so since without them altogether the particular language concerned cannot be produced at all. Others are often repeated because of established associations of form, content, or order, or all three. That is to say, there is a structure of frequency of occurrence: some of the constituents occur rarely, others frequently; and there is a constant scale of variation between the number of words (rank) and occurrence (frequency); from one third to two thirds of the total occur, in any continuum of discourse selected for examination, once only, and there are many lexical items that (in the given continuum) do not occur at all. Only a complete dictionary, if such exists, will include them all, to which new ones may be added at any moment.

Size of vocabulary, and also features of order and arrangement, are significant. It is possible, by statistical methods, to measure the concentration of vocabulary, the degree to which an author relies upon the commoner words. This has been done for the Latin theological writer Gerson (1363-1429) and for Macaulay. The method gives a rather complicated quantity or characteristic (K) indicative of the form of frequency-distribution of items in an author's vocabulary, and independent of the size of sample within reasonable limits. K, the formula for which is $10^{-4}.W(K-1)$, where W is the number of nouns in the author's vocabulary, turns out to be 35·9 for nouns in Gerson and 27·33 for nouns in Macaulay (27·2 in the *Essay on Bacon*); in other words Macaulay depends less on a commonplace vocabulary. Still they are close enough together for comparison; K is far higher (84·2) in the *de imitatio Christi* of Thomas a Kempis (*c.* 1380-1471), and higher still in the English version of St John's Gospel whether Basic (161·5) or the Authorized Version (141·5).

A sample of Gerson containing 1,754 different nouns, showed 8,196 occurrences of them. One noun (*Deus* 'God') occurs 256 times, and 804 nouns occur once only. An extract from Macaulay's *Essay on Bacon* long enough to contain about the same number, namely 8,045 occurrences of nouns, includes 2,048 different nouns. One noun, this time *man*, not God, occurs 255 times, and 990 nouns occur only once. 'God' may be a dynamic and emotive word, not a doubt of it; but in Gerson its semantic content is at least no higher than that of Macaulay's *man*; for the higher the frequency of occurrence of a word, the lower its semantic content.

Another way of looking at the framework of expectation of occurrence may be illustrated by these quotations from Marlowe:

(*a*) Confusion X upon their heads
(*b*) Revenge shall X upon thy head
(*c*) Vengeance X upon you both
(*d*) Arrows X upon thy horse
(*e*) Confusion X on him
(*f*) Victory X on me
(*g*) Mischief X on Charles and thee

in which X (*light*) is determined by the rest of the sequence. In the first four the frequency pattern is identical; and again in the last three, except where the proper name (followed by *and*) produces a rapid drop succeeded by a rise back again to the same level as in the other two. The sequence is a matter of transition probabilities in the structure of the language. The statistical average is the result of a process in which an individual utterance is averaged into all the utterances of a single speaker and these into all the utterances of all speakers, the language in short, which thus is seen to be a sequence of entities, an estimation of the probabilities of which is identical with the probabilities of morphomes and words. The formula is given as $p_n = \cdot 1/n$, where p_n is the probability of the nth most frequent word. The frequencies of the first word in each of the seven lines quoted from Marlowe vary within a very narrow range; for all the rest (since X is identical in all) hardly at all (except for the low frequency proper name *Charles*, and the high frequency conjunction *and*).

The longer any sequence is, the more likely it is that the identity of any given component is determined by that of the other components. As the sequence proceeds the determinacy at first increases rapidly and then drops off abruptly, and so on; as the sequence is extended the process is repeated in wavelike fluctuations corresponding to segments which function as units. Sequences of more than a few phonemes may be described in terms of higher order units which may be (a) morphomatic (that is, constituted of cohesive groups of phonemes with strong internal statistical influences); (b) functional. The latter involves contextual situations and often also contextual oppositions. Now the phonematic units within morphomes are more restricted than those which are transitional between them; but the contextual situation determines X more strictly than definition by reference (i.e. the verbal definition given by the dictionary), and having predicted the phonemes $l/_r$ or $p/_b$ either of which, and a number of others, gives a good statistical fit to the postulated dip in the theoretical fluctuation or wave (frequency distribution), the expectation of occurrence is fulfilled with *light* (but not *right* or *bright*), not *rest* (or *roost*), not *perch* (or *bear*), not *land* '(up)on thy (their, you, him, me, Charles and thee)' and the rest. The qualitative feature will be considered below. If only one phoneme is possible, determinacy is near to 100 per cent (as for i, '*gh*', t or $[a\underset{.}{i}t]$, after l in this example); if any phoneme at all (this is a gratuitous assumption, not truly theoretical, and not actualized, since phonemes are not equally probable), then 0 per cent. All the curves show a pronounced, if irregular, oscillatory pattern, though many of the cyclic curves are complex, bimodal or multimodal. There is a very high determinacy-pattern of long, technical, and learned words, of which the sequence is almost wholly determined by its environment and makes a correspondingly low contribution to distinctive value, its 'information' value is low. This confirms the poor opinion held of 'big words' by the man in the street and is justified also in terms of economy (the principle of least effort), which is the reason at once for 'clipping' (e.g. *bus* for *omnibus*, *Beth* for *Elizabeth*, *taters* for *potatoes*—other such mutilations are *gym*, *grad*, *lab*, *pub*, *soph*, *phone*, *Mac*, among many), and perhaps for the mass butchery of words that has gone on in Russian since 1917.

The same procedure may be followed with Marlowe's

> Threads which spider's slender foot draws,
> Fastening her *light* web some old beam about

or *light* (noun, of the day or sun; or a shining body, a source of light) and *light* (adjective, *light* blue, or 'not dark' a *light* room), as well as *light* 'not heavy' as in 'light web'. Etymological differences enter into some of these distinctions, but to many speakers there may well be a conviction of synesthesia. It has been observed that when synesthetic transfer occurs (as in 'chromatic scale', from colour to sound), the shift is most frequently from less to more differentiated levels of the sensorium, that is 'warm colour', not 'coloured warmth' (Wilde's 'green thirst' is bizarre). The ratio between the two types varies somewhat (3:1 in Longfellow, 12:1 in William Morris, and about 5:1 in Oscar Wilde and his followers), but the relative proportion is always in the same direction (transfer from less to greater differentiation). Even in elaborate literary work, as a survey of English poetry from 1540 to 1940 shows, are found terms (for example, *fair:bright:dark*) that are steadfast in their frequency distributions through five centuries, but changes occur in the morphomatic ratios such as to indicate a restoration of equilibrium after a temporary disequilibrium. Actually the statistics for prose are in agreement; yet the selection and its variation from century to century are related to language in use. A comparatively small part of the vocabulary makes up the large part of usage, and is distributed over the same terms and morphological features, whether in prose or in poetry—even in telephone conversations—and in all the languages, ancient and modern, that have so far been examined. There is, therefore, a selective emphasis which varies only within narrow limits, proportionally, quantitatively and qualitatively. Poetic choice participates in the general choice, and there is a dominance of equilibrium over long periods of time, notwithstanding the most thoroughgoing historic reconstructions of pattern. The conclusion is inevitable that subjective criticism, which seeks to establish features separating prose from poetry, or one age of literature from another, should seek its proofs in form, not in content.

Many of the statistics already available have an application to pedagogical problems. For example in modern Spanish the present indicative, the infinitive, the preterite, the past participle, the imperfect indicative, the future indicative, and the preterite perfect show frequencies of 3764, 1757, 1141, 1121, 697, 235, and 1, respectively, out of a total number of 9394 verb-forms counted in 1350 random samples taken from over 300 writers, over 100 different subjects and all genres, in a comprehensive count made a few years ago. It is obvious that the emphasis now given to these verb-forms in grammars and in classroom instruction is out of accord with these findings.

A totally different problem, that is being vigorously attacked, arises in connexion with the mathematical theory of communication (that is, communication theory dealing with systems of transformation of information from one medium to another); this is the problem of organization of knowledge and the storage and recovery of information. This is a matter related only remotely to our subject, the one point in common being communication theory, and, through it, the similar problem of machine-translation, which is also a question of transformation from one system to another, and of storage and retrieval of information. Language, whether spoken or written, and documentary problems alike carry information; that all these have certain aspects in common affecting their transmission and utilization is obvious. Both machine-translation and information-coding are practical applications of the theory of communication, and both use the concepts of probability and choice. Rejection of material not needed at a particular point is subject to statistical rules, and presumably the human brain, in its organization of knowledge, or in making a translation from one language to another, performs the same operations of classification; the machines furnish a 'model', so to speak, of these operations. We have a transformation that operates between the machine-language and informational language (in translation) or between it and the intellectual content of the original documents (in recovering information), from one to the other. In the second case the coding 'talks about' or locates, does not transmit, content. Take yet once more the matter of temperature: in the one case the coding indicates where information about temperature is located or answers that question only, in the other it translates the content of a statement about temperature. Binary choices, using a system of binary numbers (also known as dyadic numbers), are made. Each successive step asks a question that is answered yes (1) or no (0). Three such questions and three answers, requiring three binary digits, specify a unique choice among eight equally likely choices, for $8 = 2^3$ or, mathematically, if we have N choices, the number of digits required (N being a power of 2) is $\log_2 N$.

Communication is identical in purpose and subject matter whether it is face to face, or over the telephone or radio, or by telegraph. A difference enters if it is a matter of grammatical analysis, but it is a difference of subject matter, not of principle. A morphome occurring in a document may be coded alphabetically (both ways), by language, by area, and by its descriptive or historical features or by both. These are subdivisions of description and analysis, each with a technical vocabulary of its own which makes up a metalanguage (that is a language about a language), that has its own pattern, and this pattern can be coded just like the pattern of the original language in virtue of its units and their combinations. The coding (for example on cards, or film, or magnetic tape) is controlled by a statistical technique which may be formulated mathematically and which determines the subsequent selection or rejection of a wanted item or combination of items. Messages have then been transformed into configurations, and these in turn are subsequently called upon to find and restore the messages. There is a logic in this kind of solution of communication problems; but 'information' theory is the reverse solution from that of symbolic logic, even though both 'information' theory and logical statements of the structure of a language dispense with semantic reference, and even though all three—language, 'information' theory, and logic—have to do with generating all possible sentences, i.e. permitted sequences of the language.

In the case of English, it has been calculated that the number of possible different essays of 4,000 words each, is 10 raised to the power 8000, without any violation of permitted sequences of phonemes, permitted morphomes and permitted orders of their arrangements. So 'information' theory; but symbolic logic deals with limited samples of a language and seeks to derive from these its categories and grammatical rules.*

Superficially the recurrence of similar or identical segments of the stream of speech appears to occur at random. But tabulation of relative frequencies of phonemes and morphomes and of permutations and combinations of these shows that the distribution is not accidental. Examination of correlations in sequence, i.e. of theoretically potential permutations of two or more units, but not sequences too long (e.g. the entire works

* See Appendix 10

of a voluminous author) to add further significance statistically, reveals determinacy. There is no agreement at all, but the widest deviation, between realized or actual and potential sequences, which increases by a constant factor in geometric progression—that is the other components more and more determine the occurrence of any given component, the longer the entire sequence. In the wavelike fluctuations seen when a sequence is plotted in terms of relative frequencies of the units, are revealed segments of greater or less complexity, and from them it is possible to predict any given sequence and to calculate the total number of permitted valid sequences for the language in which each unit has a meaning in virtue of the determining components by which it is preceded and followed. The functional saturation, that is the point at which actualization is exhausted, for sequences of a given number of units, may be stated as a somewhat complex quantity, variable from language to language, but constant for any given language.

The technique of contrasts assumes a frame of reference of a certain magnitude, e.g. for phonemes the frame of reference is a morphome or word. But contrast often occurs when similarity of function coincides with difference of form, and therefore it is reasonable to suppose that quantitative measurement should be attainable for both. The relative frequency of occurrence is an index of the probability that a certain sequence will recur; accordingly a deviation in the index indicates the presence or imminence of corrective change to restore equilibrium. If a given sequence admits a functional contrast, this may be reduced to a 'yes' or 'no' choice, and the frequency of a functional opposition may be stated as a probability of theoretically permitted contrasts. Working with morphomes or words within a sentence as the frame of reference, we have contrasts of functional significance as between extremes of homonyms and synonyms, or of differentiation and 'identity' reflected in varying degrees of semantic specialization.

Here we reach qualitative criteria, the relationship implied in linguistic symbolism such as the commonplace observation that apparent synonyms actually reveal functional variations, whereas homonyms occur in contextual variations, that is in complementary distribution. A system approaching homonymity is purely theoretical; selection will reverse a process of

THE MECHANICS OF LANGUAGE

assimilation the moment communication is impaired. For example, identity of the Latin morphome genitive plural feminine *-um* (from Indo-European *-āōm*), accusative singular *-um* (from *-ŏm*), genitive plural masculine *-um* (from *-ŏŏm* or *-ōm*), produced by historic variation, was overcome by selection: *-arum* (in *a*-stems, from the pronominal pattern), *-ōrum* (*ŏ*-stems) and *-ium* (in the *nt*-stems, e.g. participal substantives like *amantium*, *sapientium*, *parentium*, from the *i*-stems), leaving *-ŭm* accusative singular (*ŏ*-stems), and genitive plural only in consonant stems (*consulum*). The normal equilibrium is restored between form and function after disruption by the excess frequency, actual and potential, of occurrence of *-um*. This is a restoration of the level of energy of the system, a negentropy or revivification, a restoration of orderliness. The procedure is not reversible; *-arum* and *-orum* and the rest disappear entirely in the end (as in French), but they never at any time return to *-um*. So in phonematic changes: intervocalic *-s-*, if it becomes *-r-* as in Latin (450-350 BC), is never split up again into the original distribution of *-r-* and *-s-*; it never returns to *-s-* at all. A final Indo-European *-t* that disappears from the Greek verb and other forms was never restored. Alleged examples of reversal like Attic Greek *a* (after *r*) are unproven, or are only apparently due to reversal (final *-t* in Latin secondary tenses is no phonematic substitution, for *-d* remains in *sed, haud, ad, illud* and many other forms). Determinacy is not complete, which would give an 'ideal' probability of 1·00 for any form in any context. This would be the absurd situation in which everyone had learned everything by heart in advance, as in a set speech, and is contrary to the 'stream-of-speech' concept; determinacy serves the principle of least effort, economy of transmission. The function of reference rules out a condition of positive entropy. In fact a theoretical entropic degeneration might be imagined to appear in the vocal activity of an infant that has not yet learned to talk about anything, but merely babbles *ma ... ma ... ma*, or *da ... da ... da*, or *goo ... goo ... goo*. But, as in the processes of organic life, we have negentropy (a term coined by L. Brillouin in 1951); the entropy of 'information' theory corresponds to negative physical entropy. Whether a net gain in entropy is intralinguistic historic variation as a language passes down through successive generations and therefore a loss in entropy is extralinguistic, and selection of new forms partly imposed from without by new extralinguistic conditions, is open to discussion; it is at least probable that it is due in part to the demands of symbolism, a condition of the fulfilment of linguistic function (communication). Even from the psychological point of view that behaviour is reaction to environment, still intelligent behaviour controverts this view, and intelligible communication leads one to classify variation according to origin in individual nervous systems at least as much as in environment. If we ignore the psychological argument, it is possible (on a strict linguistic basis) to interpret 'extralinguistic' merely in the sense that causes of innovation are not apparent, or have not yet been intralinguistically discovered. The assumption that language fashions other human activity either begs the question (for what then fashions linguistic activity?) or implies belief in magic. It seems more likely that inherent tensions and instabilities are at work; material, social, cultural, even technological, factors would be established only if a closer correlation of linguistic and cultural evidence than yet appears were to be established.

Emotional factors are sometimes dependent upon mental disorder; but in the use of language in propaganda, in advertising, and in poetry, they are significant for normal variations. A relation between frequency and affectivity is demonstrable, as in the formal (not semantic) features that distinguish poetic discourse, which in content is not distinguishable from prose paraphrases. Low frequency goes with high affectivity, as witness also oppositions such as cliché:taboo, commonplace: endearment; whereas gossip:scientific discourse, or small talk: witty style, occupy a middle ground. This is obvious enough —but it has also been proved by actual proportions of frequency of occurrence. Again the number of undetermined variables is neither high nor arbitrary; it is the number of determined variables that is high.

Written material in a totally unknown script usually seems to present an unsoluble problem. In famous cases, like Egyptian hieroglyphic or Persian cuneiform, the first step was actually a lucky guess, which proved to be correct, that certain segments might be royal names; the second was taken with the help of an actual translation into a known language (the Greek of the

Rosetta stone); or, what amounts to the same thing, if afterwards justified, the hypothesis of kinship with assumed cognate languages already known, contemporary (like the other Indo-European languages with which the old Persian was compared) or of later date (Egyptian compared with Coptic). The reading of the script of many but brief inscriptions found at Mycenae in Greece and belonging to the middle of the second millennium BC (Linear B), which was accomplished in 1953, rested more heavily on the known fact of relative frequency of distribution of linguistic units (phonemes). Only if a proposed decipherment satisfies this requirement can it be accepted as correct, for neither random guesses nor mere chance will lead to its satisfaction. Acceptable translation based upon this prior condition is looked for, but translation is not in itself the proof. Adequate proof is afforded by the statistical relationships of the units of the decoding or transcription. Since in this instance the statistics agree closely with those implicit in the structure of an early Greek dialect (early Achaean), it was certain that the transcription was essentially correct, even before translation was attempted, and in defiance of prior, archaeological dogmatism (that the text could not be Greek at that date) which had long hindered decipherment.

Translation by machine, to be completely successful, that is to be independent of restrictions of subject matter, or the reader's previous knowledge of it, length of text, size of vocabulary, the human aid of pre-editing (of a document to be translated) and post-editing (of a translation) demands structural and statistical techniques in terms, not of phonemes but of morphemes, and of the orders of their arrangements, for *both* of any two languages concerned in a particular version, that is not only of (say) Russian but also of (say) English, if the machine is asked to translate Russian into English. No such information is available for any language. A human translator has the necessary circulatory pathways established already as patterns of neural activity by virtue of being bilingual.

It appears likely, simply in terms of regional examination of the human living brain and its functioning that speech and 'thought' are very much connectible. Language to a tremendous extent is a matter of habit—if it were not, communication would be impossible; but the areas of association on the basis of which

most of our linguistic and non-linguistic behaviour is to be
accounted for, the socio-personal areas, are so closely linked
(see the diagrams at p. 78), that cerebration, if done
symbolically, with both the outside universe and inner 'experience' as a unified frame of reference, is done with linguistic
symbolism, or at least within a system of operations based on
linguistic symbolism. We must ask ourselves, therefore, what
structure of language is best suited to this purpose, and one
answer, for which there is a good deal of evidence, is that
morphomatic and verbal (word)—not phonematic—coding is
best adapted to the requirement; that language is a message
purposively, that is by adaptation, generated in such fashion
as to be encoded and decoded word by word with the greatest
economy, i.e. on the principle of least effort, implying a matching of neural (including cerebral) and motor activity. The aim
then becomes to produce a theoretical model of information
which brings the structure of language into harmony with the
presumed processes of the brain. This is a different undertaking
from that of the communications engineers' theory. Given the
structure of language, the coding process, and the criterion
of economy of matching, a mathematical deduction from the
structural and historical data proves their compatibility. The
symbols of language are conventional and qualitative; the
mathematical deduction shows that language is and must be
structured in sequences of units (morphomes or words) such as
to provide a statistical distribution law for the relative frequency
of occurrence of these units. This turns out to be in agreement
with the statistical data *previously* assembled, subject to some
corrections applied to the small minority of words that are
used most frequently, and to the very large number of words that
are used once or twice only, or at most very rarely. This used
to be stated as a simple formula, subsequently refined, $f \cdot r = \kappa$
(frequency multiplied by rank is constant) but further corrections were necessary at the two extreme limits of frequency
(very high or very low) where the simple formula has been found
to break down. How do the levels of phoneme, grapheme,
clusters of phonemes, morphome and groups of morphomes compare with the cerebral process? An answer to this question has
been offered by the mathematician Benoît Mandelbrot which
deals with the weakness of the simple formula $f \cdot r = \kappa$. Since

the overt language is replaced by private substitution of neural impulses, it is necessary to suppose that a continuous incoming string is segmented into smaller units, each of which is recoded separately. At this stage not only the overt pro-presentation has been lost, but presumably also its elements as separately identified in the overt pro-presentation; for them a 'tally' is substituted, and the message is matched or 'fitted' if the work of decoding (and encoding) is the least costly of effort possible, is automatic, that is to say if the matching relates both the symbol (and its referend), *and* the statistical structure, to a corresponding coding. The most elementary structure is phonematic, but matching and historic variation obtain at all levels. Hence the hypothesis is advanced of statistical averages in which (to repeat) the single utterances of a single speaker are accommodated to all the utterances of that speaker, and these into all the utterances of all speakers, just as the theory of games proceeds from a single game (for example, of chess) to a set of games by one player and finally to all possible games. We end with a mathematical theory of the 'play' of communication, as if communication were a game of great skill. Modern electronic communication is indeed a matter of extraordinary skill. Pro-presentative communication excludes items which are not conventional or standardized but liable to continuous alteration, for then each and every referend would require a different sign peculiar to itself. But this would be uneconomical and excessively costly of effort, if not altogether beyond even human capacity of differentiation. It would be like picture writing in which there is a separate picture for each and every referend, which again is impossible for any but simple concrete referends and the simplest and briefest combinations of them. Only symbol *and* system together, that is a systematic symbolism, can satisfy the requirements. This was made possible by the capacities of simple units to combine into complex strings, accompanied by the standardization of the elementary but conventionalized symbol-referend relationship, in short by the invention of the word. The history of the alphabet is a parallel development, from the non-standardized imitative coding of pictographs, through ideograms and logograms, to syllabary and eventually symbolic and conventional alphabetic spelling. The utterance is progressively freed from the perceptual context as it becomes less and less dependent upon explicit reference, no matter whether the utterance is long or short. It is no longer identified with the immediate context of situation but detached through the selection and variation, permutations and combinations of the conventional and standard units of utterance, that is of words.*

There are other statistical relationships that give a good fit as well as the rank-frequency distribution; namely length (or size) and frequency, determinacy, content, perspicuity and frequency. A special case is that of the so-called *hapax legomenon* (word of unique occurrence), which statistically does not differ from words of low frequency. The *hapax legomenon* (for example in Aristophanes) is usually a word of unusual length; it is virtually equivalent to a phrase or clause. Extreme examples are the long compounds of Sanskrit, where even elaborate logical statements may be 'coded' into two very long words, by which the concepts are symbolized just as effectively as by the symbols of modern logical syntax.

The true interpretation of the statistical formula is, I believe, both historically and descriptively, given in terms of my theory of selective variation. It gives an 'informational' theory of linguistic structure, contrary to the procedures of logical syntax in which the atom is $\bar{p}$ (the proposition), and contrary to that of the telephone engineers. These latter set themselves the problem: find the least costly method of coding for a given message; not, the coding having been given, distribute 'information' among the available units in such a way as utilizes fully the capacities of coding, and to satisfy the criterion of economy. This (Mandelbrot's) ' "informational" theory leads to the actual distribution of information among the words of the language; these are postulated to be there, but without meaning, without any relation to anything else'; further, this 'model of language is fully analogous to the perfect gas of thermodynamics'. This latter result is the one found also by the communications engineers whose solution is to the direct problem of statistical matching, Mandelbrot's to the inverse problem. Both give almost identical percentages of 'redundancy' for English.

The theoretical considerations appear not to be affected by the medium of linguistic communication. It may be a natural

* See Appendix II

language, written or spoken, of no matter what family or type or age; or radio, telephone, or telegraph; or 'acoustic', encoded in sound wave, when Fourier analysis reveals signals compounded of a certain range of frequencies.* The same definition of quantity of 'information' results, but instead of the sine waves of Fourier analysis, linguistic units—phonemes or morphomes— are used. It is important, however, not to confuse the complex frequencies of Fourier analysis obtained by electric filters with the statistical frequencies of distribution, that is relative frequencies of occurrence.

An accepted model of communication goes like this:

$$signal$$

$$source \longrightarrow message \longrightarrow \square \longrightarrow message \longrightarrow destination$$

The signal may be disturbed by interference of any kind. It is produced by the speaker, and received by the listener only when encoded and decoded in the agreed manner, for example a language, or Morse code, or electrical impulses over a telephone wire or radio. Coding involves the sequence of automatic choices, phonemes and the rest, permitted by a given linguistic pattern and their emergence as signals. In the human being this is performed as a motor activity in speech and writing. The 'choices' (i.e. selection) and their sequence manifest at any particular occurrence a high degree of determinacy, which is given in part by the nature of the 'information', but also by feedback from previous utterances, heard and spoken, and reinforced by previous experience of them. Encoding need not be overt; the vocal behaviour may be suppressed, but it can always be produced at call. It may also always be varied in one of two ways: (a) the patterned alternants, e.g. *wife* as a noun, but *wive* as a verb or, if a noun, only before -s (and followed only by a plural verb form *are*, not *is*), but not after s- (at least not in modern English, or with the same meaning)— or, very rarely, departures from the pattern, which may be incipient historic change, as *breaked* for *broke*; and (b) historic change as *helped* for *holpen, got* for *gat*. Variation is a necessary part of the code, as much as selection, both in its contemporary usage and in its historic development.

The code, then, is systematic. The systematized recurrent

* See pp. 125-128 and Appendix 3

features are words and arrangements of words, morphomes, phonemes and any other features, within the types and patterns of a language. Decoding is the reverse process, perception of the message and discrimination among its components. However, all members of a speech-community act indifferently and by turns as speaker and hearer.

'Communication' theory quantifies these processes regarded as the telephone company's commodity. Its importance to linguistics is that it furnishes a good model of language as a status, from which it may be argued that all languages, ancient or modern, must fit the same model. This is also concluded from structural linguistics, as well as from historical and comparative linguistics.

The source and destination of a message are respectively the speaker's and hearer's brain. The message is made up of discrete units transformed into continuous form (speech waves) by the transmitter (the speaker); the signal is normally mixed with 'noise' (interference) in the channel, e.g. actual noise, a foreign accent, a bad cold; it is picked up by the receiver (the human ear) and decoded back into discrete units at the destination. Conditioned probabilities in language are high, as shown by the statistics of language, and thus make language, mathematically considered, a stochastic process; moreover they are determined by preceding events (this is called a Markoff process); finally it is ergodic (on this term see the Glossary). The mapping of the continuous signal into discrete units has been shown to be a matter of quantification, greatly aided by the fact that language is such a highly ordered sequence of events. A sudden decrease in the probability of a unit (and therefore increase in the amount of 'information') indicates a boundary (e.g. of words or morphomes) in the sequence. 'Information' is concerned with making adequate choices, that is accepting or rejecting a given item out of a finite number of items, the probabilities of which are not equal.* This, it appears, is just what is done in language, and in a manner analogous to the open or closed switch of an electrical relay.

Selectivity is a necessary condition of the dynamic balance or equilibrium of language, and shows itself in statistical regularity; variation is a necessary condition of pro-presentation,

* See Appendix 12

symbolism, and a product of its demands, as well as of the conditions under which language is historically transmitted. A linguistic status is achieved by the constant interaction of variation, which is destructive of the system, and selection, which is therapeutic. In this way a pattern is maintained, but its structure is different at different times (compare modern with Old English) and in different languages (compare English with Paiute). The negentropy of language means that the status is not allowed to run down to a prolonged 'moo'; the function of reference (symbolism) checks entropic degeneration, selection repairs unlimited variation. By using verbal formulations as surrogates for infinitely numerous and complex memories of experience it is possible for man to respond effectively to a far wider range of phenomena★ than would otherwise be possible. As 'storage' increases we modify our formulations in the interests of consistency. In scientific fields, a high degree of precision is reached; in the emotions, verbal 'magic' may operate, supported by mistake, incoherence, inconsistency, and imprecision. But emotion and imagination are not ruled out of the human operation. It has been asserted that inculcation of synthetic emotions into electrical computation machines is quite a conceivable future development. Emotional reactions result from warnings sent at high speed by glandular secretions, and are therefore a form of intrapersonal communication. Man has more input channels, more computing units, and, more output channels, which give him the ability to perceive pleasure and pain, suffering and happiness, to exercise imagination and to show originality. It is the symbolization of these sensations, not the sensations themselves, that is subject to law and theory. But they may yet be made subject to 'control'—in the sense of guidance and prediction of the results which they will engender.

Forecasts are made from time to time of machines that will 'compose' in traditional literary forms. More likely at present is the possibility of predicting the way a language is going, and of extrapolating backwards to a former status, and so of discovering former relationships (for example, of Indo-European with Semitic) now only guessed. The actual state of a system governed by statistical laws and following a predetermined course must be related to its subsequent state by equations

★ Appendix 10

identical with those which relate it to its previous state. The development of mathematical linguistics is opening a new field of inquiry, and may rightly be expected to bring greater order into a subject, which, treated subjectively, has been and still remains chaotic.

XII

LANGUAGE AND LIFE

AMONG the Cuna, a homogenous group of American Indians who occupy the eastern part of the isthmus of Panama and northern Colombia, and who have maintained their own language and way of life, despite contact with Europeans since the end of the fifteenth century, most animals and plants have different names for use by day and by night. But there are no names for days, or for divisions of time less than a month, and nothing to correspond to a past tense. Southern Paiute, a Shoshoni dialect spoken in southwestern Utah and northwestern Arizona, has means of expressing relative time, chiefly formative elements combined with the verbal stem, and also similar devices for distinguishing kind (not time) of action as durative, momentary, terminative, progressive. Think of a moving-picture film as giving a progressive picture of action in its entirety, a single frame of the film a point of action; inceptive action is the initial frame, terminative either the initial or the final frame, perfective all the frames superimposed one on the other. In the personal pronouns of Southern Paiute, there are inclusive and exclusive forms for the dual and plural;* but the third personal forms introduce two other formal (that is in linguistic form) distinctions, between animate and inanimate, and visible and invisible, of which that between animate and inanimate is found also in certain plural forms of nouns Some early Indo-European languages have a multipersonal generalizing form meaning 'people in general' designated by a suffix reserved to this meaning. Greek and Sanskrit have a peculiar so-called 'middle' voice, to describe what may be called a 'boomerang' or reflexive action, especially of bodily functions and emotions. In Welsh and Irish there is a special form to

* See Appendix 9

express equative degree ('same as') as well as comparative ('more') and superlative ('most'). Bantu distinguishes animate and inanimate by grammatical devices.

Such illustrative detail is endless, repetitious or peculiar, discordant or in agreement, partly congruent and partly not; yet only a small number of the languages of the world have been observed and described accurately enough to give a basis for definite statements of their usage. It is only when there occurs a distinctive form which carries a distinctive function that attention is directed at such matters as the presence or absence of this or that particular grammatical category (gender, number, case, tense, voice, mood and the like) in a particular language. Further inspection frequently leads to the conclusion that what at first glance seems to be missing, since there is no distinctive form, may be and actually is expressed in some other way, e.g. an entire phrase. But this is not to say that every variety of content of expression is to be found in every language. There is, however, nothing to prevent whatever the content of Hopi or Eskimo or Aranta expresses from being put, for example, into English or French or German, provided that the effort is made. Those experts who know Hopi or Eskimo or Aranta, and who begin by insisting that this or that feature is incapable of English expression, always end by explaining it in English. Evidently they are confusing what is habit in the two languages which they are comparing, that is the formal equipment of grammar, which may be quite different and may even have some category or other totally wanting; and what is choice, the things that speakers of different languages may or may not have occasion to say at all, which again varies from one language to another. The argument is of a hypergrammatical character, and much of the theoretical discussion that has gathered around it mere hairsplitting.

Parts of speech are the maximum word-classes of a language, deduced from its syntactic constructs, each class being defined in terms of the functional meanings which it fulfills. Broadly put, both parts of speech, whether formally distinguished or not, and the grammatical categories which they sustain, are functional. Sweeping generalizations are risky. It has been said, for example, that nouns may receive formative elements of case, but verbs may not; and that verbs have formative elements of tense, that nouns have not. Yet temporal pronouns are found in Melanesian where pronouns also have distinctions of mood. Hence many of the supposedly exclusive categories apply only to certain languages or groups of languages. It is better, therefore, to insist upon the formal aspect of grammatical categories, and to specify in each case the language concerned, avoiding anything that approaches universal grammar except so far as a logical system may be devised that will generate the features of a given language, and this task has not yet been completed. Distinctions are not always clear cut; for example, both pronouns and verbs often show features of person, gender appears in the Semitic verb, in the second person singular; number is common both to nouns and verbs in very many languages; voice in the verb varies with case in the noun. The connective verb, e.g. Indo-European *esti 'is' (to be distinguished from the substantive meaning 'exists') has verbal, personal or pronominal (-ti 'it'), and (since it may be entirely wanting, as in Latin herba uiridis 'grass is green'), zero forms. Moreover a form such as esti and the conjunction are functionally identical, since one joins morphomatic constructs, the other syntactic constructs. Categories, then, have a subconscious basis, actualized in the formal types of utterance, or simply in the utterance (if formal distinctions are wanting); to regard them as a fixed quality of language is unjustifiable generalization, and minimizes both the differences between languages, and the overlapping of functions within even one language, without leading to valid or even practical broader conclusions. How can a formal theory of parts of speech refer to Chinese or Aranta or Eskimo, all of which lack the necessary formal apparatus? A given concept is pertinent to different languages, therefore, in different degrees and in different ways.

Correlation between grammatical categories and natural categories, e.g. tense and time, case and locality, gender and sex, is apt to be incomplete. French with only two genders, German with three but 'unnaturally' distributed, a language with six formal genders show the discrepancy. Case forms sometimes mark logical, and not purely local relations. Number is not always logical, for example wheat but oats, or in Lithuanian dumaĩ (plural) 'smoke', save in so far as there may be a designation of mass in respect of constituent particles; nor is formal agreement—in Latin *exercitus* (singular) is often construed with a plural verb. Finally, form itself is not consistent—genitive singular in Latin is *-ae*, *-i*, *-is*, *-s;* or consider *-i* which is genitive, locative, dative singular, or nominative plural, or passive infinitive, or first person perfect active indicative, or imperative. The complexity of functional classification is very great, and not always amenable to the technique of substitution. It follows that grammatical categories are by no means absolute or exclusive; they are in fact as complex as life itself, even when not directly related to life or to nature; it also follows that the degree and abstraction of pro-presentative features vary considerably from one language to another, both by their presence or absence and also grammatically, all the way from simple appositional arrangements to complex inflexional patterns. Fundamentally, from a strict linguistic point of view, grammatical categories are concerned with formal interdependence of relationships within a system. A particular system determines the function of a particular category. For example in Bantu there is a separate prefix for each of the following categories: people; spirits; natural pairs; liquids; tools; languages; customs; usages; animals; mass meaning; abstractions; diminutives; augmentatives; depreciatives; and locatives. The distinction between quantity and quality is not always made formally, but when it is, one result is that men, elephants, horses and cattle are treated as persons, but 'small' people as women and children and slaves are considered things. In the Hamitic Bedauye dialect, *šà* 'cow' (which is important to a tribe of herders) has wandered into the person class (masculine), but if it is a question of the flesh of the animal (a distinction like *ox* and *beef*, *sheep* and *mutton* in English), then *šà* goes into the thing class (feminine).

The conclusion, for which there exists abundant evidence of the kind already given, is that life fashions language; that different languages develop their respective systems of symbolism and categorization by procedures of selection and variation; that categorical oppositions or contrasts may be stated in terms of binary choices; and that substitution plays a large role (e.g. a pronoun is a linguistic unit of which the referend is disclosed only outside the syntactic constructs in which it is used).

The assertion that grammatical categories or large-scale pat-

terning impose compulsion upon action is not justified historically, since again and again it is precisely language that has
pointed a way out from restriction on action, and opened the
door to new action. There is nothing to show that concepts
such as time and space have been *imposed* by language. It is
said by physicists that the concept of motion is older than that
of time, and in so far as Indo-European languages have developed the category of tense from that of aspect, which seems
to be the fact, the assertion has some truth in it, even linguistically viewed. Similarly, a symbolic expression of 'rapidly' passes
easily into that of 'presently, soon', even though tomorrow
never comes. But a civilization of timepieces, railway and
airplane schedules, or delayed action bombs, is bound to place
emphasis upon time. If the question is put, whence did language
get the category of time, the answer can only be, from the
external world. Concepts are related to sensible experience,
if not logically derived from them, and the observation of things
in motion (aspect) leads directly to that of time (tense). In
the same way, the contemplation and handling of solid objects
leads to the notions of configuration (how do you know what a
sphere is?) and of spatial relationships—in particular through
realization of an interval between two solid objects at a distance.
Space is seen as filling the interval or intervals between two or
more solid objects, and here is precisely the symbolic value of
the Indo-European category of case, e.g. locative, ablative,
accusative, even the genitive. The story of the discovery of
the outer planets of the solar system suggests that in certain
situations the structure of language tells us something about
the structure of the universe. How else are propositions to be
maintained or denied? Or must we abdicate, and hold that we
have knowledge only of language and of nothing else? In a
storm at sea we trust the meteorological language of storm
warnings, and expect the captain to heed them, and get out
of the path of the hurricane.

If tomorrow never comes, 'day' should have no plural, and
so (we are told) the Hopi do not say 'he stayed ten days' but
'he left on the day after the tenth'. But the Latin way of
reckoning the date is absolutely the same (*ante diem decimum
Kalendas Iunias* 'nine days before the first of June', literally
'on the tenth day', i.e. May 23), and the linguistic argument of

a fundamentally different concept of time in Hopi and Indo-European falls to the ground, in this and in all the other linguistic evidence held to prove the contention that language imprisons man. It is expression that varies, whether historically in one and the same language, or in different languages. There is usually an empiric test available; when observation is corrected, so is language, to match observation. Newton was not the last word. There is no obligation to act about situations in a certain way as a consequence of the way the situation is talked about; for if the act is unsuccessful, then talk is modified to suit experience. Contradictions appear not because verbal expression dictates behaviour, but when it is followed by no behaviour at all (or by contradictory behaviour); verbalism, the utterance, is then taken to be enough, and behaviour stops short at mere verbalism, as with the injunction to love your enemies, or else is falsified and then you go to war. It is not linguistic symbolism that is at fault, but non-linguistic behaviour. Those symbols in fact are most effective that are unemotional, such as x, y, z; or discussion about the properties of triangles, or the value of π (3·14159). It may be objected that much of language is not amenable to such precision. This is not true; it is man that (so far) is not amenable, and now he is faced with a new linguistic crisis, similar to those presented to the Greek sophists, to medieval scholasticism, or to eighteenth century epistemology. Language, since it is neither static nor inflexible, is a way to that which is yet to be known; not a form of bondage, unless we voluntarily place ourselves in bondage by arguing (for example) that classical Greek is more highly symbolic (for us) than twentieth-century English. We can and do criticize language, which is not, therefore, outside our critical consciousness. The contrary view simply fails to distinguish between the 'how' and the 'what' of linguistic expression; it identifies habit and choice, and could be true only if the entire universe were a solipsist myth. But language eliminates solipsism: 'I' (X_1) is objectified as 'me' (X_2), 'us' is 'me' (X_2) as well as the onlooker (Y), and the third person objectifies both (Z). 'You' (Y) and 'he' or 'they' (Z) are objective, contrasted with the subjective 'I', and everybody is Y or Z as well as X by turns. 'We' occurs variably, as a chance collection of different 'I's', in the classroom, in the subway; but it is not the plural of 'I' (i.e. many instances of 'I') as 'houses' is the plural of 'house'. Even in grammar the symbol $I:we$ is as different formally and etymologically as the referends themselves are biologically. Language is an emergent conceptual pattern that, if unfettered by a dead tradition, solves its own problems; modern attempts at intelligibility and coherence, amid new problems, are like what people have been doing with language all along through recorded history. In a crude way trade-names are more enterprising than the stereotypes of 'literature', and the linguistic capacities of professional philosophy often inferior to those of human beings in general. We can always choose; even if we refuse to make a choice, that is to choose not to make the choice, and doubt must end in the doubt of doubt. Language, then, is not only the mould in which 'thought' may be cast, it is also the medium for its transformation. It is no support for a doctrine of a fractional nominalism, a discordant fraction at that, appropriate merely to each linguistic type. For example, a supposed division of nature into events and objects on the basis of grammar loses all cogency when it is realized that formally and historically the distinction of *noun: verb* is indefensible. Linguistic form or habit is largely a convenience, and 'it rains' is a ribald joke to Aristophanes ('Zeus sends the rain'), but a noun ('rain-there') to comparative Indo-European grammar just as to modern Hopi grammar. As for the contention that a class-label is apt to be too large or too small, even English distinguishes between the tail of a rabbit (*scut*) and the tail of a fox (*brush*), or a gathering of geese, partridges, or porpoises. To say that 'Hopi' physics is different from 'Standard Average European' physics (whatever these varieties of physics may be) is a curious error; there *is* no 'Hopi' physics at all. Language is, or may be, concerned with formulation in process, and therefore rarely if ever completed. Its symbolic character depends upon its capacity for selecting, for habitual use, what it needs from a great repertoire of possible linguistic symbolizations and formulations, and for varying both of these, also at need. It is, moreover, the temporary limitation of pattern that makes possible the choice, the new step forward, namely through new and often highly individual recombinations of 'evidence'.

Since the ear cannot be closed nor the tongue stilled, there

228

LANGUAGELANGUAGE

is nothing for it but selection. This is true even at the lowest level of rough phonetic approximations—too 'good' an ear is a 'bad' one, that would never succeed in sorting out distinctive features. Structure and pattern come from gradual emendation of language conceptually as well as formally: 'follow' becomes 'see' (follow with the eye), or 'say' (make to see), and 'man' (Old English *sec3*) comes from 'comrade, follower', all derived from a root *sequ*, 'to follow'. Until the atom was split, there was no expression 'fissionate', just as no fence 'ran' before a fence was built. It is not beyond the capacity of language so to remake itself as to bring current philosophical and scientific views of 'reality' into verbal (not merely formulaic) language. Concrete spatial terms, for example, have often become non-spatial before now, as *religion, superstition, principle, fundamental, comprehend, understand*. Language is not merely a self-contained symbolic organization; it is also imaginative, creative and emergent. This is at once its strength (in progress) and its weakness (in error). It has its inconsistencies as well as consistencies, its wisdom as well as its folly; and it is impossible to reject this dual 'purpose' without wrecking language. But language has always succeeded in clarifying its own components in the past, and there is no reason to suppose that it will fail now. Its evolving symbolism is a process of self-renewal, which is life, a process of self-emendation, of self-correction. Standardization and specialization are inhibiting, and in the end fatal; man need not bend to linguistic circumstance, but may easily bend language to his needs.

As a step in the cosmic process, of the evolution of the world and of life, language is a comparatively recent stage in the development of consciousness, that particular kind of awareness of environment in the truly human being which sets a problem only to be solved by articulate and cumulative language. Biologists characterize life as structure and activity. Now, to repeat, language is not an organism, but it *is* an activity of the human organism and partakes of the nature of organism by the very fact of structure. In some sense its structure corresponds to the structure of man's life and of his world, particularly in the manner in which it holds time and space within itself, differently as different languages conceive these forms, each language being a sort of duplicate partial world contained within itself. The factors of this duplicate world are not the entire universe but are selected, for no individual has an input capacity for information so vast. To cope with as much of it as human knowledge does, even by the subdivision of 'labour', is achieved by systems of symbols that have become more and more comprehensive through a cumulative and unifying, but at at the same time economical, process. Vocal symbolism is a superior system to others by its precision, and by its carrying power (especially through modern methods of transmission) in all possible directions and in the dark. Musical sound lacks the precision of language; the arts, like sign-language, or writing, require the medium of light, and also lack precision. This is where even television fails or a moving picture, unless accompanied by voice; and also illustrations unless accompanied by words. Some of the popular picture magazines of our day have already regressed, backwards into a semi-inarticulate stage of the infancy of man. A portrait of Oliver Cromwell may show the shape of his nose, but says nothing about who he was, when he lived, what he did, why and where and how he did it, and what the result of it all was; and no picture or diagram by itself communicates much scientific or mathematical knowledge. A painting by Constable may show no single animal in view; but language—any language—may tell me or anyone, observing the same meadow, that the cattle have gone into the barn. The observer, when he sees the cattle crossing the meadow, sees the same picture, no matter what his language. But his language will use in the case of each observer its own symbols, and especially will distinguish somehow between the cattle now *are*, and the cattle *were* or *will be* in the meadow, putting them back so to speak into the meadow of Constable's painting. Language is thus a recent (and so far the latest) stage in evolution, it might almost be said in cosmic evolution, which has been brought to the stage at which it may be exercised imaginatively and even prospectively so as to anticipate the future course of events and their outcome. It is as if the natural world, and all its significance, were being caught up more and more into a counterpart of symbolic language, and then stored in a great world library by means that are both purposeful and self-determining. Spoken language is fleeting; it may be recorded on disks and tape—perhaps the libraries of the future will contain these in continually increasing number and bulk. Meanwhile, 'in black ink' all things 'may still shine bright'.

Language has to do not solely with external events, experience and behaviour, but also with understanding, intellection, 'mental'* events. Some phobia or other, for example, is not completely accounted for, if it is regarded simply as a cluster of conditioned reflexes; for identical experiences do not necessarily produce the same, or any, phobia in everyone who undergoes them. Thus the individual interpretation put upon the events must play a part in the outcome. Similarly, in the way the pattern of a Maltese cross or the schematic representation of petals of a flower is 'seen', there is an element which is indeed subjective, but not therefore irrelevant to the interpretation. It is in this sense that man may be said to 'fashion' himself, guiding his own impulses and forging his own purposes—for example, deliberately directed toward progress in *this* world, not in another, future world. It is characteristic of all attempts to put the notion of 'immortality' into linguistic symbolism that either they are negative (like *immortality* itself), or vague (*eternity* 'an age long', the inadequacy of which led to *sempiternal*, which is no better), or not what is meant (*perpetual, reincarnate*), or susceptible of widely varying exegesis; moreover, these negative expressions are, in Homer or the Rigveda, reserved for the gods—only apotheosis confers immortality. Even the meteorologist's prediction of tomorrow's 'highest' temperature is based on today's and yesterday's readings of temperatures and of other conditions over extensive contiguous masses of land and ocean. Statements concerning the future are interpretations of the regularities of the past. Observation and analysis of experience stop short without the intervention of yet further events, namely, a 'mental' interpretation and a pro-presentation by means of symbols, whether in a meteorological map or in articulate language. There is foresight of an end. To this, at least where human activity is concerned, purpose to achieve an end is added.

History and literature may be regarded as constituted of three similar steps: in these also interpretation is preceded by

* For the justification of this term, see G. Henrik von Wright, *A Treatise on Induction and Probability*, London 1951, p. 269.

a record or story (observation, the statement of events) and by an analysis of experience (as in tragedy) or an artificial extension of social memory (as in history), as preludes to inference. Criticism, however, is faced by a peculiar difficulty in that it assumes, and especially when it sets out to teach criticism, that the knowledge already exists. How is it possible to read a page (or a book) about how to read a page (or a book) without having first learned this art?

The fact is that there is far greater variation in the human response than in non-human, and no such consistency in animate as in non-animate properties. 'The burnt child dreads the fire, a burnt poker does not'. As for the cat which never gets itself into quandaries, it may be answered that while a cat is perfect for cattish purposes, it is not good for much else. The enormous variety of recombinations of what is known, the constant possibility of intelligent and novel steps within an old framework, as the very nature of human activity, these are a matter of linguistic social inheritance. White mice and pigeons, like cats, have stereotyped invariant responses, social in part, but not linguistic at all.

But in human beings inherited patterns and stereotyped impulses, for all their worth on occasion, may also stand in the way of increased intelligence in the use, and fuller control, of linguistic responses, as when we shelve our responsibilities upon metaphysical absolutes or a mythical pantheon. For many, the attitude remains the same, in purchasing a charm over the counter of a drugstore, that it was in the Middle Ages, in buying a charm from the priest. Allegorically it was the spoken word of God that formed the world in seven days ('God said . . . '), or 'In the beginning was the word', or rather 'a plan' (λόγος). This implies a deliberate choice of the appropriate utterance as the decisive factor, a conscious formulation of values and verification of the validity of concepts, perhaps even an estimate of their effect when put into practice. Often enough in the past the accepted doctrine of one age had been derided as 'nonsense' in earlier times, a relation that seems likely to be repeated now in the promises of greater synthetic grasp, balance and judgement, finer acuteness of perception, and a higher level of performance that biologists and communications engineers alike seem to forecast. The rejection of a geocentric universe, or

of the dogma that the earth is flat, were victories for theories
that had been condemned as 'nonsensical'. The obstacle had
often been linguistic, in the difficulty of inventing and defining
new, or of redefining old, symbols. It follows that there is a
compelling obligation to use words in a certain way, an obligation that is rarely if ever declined in scientific experiment and
theory, but is constantly evaded by obscurantists in religion,
in politics, and in criticism, and frequently even in the law.
Abuse of the pro-presentative power of language ends by de-
priving the symbol of its value: to cry 'wolf' (or 'tiger' or 'bear')
as a mere empty threat, or for the sake of excitement, opens
the way to actual danger when the warning is no longer heeded:
hence *tiger* is a taboo word in parts of India. Language tends
to redesign itself, and from a strictly linguistic point of view,
it makes no difference what current theory may be, since one
characteristic of language is to develop new functions, to symbolize—not to copy— 'nature'. Not only in philosophy, but
in all its expression, language needs to be 'well made', in the
sense that its constructs, while symbolic, shall be also creations
of intelligence, not of mysticism or nihilism or negativism.
Chemistry is a better language than alchemy or black magic,
astronomy than the incantations of superstition, supposed to
ward off an eclipse or its imagined possible consequences. But
there can be no finality; to seek it is delusion, and to impose
any doctrine as final and complete is, to that extent, to induce
a total paralysis of language. This disease of language has
threatened man in the past, and fears aroused by the impact
of recent discovery and invention seem likely to lead to attempts
to revive it. But fear of 'machines' is irrational; a machine is
an extension of 'mind', which can control what it has made.
'To believe otherwise is to abdicate.'

Language as an emergent symbolism cannot be static; since
it is dynamic it may on occasion be erratic. But those who
believe it to be the source of all human error, because it is and
must always be in a process of adjustment so long as it is
spoken, make the mistake of regarding it as a straitjacket, as
if it were all habit and no choice. Over long periods of time
language has been liberating more than inhibiting, and its
liberating qualities, which are vastly the more important, are
precisely those which have been forgotten by some modern

theorists. Belief in the mechanization of man is perhaps a derivative from the background of a highly mechanized environment, but if man must be thought of as a 'machine' then it is he himself who has made the machine and who must keep it in repair and under control. Within certain limits, he has the power of choice, and it is the faculty of choice, not the limitation, that is the more important, above all in language, today as in the past and in the future, as a *linguistic* as well as a social responsibility. The fact is that every language has infinite possibilities of symbolism—there is no necessary bipolar distribution of events and objects in terms of verbs and nouns, most languages have more than one symbol for the same object (like Greek δρῦς and φηγός 'oak'), or the same word for different objects 'snow, cold, ice' (so in Indo-European as illustrated by Latin *gelu* 'cold', *glacies* 'ice', Avestic *garᵊnu-* 'snow [?]' all from the same root)—these features are no prerogative of Hopi or Aztec; the number of possible combinations of words is not infinite, but it is enormously large in any language, and the range of symbolism is thereby enlarged almost without restriction. Progress in language is basically a question of keeping pace with non-linguistic events, not of reducing language to logic, which would then become a dead hand, by making language definitive. If falsehood and error and at times folly are implicit, this is the price to be paid for pro-presentation; only if language were static would it be possible to confine its values to denotation and extension, excluding connotation and intension. True, an accumulated intension is a fruitful source of ambiguity. But this risk is unavoidable; and if it compels a reshaping of expression from time to time, it becomes beneficial. Linguistic meaning is enlarged by the very circumstance that words connote as well as denote, thereby giving new points of departure. If the Klamath Indians (in Oregon) really have no general term 'to run', but only for different kinds of running, that is a defect, a shortcoming. It means that there is no real abstraction. Fortunately language is not static; it may lag somewhat, but in the long run it is a historic continuum that keeps up with the continuum of events, or with the observation and interpretation of events, for words can be created at will (e.g. *thermometer*). Yet neither the vocabulary nor the syntax of a language is haphazard; its very regularity and its constant advances are a good proof of 'reality', and of our increasingly improved command of it.

Meaning is the first and most specific problem for any philosophical basis of language, the nature of the relation between words and their combinations and that to which these refer. This book has sought to show that language may be described in three different ways: (1) as a series of physical events in sequence; (2) analytically, as discrete units, morphomes and phonemes; (3) semantically. The first is the concern of phonetics, the second of linguistics, the third of semantics. Language is thus connected with reality at both ends, the phonetic and the semantic; but structural analysis shows it to be systematic. This is why language is a code, a system of symbols or a systematic symbolism. And that is the simplest answer to the question, how are words related to their referends, namely by pro-presentation, the third dimension of language, which mediates between expression and symbol, between form and content. Expression is merely a sensuous sign, heard or seen; and analogy the link between sign and symbol. Most words seem to have a physical reference in origin; their analogical or metaphorical extensions give them new reference, and even a generality which may reach any degree of abstraction; gradual 'emendation', or selective variation, gives them and their combinations one with another the structure characteristic of a particular language.

Phonetic varieties, which are infinite, coalesce into a strictly limited number of phonemes, of the possible orders of which a given language uses only a small submultiple. The morphomes of a language are finite in number, and may readily be catalogued exhaustively. The number of morphological constructs of morphomes is again a small submultiple of the number of forms. Similarly with form-classes, categories, and parts of speech. Yet these unite into a very large number, so large as to be practically without limit, of possible combinations in continuous discourse, and cover all that we find to say. Further, it is possible to escape the distracting complexity of things by selecting what is for the moment significant, but in the totality of utterance to comprehend the universe, to see it as a whole and so resist the frustration and negativism of the finite mind. Not only are all intelligent steps (and some that are not) taken in this way, but the procedure is fundamentally one and the same in science, in philosophy, and in letters. The correlation of symbol and referend is the product of the versatile discriminatory capacity of language, which has made and can continue to make man as an intelligent being. Beings which continue to repeat unsuccessful behaviour not only are not intelligent; they become extinct, like the dinosaur, the Tasmanian. Perhaps this is what is happening in the destruction and slaughter of modern warfare—we persist in our unintelligent but 'normal' responses. It is high time to exclude once and for all deliberate nonsense, untruthful propaganda, religiosity and scientism, cretinous advertising and moronic broadcasting. Those who are actuated by profit should understand that profit accrues to the proper use of language. Misuse of language breeds illusion, and illusion is always damaging, either directly or through the later process of disillusion. A clever work of fiction has portrayed communists as ants, fascists as piranhas, professional politicians as howler monkeys. It might well have gone on to condemn some products of wasted education as trained mules; or, to change the metaphor, the fine talk and fine writing of modern critics, as Plato did the sophistry of his contemporaries, as mere confectionery. For language may also culminate in estrangement, notwithstanding good intention.

The linguist who takes science to be no more than a form of linguistic behaviour, and not about things, at the same time condemns his own linguistics as a form of linguistic behaviour, and not about language. The former tells us about the linguistic behaviour of scientists, the latter of linguists. But this view is untenable. Language, and particularly scientific language, assembles reminders for particular purposes. This is close to the existentialist view that all knowledge which does not relate itself to existence is contingent and non-essential, though that view does not take the further step that there is an obligation to use language, not to misuse it: 'let your communication be Yea, yea; Nay, nay', without any hedging or dodging, is an injunction addressed to human beings, but so far performed better by their machines, which now promise soon to be able to check and verify inferences, and to predict the outcome of action with precision. In industry there is often a failure of the human element, working with complex systems of machines, as a result of imperfect communication. It is important not only to make available enough information to an operator, but also to avoid unnecessary complication of the task by providing too much or irrelevant information. Once more we are reminded of Plato, who defined social justice as 'minding one's own business' (τὰ αὐτοῦ πράττειν), no man being set to perform tasks either above or below his powers, which Plato thought was the most fertile source of misery and crime.

The entire doctrine of language set forth in this book is based upon the view that there is a limit of tolerance in linguistic function. This is the notion underlying relative frequency and selective variation as the controlling factors of the use and the development of language. Input limits vary, as Plato would have seen, from one man to another. We are now told that there is an analogy between mental disorders ('nervous breakdowns' as they are popularly known) and the failure of a digital computing machine that is overloaded with input instructions so excessive that the 'memory circuits' are unable to carry instructions adequate to cope with the situation. This has been called the traffic problem of the nervous system, that limit of each organizational form beyond which it will not function. Control of body temperature is normally automatic, like the control of a heating unit by a chronotherm servomechanism—the comparison is of the crudest sort, no doubt; yet there is a certain unity of 'knowing' between the verbal expressions concerned with temperature (*refrigerium, thermometer, heat, cold, it is hot* [*cold*] = *calet*[*friget*]), recordings of temperature, the activity of putting on or taking off clothing, bodily homeostasis (of temperature), and the goal-directed activity of a servomechanism.

Linguistic events are statistically determined. By contrast much of the rest of human behaviour appears disorderly, even self-destructive, for example in modern warfare; left to itself, the total amount of disorder in nature is said to be steadily increasing—the clock is running down, unless, indeed, there is a force that rewinds it which has not yet been discovered.

One of the great difficulties in any treatment of language that seeks to be scientific is the closeness of the data to the observer: language is part and parcel of him, like other forms of human behaviour. In comparing verbal with non-verbal behaviour, therefore, identical disability obtains. It is also the case that the two are often correlates of the same situation. Perhaps the most obvious conclusion from a comparison of the two, indeed it is a commonplace observation, is that language, in our time at least, is working badly everywhere except in scientific discourse, and even there the scientists themselves express their own misgivings from time to time. So far then as 'meaning' is, or is intended to be, goal-directed activity, it is proper to compare utterances with non-linguistic behaviour. The great gulf between the two is that whereas language as such is orderly, the use of it, and still more, other forms of conduct, do not show any such orderliness, or in anything like the same degree. A linguist may perhaps be allowed to suggest that if the human race has developed a form of conduct which in itself is characterized by almost mathematical regularity, and if each normal human being is capable of acquiring this form of conduct and of using it, in part, but far from entirely, in an automatic way, then it would seem possible, at least theoretically, for him to learn the same kind of orderliness both in all his use of language and in all his other forms of conduct at all points.

The universal technique of talking is normally carried on within the permitted pattern of a language—or not at all. Comparable behaviour might be postulated as a condition of a reasonably successful conduct of the rest of human life— for example, of obtaining food and shelter, of survival. It is no use to depart utterly from the pattern and expect to stay alive, outside an asylum for the insane. But the rest of human conduct departs widely from the standard of this technique. Yet again and again, practice in many fields of human activity, technique, has been improved until it approaches a theoretical ideal—in sports for example. One dominating feature of language has been shown to be controlled selection and variation: is this a clue to the answer to the human problem? Beginning with the use of language? And then passing on, through it, to the control of other activities? These are difficult but basic questions, which as yet can only be asked, not answered. But so far as language is capable of adaptation to environment, as its history shows, the situation is not entirely hopeless; the problem itself has become acute through the enormous and enormously rapid change of environment of the present and immediately preceding generations as compared with the conditions, economic, social, political, national and international, and all the rest, under which *their* predecessors lived for many generations—perhaps as far back as the close of the Stone Ages, certainly as far back as the earliest practice of irrigation and agriculture. We are living in the midst of a 'technical' revolution, in trying but exciting times. Language is still far behind, appropriate more to the middle ages than to our own age, adaptation to which it will have to work out for itself and at the same time try to keep up with the still newer and more accelerated changes in environment which seem imminent. This cannot be done by a return to the past, an answer that is continually urged upon us by the humanists. Human conduct is, in a sense, a skill that is acquired and can be taught; but it is not historically reversible and even world-wide catastrophe will not restore a garden of Eden, should a solitary Adam and Eve survive to inhabit it. They would speak some modern language, with all its accumulation of knowledge and stored experience, not the first human vocables.

Improvement of the technique can be hastened by deliberate study and perhaps put into practice effectively; we need not await the slow adaptation such as has taken place in the past in historic linguistic changes. The great difficulty is that it is not quite the same sort of problem that a chronotherm, for example, has to deal with, or even the person who feels cold or hot; but more like the involuntary control of homeostasis which keeps the bodily temperature even, independently of the temperature of a room or of the outside weather. It is a question of whether the self-stabilizing control of language as system can be extended and harnessed to the contemporary use of language socially, and thence to all those forms of behaviour to which linguistic control may be applied, and which make up a large part of the entire repertoire of human conduct. Language, as was said at the beginning, touches everything that we do. Here is its overwhelming importance, and also the overwhelming importance of understanding language, in order to improve, and perhaps hasten, the adjustments which it *must* make, the sooner the better, to its present environment, not least in its relation to the discoveries of other scientific disciplines, for which, as also for those disciplines that, by a false and unjustified antinomy, are called as it were par excellence the humanities, language is a common ground, and thus is able to reconcile and unify human knowledge. The somewhat satisfactory state of orderliness which men show in small day-to-day affairs is the goal at which to aim in larger undertakings that affect humanity as a whole through long-range chains of events on a large scale. Some of us run our personal and family affairs, even our businesses, with reasonably good order; from economics (in its etymological sense of 'the science of good order' in a household) to 'anthroponomics' is a long, long way, but it is language that will chart the path of escape from human bondage. This view is neither pessimistic nor optimistic; it is based simply on the observation of words and their ways. The fundamental features of language which this study has attempted to explain are: pro-presentation; selective variation and adaptation; the principle of binary choices, linguistic 'negentropy', input-output feedback (on a multilingual as well as monolingual level); that meaning ('goal-directed activity') is what you do (or at least what you intend), if not always what you say, even though what you say is part of what you do; and above all that the patterned order of language gives hope for establishing relative good order, to which man can never be in bondage, in the place of widespread disorder in human affairs, to which he must always remain in bondage.

Some minor practical aims, since it is a test of theory that it should bear on practice and have some relevance to the contemporary scene: Confucius, it is told, was once asked what he would do first if it were left to him to govern a nation. He replied: 'to correct language . . . If language is not correct, then what is said is not what is meant; if what is said is not what is meant, then what ought to be done remains undone; if this remains undone, morals and art will deteriorate; if morals and art deteriorate, justice will go astray; if justice goes astray, the people will stand about in helpless confusion. Hence there must be no arbitrariness in what is said. This matters above everything.'

We do not know how our language will be redesigned—that is emended or corrected; redesigned it must be, and if left to itself it will redesign itself, however slowly. One philosopher, with this problem in mind, suggested, as an example, 'green greens me'—not 'the grass' (or whatever it is) 'is green' (which is not true, chiefly because it is contradicted by the theory of light, but also because a red pigment of what has been named leghemoglobin, said to be nearly indistinguishable from the red pigment hematin of the hemoglobin of human blood, has now been discovered in plants). But it is impossible to foretell these things; all we can be sure of is that so long as spoken language exists it will, sooner or later, adapt itself to the needs of the speakers. Language has a primary function in the organization of this world's work, in teaching and learning (in particular of languages), in the correction of faulty education (especially since so much of education is the transmission of verbal habit), in giving better insight into human nature as well as into nature at large, in better control both of linguistic and non-linguistic conduct, conceivably in the perfection, and in the not very distant future, of usable translating machines. This may seem poor stuff compared with chemistry, physics, medicine, engineering, commerce, and all their tremendous achievements and applications; perhaps linguists would be better employed doing something else. But, over all, there still remains the love of learning, the wish to know, be its practical outcome obvious or not, great or small, the 'consolation of wisdom'. Such are some aims of linguistics; there are no doubt limitations to knowing, since man is himself involved in the knowing; but every step that can be taken out of the darkness and into the light is its own justification.

Memory of the past gives expectation of the future, the faculty of anticipation, almost an organ of hope. For old habit can be broken, and new habit formed, deliberately and intelligently, importing linguistic into technological revolution. But the spoken word (λόγος) and the reading (*lego*) of its written equivalent are both of them fundamentally also the exercise of choice at every step—choosing not only the right sounds and combinations of sounds but also the right words and combinations of words to fit the continually emerging patterns both of language and of life.

APPENDICES

1 (p. 65): *On Degrees of Linguistic Relationship*

THE statistical method of the so-called 'tetrachoric R', using the Q_6 formula, is valuable in revealing the degree of correlation ('relationship') between languages which may be suspected to be historically akin, provided a sufficiently large number of elements be included for comparison. But there is not necessarily the same coefficient of similarity in all of a group of related languages one to another, i.e. in respect of the linguistic features which they do or do not share. Nor is there any reason in the historical development of languages why there should be. In comparing dialects correlation methods may be used to show how much the bilingualism of frontier districts, or the polylingualism of an interlingua may safely draw from different languages. The inventors of artificial interlinguas seem to be unaware of this important procedure, though they have paid some attention to the expression of 'universals', concepts such as indication, totality, the relational complexes of starting-point, passage-point, and ending-point; comparison or grading, singularity and plurality, and such like; numerals, clock-time, ratio and proportion, composite wholes, and some others.

2 (p. 108, 122): *Phonematic Efficiency*

IF the distinguishing feature that discriminates between words is restricted to a single phoneme (like English *at: it, lack: lick, be: by*), the longest series of words so distinguished in modern French is six if the vowel is initial, seven if medial, and ten if final; in modern German the figures are five, seven, and six; in English eight, nine, and eleven. If the distinguishing feature is a single consonant (like *low: mow, letter: leather, league: leak*), then the longest series of words so distinguished in French is fourteen if initial, seven medial, and eight final; in German twelve, ten, six; in English fourteen, six, nine. But all these types are of words of comparative frequency of occurrence, which play a large part in the mechanics of these three languages. If the fullest possible use had been made of the resources of the languages, then, with words which *might* have been distinguished by a single phoneme only, as compared with those which actually are so distinguished, we have, as the longest series of words (standard pronunciations):

	Consonant and Vowel		*Consonant*		*Vowel*	
	possible	actual	possible	actual	possible	actual
French	105	52 (49.5%)	57	29 (50.9%)	48	23 (48%)
German	99	46 (45.5%)	66	28 (42.4%)	33	18 (54.5%)
English	123	57 (46.3%)	72	29 (40.3%)	51	28 (54.9%)

	Consonants	*Vowels and Diphthongs*	*Total*
French	19 (54.3%)	16 (45.7%)	35
German	19 + 3 = 22 (66.6%)	8 + 3 = 11 (33.3%)	33
English	22 + 2 = 24 (58.5%)	9 + 8 = 17 (41.5%)	41

Note to Table

No account was taken in these calculations of the relative frequency of occurrence of phonemes. Thus the proportion of *t:d* in English is 7.13: 4.31, of *m:n* it is 2.78%:7.24%. There is evidence to suggest that the distribution varies slightly in poetry as compared with prose, a further indication of the importance of form in poetic discourse.

Homonyms, that is words identical in sound but different in meaning, are bound to occur in series of words distinguished only by one phoneme (e.g. *lark* 'alauda' [skylark] or 'jest'; *be* and *bee; bow* and *bough; by* and *bye; bier* and *beer*). English shows 37 such, French 36, and German 17, which corresponds to the proportions of the actual cases in the table above.

Moreover, distinctions are made more often by the contrasts of more than one phoneme at a time, e.g. not only *pin: pen* (one unit) but also *bin: pen* (two units) or *bell: pin* (all three units), still only with labial consonant (*p:b*), vowel (*e:i*), and resonant (*n:l*), or most simply consonant (C) : vowel (V) in the arrangement CVC.

The figures for French, German, and English respectively, of words consisting only of consonant plus vowel, are about 115:30:120; of vowel plus consonant, they are about 30:26:50. These figures show that German disfavours the extreme type of monosyllabic word CV or VC, and this is the case also with regard to monosyllabic homonyms, for the greater the tendency to monosyllables, the greater the number of such homonyms unless there is some counter force. Further, the proportions of the types CV:VC are 5:1.3 French, 5: 4.3 German, and 5:2 English. The position of English, intermediate between the two, is due to surviving consonant inflexional endings such as -*s* third singular (*goes*) or plural (*foes*) and -*d* past tense (*loved*) compared with French and German which have fewer and more respectively. French and English both make great use of the contrast between voiced and unvoiced consonants (*v:f*), both initially and finally. German uses the contrast between long and short vowels, especially in stressed syllables, where it is effective in all the vowels that occur in such syllables. English is remarkable for its wealth of vowel phonemes (including diphthongs), and the extensive development of homonyms—puns are easy in English, and correspondingly despised.

The English phonematic system shares some features with German, others with French. This is historically true also, for English is genetically related more closely to German, but its linguistic ancestors were for a long time members of a bilingual milieu. It is barely possible that a single non-Romance and non-Germanic factor worked towards a contagion, if not precisely an affinity, namely the Keltic substratum of both languages. Current opinion discredits the likelihood of such an answer. But the evidence has never been sought.

3 (pp. 123, 217): *Spectrographic Analysis*

IF the two stock utterances, *cameras cost too much* and *can't do it* are recorded on magnetic tape, the investigator exchanges the initial elements, by cutting the tape, exchanging the units and recombining the tape, until he finds that he is cutting a segment of such length that the speaker will accept a playback recording as a repetition of what was originally pronounced. This may be shorter than is desirable—it may give only the burst of the initial [k] instead of the accompanying aspiration [h] which together with it makes up the initial phoneme of *camera*, *can't* [kh] or [kʰ]—but it will never be too long. A different sequence, e.g. *can't* . . . and *ken* . . . is a guarantee against getting a sequence that is too long (i.e. includes part of a second element), but the element (*a:e*) that follows the first must be close enough to it to prevent mere positional variants (e.g. in *kin: cot: cut: cool: queen*) from being rejected as repetitions of the same phoneme; in nearly all dialects [k] and [q] were distinctive, except before *o*, for it was possible for Cicero to relate a pun on *coque* 'cook' and *coque* (i.e. *quoque*) 'also', though Latin *quinque* 'five' gives rise to French *cinq*, Italian *cinque* but Sardinian *kimbe*. When, therefore, we have to deal with the summation of particular coincident movements of speech organs, we have to be careful to keep them together in one concurrent bundle as one phoneme, since the sums are not contrasted. The resulting segment remains a 'minimum' unit. It is precisely because phonematics and morphomatics deal with minimum units (phonemes and morphomes) that, important as these branches of linguistics are to linguists, they appear sterile to the layman, in contrast with glossematics which is concerned with significance on a more obvious plane. Phonemes and morphomes (minimum forms) have a status which is only relative; they result from the reduction of the stream of speech to its elements for purposes of analysis. Each phoneme has its own characteristic marks.

it is an atomic structure, but remains a minimum unit relatively to a morphome, a molecular structure. Morphomes, though compound relatively to phonemes, are simple relatively to words, clauses, phrases or sentences.

The multitude of phonematic segments are grouped into phoneme classes by the procedures of complementary distribution and free variation. Those segments which share no environment, found by inspection of the recorded samples, and which are phonetically similar, go together; those which alternate freely in a given environment, without change in response, also go together. These are found, in a modern spoken language, by having a native speaker reproduce utterances so that it is possible to observe what variants are present, and then the investigator repeats the utterances with what he thinks is random variation to see whether the informant will accept the element in question as repetition, using (if possible) also the technique of cutting samples on magnetic tape, and substituting the segments one for another. Phonematics, besides being a first step in analysis, and besides the prime contribution which it makes to the discovery of the pattern of a language, furnishes the best possible method by which a language, once it has been mechanically recorded on magnetic tape or disks, may be reduced to an unambiguous written form.

4 (p. 139): *On Morphomatic Analysis*

THE basic principle is comparison (same, similar items) and contrast (not the same), or binary (yes-no) oppositions. When samples are random, and sufficiently large, they are typical of the whole dialect or language; apparent complexity is due merely to the large possibilities of permutation and combination of elements. Actually the forms of a language are finite in number, and they belong to quite small numbers of classes of constructs, parts of speech, categories, and arrangements of order. In English nouns and verbs form plurals, if at all, by different devices (*book: books; I was: we were; he loves: they love*), but Turkish uses the same *ler* both for nouns and verbs. In English a pluralizing device ends the sequence; in Turkish *ler* may occupy either a final or a medial position, e.g. in the word (*ev-ler-in*). A final formative closes the process (English plural *-s*, Latin passive *-tu-r*); but several medial formatives may be added one after another. Latin *socius* 'comrade' contains a root (*sequ-* or *soc-*) plus a suffix *-io-*, but *societas* 'society' has a further suffix *-tat-*, and then the *-s* of the nominative singular (*societat-is* gen. sing.). There is in early Indo-European languages usually a fixed pattern not only in the forms of the suffixes, but also in the number in sequence that will determine whether the result is to be a noun or a verb: e.g. I.Eu. has a root *$\ast\underset{}{i}eu$-* (Sanskrit *yu-* 'join'),

Whatmough   9 Feb. 1934

o   l   d
a   l   d   d

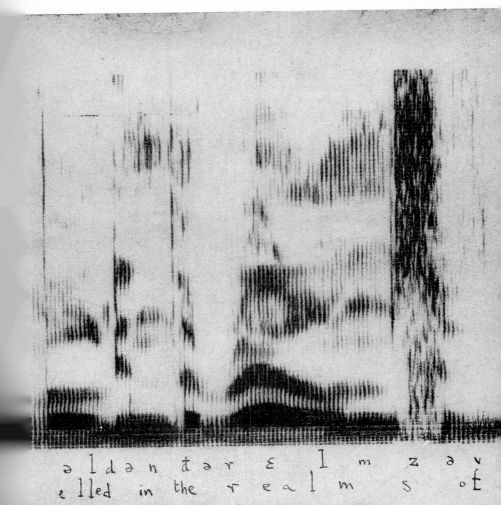

ə l d ə n t a r ɛ l m z ə ʋ
elled in the realms of

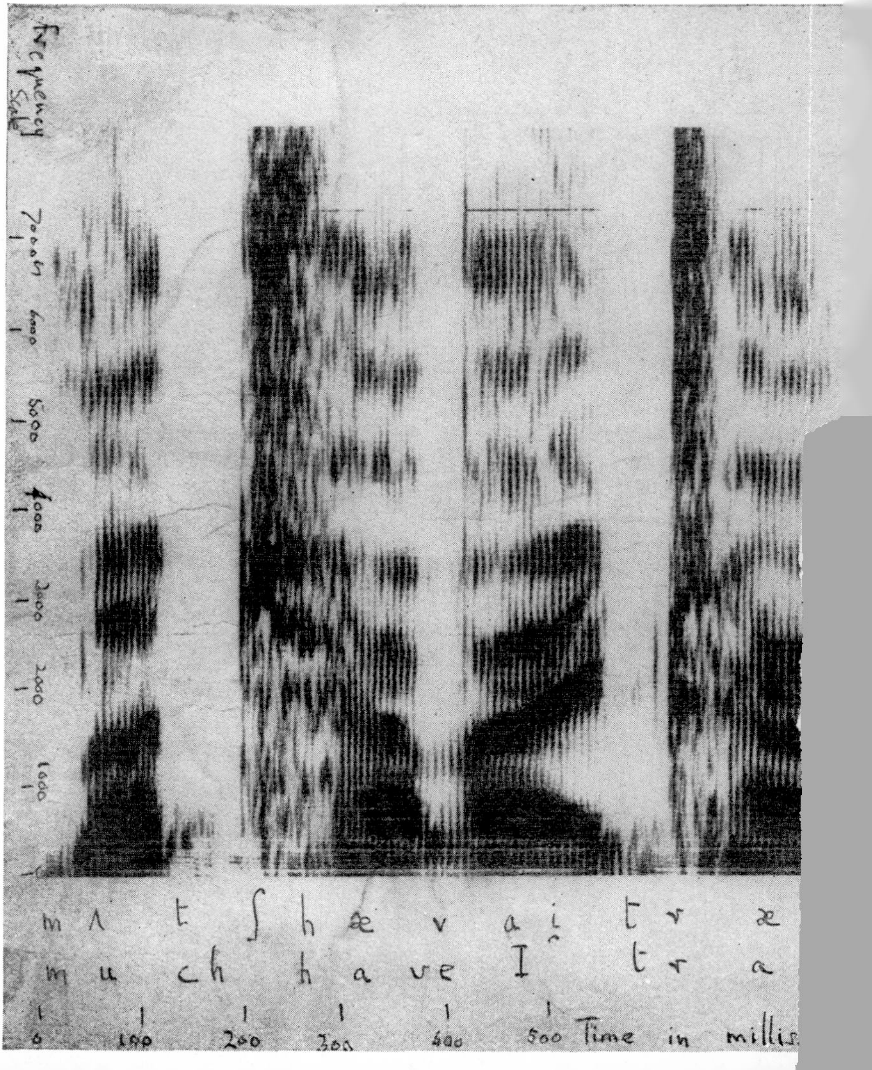

Frequency Scale
7000
6000
5000
4000
3000
2000
1000
m ʌ t ʃ h æ v a i t r æ
m u ch h a ve I t r a
0 100 200 300 400 500 Time in millis

then *ieu-eg- has the variants (i) ieug- (Greek ζεῦγ-ος 'span, pair [of horses]'), (ii) iug- (Latin $iugum$, English $yoke$), in either of which -$n(u)$- may appear (Latin $iungo$ 'join', Greek ζεύγνυμι 'join') and (iii) $iueg$-, again with -n- as in Sanskrit yu-n-$ák$-ti 'he joins' (the a is I.Eu. e, -k- I.Eu. -g- before t, thus *iu-n-$ég$-ti, *$iunékti$, $yunákti$); but to ieu-eg- may be added -e/os - as in ζεῦγος (sg.) 'yoke', ζεύγεα (plural) 'yokes' from *ζεύγεσα (Latin $iugera$), and -men- (cf. $nomen$) and -to- in Latin $iouxmenta$ (sixth century BC, x is from -g-s-), classical $iumenta$ (plural) 'beasts of burden', but beyond the stage of root plus suffix plus extention there is a slowing-down process that prohibits a further extension for the formation of anything but nouns, i.e. verbs are not formed at this stage, and there is nothing approaching polysynthesis. The whole process is almost entirely abandoned in a modern Indo-European language such as English, which, by giving up formative elements in favour of separate words (e.g. Latin dic-s-er-u-nt 'they have said', dic- 'say', -s- past time, -$ēr$- multipersonal, and -u-nt plural, but English 'they have said'), has freed itself from troublesome appendages, in a manner that has been compared to man, with a sword that he may take up or lay aside, as contrasted to a swordfish, with its sword permanently attached to its snout. If electronic symbolization, dispensing entirely with linguistic patterns and substituting its own, leads to a satisfactory interlingua, then a process will have been evolved that will be really worthy of the term 'etherealization'—getting up off the ground and into the air.

5 (p. 145): *Analysis in Syntax*

A stock example:

$$
\begin{array}{ccc}
A & B & \\
\left.\begin{array}{c} The\ king\ of\ England \\ John \end{array}\right\} & \left\{\begin{array}{c} opened \\ prorogued \end{array}\right\} & Parliament
\end{array}
$$

Either A or B may be isolated as a 'focus', leaving either B or A as its 'environment'. Then

$$
\begin{array}{c|c}
The\ king & of\ England \\
x & y
\end{array}
$$

(not *The* $\mid$ *king of England*, for $\overset{0}{nil}$ + *king of England*

does not occur in the environment of B); x is called the 'nucleus' and y (which is dispensable, as if

The king + $\overset{0}{nil}$) is called the 'satellite'.

The relationship between any two segments at a particular level of analysis may be that of (i) determination, when $m+n$ . . . presuppose $a+b$ . . .; (ii) dependence (a and b or m and n presuppose one another); and (iii) aggregation (when $a+b$ . . . occur without presupposing $m+n$ . . . and vice versa). Different foci in identical environments are in free variation with one another; if they have some environments in common they are contrasted; if they have no environments in common, they are in complementary distribution. In all this it is always necessary to be satisfied with representative samples of a language; and also to apply the principles of comparison (same : different) and distribution by turns; the two criteria are not coincident, but if they conflict appeal to meaning usually settles the matter, since syntactic meaning is a statistical measure of multitudes of experiences of different individuals.

6 (p. 147): *Monosyllabic English Patterns*

A SKILFUL, but exceedingly cumbrous, scheme has been devised to exhibit the pattern of a monosyllabic English word. Here it is; it needs so much explanation that its usefulness is limited to convincing the sceptical. We start with the assumption that such a word, in order to be pronounceable, must have a vowel (V) which may or may not be preceded and followed by a consonant (C), i.e. it has the pattern CVC, in which either the initial or final C may be replaced by zero. Thus:

1.   (i)   0
or (ii)   C-ng
    (iii) g(l), k(l), sh, d, th, f(l), b(l) $\pm$r
    (iv) h, g, t, d, th $\pm$w
    (v) h, k, g, f, v, p, b, m $\pm$y (if u)
    (vi) s $\pm$k(w), t, p(l) $\pm$r
    (vii) s $\pm$k, t, l, n, f, p, m, w

2.   (viii) V
    (ix) $\begin{Bmatrix} a \\ aw \end{Bmatrix} : 0$
    (x) r, w, y

3.   (xi) C-h
    (xii) (l, s) k, t, p, (l) b, m, f, d, s, (m) p, n (k, g, t, d, s)
    (xiii) (l, n) ch, j
    (xiv) (k, x, ng, t, d, l, n, f, p, m) th, (m)pf
    (xv) $\pm$t/d, s/z, st/zd
    (xvi) $C_a C_a > C_a$

NOTES

1.   (i)   0 means no consonant.
      (ii) Any consonant except (minus) *ng*
      (iii) Any consonant in the list followed by *r;* or in the case
            of *g, k, f,* or *b* followed by *l*
      (iv) Any consonant in the list followed by *w*. The writing
            wh is often pronounced simple *w;* if not, it is better
            written (as in Old English) *hw.*
      (v)   Any consonant in the list followed by *y* provided that
            it is followed by *u.*
      (vi) *k, t, þ* may be preceded by *s*, and followed by *r; k* also
            by *w* and *þ* by *l.*
      (vii) Any consonant in the list preceded by *s.*

2.   (viii) Vowel
      (ix) The vowel may end the word if it is *a* or *aw*. An English
            word that appears to end in *e* or *i* actually ends in
            -y; one that appears to end in *o* or *u*, actually ends
            in *w.*
      (x)   Here *r, w,* or *y* may be interpolated.

3.   (xi) Any single consonant may end the word, except *h.*
      (xii) *k, t, þ* may be preceded by s or *l; b, m, f, d, s* may be
            preceded by *l; þ* may be preceded by *m; k, g, t, d, s* may
            be preceded by *n*. This term seems inadequate.
      (xiii) *ch* or *j* may be preceded by *l* or *n.*
      (xiv) *th* may be preceded by any consonant in the list; and
            -mpf.
      (xv) These may be added after any voiceless or voiced sound
            respectively.
      (xvi) Prohibits double consonants.

Transition markers are not taken into account in this scheme. The
description made of Sanskrit by the grammarian Pānini about 300 BC
surpasses in minuteness of detail anything that has been done in
modern times. It also uses the device of zero, which is indispensable
to the technique of binary oppositions.

7 (p. 165): *Examples of Historical Change*

PHONEMES: (1) *oktau* a dual form of Indo-European meaning 'two
sets', namley of '(four) points', that is 'four fingers on each hand'
(compare Latin *acer* 'sharp', *acus* 'needle-point', or the term *acies*
'edge', and the mountain name *Ocra* 'peak'), but in Sanskrit it is
aštau, in Gothic *ahtau*, in Old English *eahta*, modern English *eight;*

(2) Latin has *uetulus* 'old', in Vulgar Latin it is *veclus* (like sub-standard English *ac least* for *at least*), Italian *vecchio* and French *vieux*. Such alternants as *was: were, seeth: sodden, freeze: frore* are the result of accentual conditions that can be accurately stated.

Instead of the *cildru* of Old English we have in English dialects *childer* (like German *Kinder* 'children'); the puzzling *Bellerophon*, as a name of a ship, was assimilated in the British Navy to a more familiar 'Billy Ruffian'; *norther* has become *north* to match *south*, and *south* is also *southern* to match *northern;* Latin *hábeo* gives (*j'*)*ai*, and *habémus* gives (*nous*) *avons*, but *nous aimons*, instead of *amons* (from *amámus*), follows the pattern of *j'aime* from *ámo*, like *parlons*, though *je parole* has yielded to *je parle*. In some of these examples reshaping in adherence to a pattern is obvious enough. Moreover the reshaping disfavours the irregular variants in inverse proportion to the frequency of their occurrence: the irregular pattern *was: were* is now endangered by the more frequent (*I*) *saw: (we) saw*, and *I were* or *we was* may come to be standardized. Change is not limited to substitution of phonemes; it is just as pervasive in morphology, so that we say *books* where Old English had *bōc* 'book' and a plural *bēc*, like *foot: feet; help, helped* for Old English *helpe* (present), singular *healp* and plural *hulpon* (past), *holpen* (participle, as still in the Authorized Version of the Bible); or in syntax, for example *he eorthan* (accusative without preposition) *gefēoll* (like *go home*), but now *he fell to earth*. Nothing is more easily observed than change in meaning. The changes are highly regular. In broad terms it may be said that spoken language changes at a *rate* which leaves con-temporaries free to communicate without disturbance; at an *intensity* which varies inversely with the ease and certainty of communication between speakers; but which is *uniform* in proportion to the degree of communication between them. From abundant evidence of widely different dates and regions, there is no doubt whatever that a lin-guistic pattern is constantly being modified regularly, and that pattern is never wanting or destroyed.

8 (p. 169): *Regularity of Development*

In Latin every Indo-European -*s*- between vowels became -*r*- be-tween 450 and 350 BC. Hence *genus* but *generis*, from an older **genesos* (the * means that the form is not actually recorded), or *meliorem* but old Latin *meliosem* (compare *melius*). After this change was exhausted, any Latin word (of later date) with intervocalic -*s*- is an apparent exception. For example, *causa* (in Cicero's time) had been *caussa* as late even as Cicero's own boyhood; still earlier it had been **caudta;* or again *rosa* is not Latin at all, but borrowed from Southern Italy. So far as phonematic substitution goes, there is a gradual, but completed, shift in the basis of articulation. Some changes occur in different times and places (e.g. -ld- or -lt- giving place to -u̯d-, u̯t- in French *chaud*, *autre*, Dutch *koud* 'cold'; and so in Osco-Umbrian, ancient Cretan, modern northern English). Regular changes appear also in other linguistic features; in the structure of inflexional forms, in syntactical developments, in semantic changes.

This principle can be observed at work in the unwritten history of languages. That form of Indo-European which developed into Greek, Latin, Sanskrit and the rest had the vowels ĕ, ē; ŏ, ō; ă, ā. Still earlier it had a laryngeal h_1, h_2, or h_3, combined with but a single vowel, namely *e*, preceding or following the laryngeal. That is to say, there was considerably less perfect shuffling in pre-Indo-European as compared with the historic languages, though no doubt pre-Indo-European strove to attain its own equilibrium. Its vowel system was as simple as that of modern Aranta or Hawaiian.

Retrograde prediction, based upon historical linguistics, had foretold the discovery of Indo-European *h*, which actually came only after the archaeologists had uncovered the Hittite records at Boghazkoï thirty-five years later. Structural research into the morphology of Greek foretold the historical development by which an ending -ă in the first personal singular of the optative mood must have been displaced by the recorded -*mi* ending. Actually a form in -*a* appeared in an Arcadian inscription discovered in 1913; but this had been predicted in 1877, long before archaeologists excavated the site of Orchomenos where the inscription was found. A comparable form, vouched for only by an ancient grammarian, was already known— but generally rejected! Similarly, in Latin, from historical patterns of different dates, it was clear that, with a diphthong *ou̯* and an ending -*om*, the word *iumentum* must have had -*g*- before -*m*-(i.e. **ioug[s]mentom*), some thirteen years before an inscription was unearthed with the spelling *iouxmenta* (neut. pl.), in which *x* is the postulated *gs*. It is confidently held that Indo-European 'roots' had the pattern consonant + ĕ + consonant, followed by a suffix ĕ + consonant (CvCvC). This is not likely ever to be confirmed by the discovery of written records, for it goes back into a period older than the use of writing by Indo-European speaking peoples; but on the ground of this hypothesis we expect to be able to find kindred of Indo-European in other families of languages.

Prediction of the direction a language is going is also possible, so soon as there is evidence covering a long enough span of time. Strong verbs (e.g. *sing*, *sang*, *sung*) are disappearing from English; extrapolation points to *c.* 3000 AD as the likely date of almost complete disappearance. Or observe the emergence of a new type of compound in English since about 1900 (e.g. *better-than-leather-miracle-covering*,

December 1950, in one of the popular magazines). Fifty years is too short a time to give assurance of the trend; astronomers usually have observations ranging over a few centuries before they decide that there is something wrong about an accepted theory, and set up a new hypothesis which must await confirmation of its predictions from suitable later experiment or observation; and linguists are in like case. But a new form of English attempting to make articulate some formulae now current in physical theory (e.g. the expression of space-time by means of a grammatical category) might well emerge along the lines of compounds of a new type.

9 (pp. 189, 200): *Social and Linguistic Correlates*

A SYSTEM of family relationships is often reflected in linguistic terms, and likewise tribal groupings (for example numerically in Gaulish ethnic names compounded with *Tri-*, *Petru-*, *Pinpe-*, *Sex-*, i.e. 'three' to 'six'); or institutions such as monarchy. A peculiar situation is revealed in the ancient Sican and Illyrian royal names *Teutos* and *Teuta* which mean 'people', as if 'l'état, c'est moi'. The Roman system of names of freeborn males (like *Marcus Tullius Cicero*) is a patrilinear and aristocratic one (the girls were apt to be numbered merely, as *Prima, Secunda, Tertia*); an uncle or cousin on the father's side is sharply distinguished from one on the mother's (in Latin *patruus* and *patruelis*, *auunculus* and *consobrinus*), as are relatives through males, blood, or by marriage (*agnatus, cognatus, affinis*), ancestors and descendants six generations up and down (*tritauus* 'great-great-great-great-grandfather' and similarly *trinepos* 'great-great-great-great-grandson'); a husband's brother has a special label (*leuir*), and so forth.

There is good non-linguistic evidence for believing that the kinship-systems of the Apache-speaking tribes reflect an old division of Southern Athabaskan into two groups, which is confirmed independently by linguistic evidence. Or again, relations between siblings of the same sex as contrasted with those of an individual with the relatives of his spouse, may be poles apart, a distinction reflected in the language which uses distinctive forms of address, and especially different terms of respect. In Navaho avoidance of the dead is grammatically indicated by a special suffix; however, the meaning of this suffix does not seem really to go beyond the designation of past time. But the Apache 'great family', with matrilocal residence after marriage, has its special terminology, just as much as the patrilinear system of descent and inheritance among the Indo-European speaking Romans.

The kinship-system of Vietnamese recalls that of Latin in its elaborate distinctions of age, agnate and cognate relationships. The ascription of age, usually avoided in English, is regarded as a compliment and not unwelcome. More remarkable is the segmentation of the immediate from a more remote audience by distinctions of inclusive and exclusive pronouns (We = 'I plus my hearers', or We = 'I plus certain environmental units', more distantly alluded to, and We = 'I excluding certain units') which has social implications. High and low status is distinguished by four separate forms of the verb for the second and third persons in Maithili (North India), the speaker (first person) assuming low status; so Italian has (or had until recently) the dignified form of address (*Ella*); and those languages which distinguish a second person singular from the plural when addressing a single individual, especially a child or close relative or a servant, clearly pay attention to certain social relationships no longer linguistically distinguished in English. The plural of royalty, of the pulpit, of the professor's chair, or of the editorial office, like the Latin dignified first person plural in the singular sense, all have a flavour of exalted status. The speaker projects himself upon a screen, steps back to admire the result, and says 'we said in our last orders, sermon, lecture, issue', or whatever it may have been. Latin can be quite pointed: 'saluta Tironem meum nostris uerbis' writes Cicero, 'pray give my dear Tiro' (his freedman) —then '*our* very kind regards', like the English 'our good friend' (who is no friend at all) checks the exuberance of the preceding *meum*.

10 (p. 209, 219): *Language and Science*

THE attempt to find a hard and fast relationship between 'physica' and 'linguistica'; or between phenomena and noumena, corresponding to a linguistic relationship between form and substance, seems to assume that language is a part of nature, which it is not. Linguistic events *are* part of nature; and that which they symbolize, at first remove (e.g. protocol or basic statements), also is part of nature. But symbolism, which must not be confused with semiology, intervenes, except in these primary situations which are a very minor part of language. For the most part we carry on with intraverbally associated words, far beyond those which facilitate an association in an extremely simple way, such as synonyms, homonyms, and antonyms. Lexical definition is not at all a frequent recourse in discourse, which must proceed at high speed, and does so among people who have never even heard of such a thing as a dictionary; or of an appeal to reinforcement of one kind or another, to bolster up the stimulus-and-response relation; or of the allocation of a linguistic unit to an experiential continuum defined by a pair of polar terms. To the speakers of a language like Eskimo sentences are not distinguished from words—sentence-noises are like elaborate, prolonged word-noises. Sentences and words alike function at least as much through relations between persons as between linguistic elements or their supposed intrinsic properties.

The limitations of word-usage are sharpest for designating the percepts of the various senses at a comparatively low level—smells, noises, or sights; and then for natural substances such as water or oxygen, or phenomena such as electricity. This is quite different from the procedure of ordinary everyday language with its immense and fluctuating variety. However systematic in form and symbolism, in usage linguistic systematization is strongest in specialized languages—logic, or mathematics, or the exact sciences like chemistry and physics. The efficiency of scientific terminology is something to be envied; take the system of prefixes and suffixes *hydro-*, *hypo-*, *per-* and *-ic*, *-ous*, *-ide*, *-ite*, *-ate* in the terminology concerned with compounds containing chlorine (or fluorine, or bromine, or iodine) and various quantities of oxygen (*hydrochloric*, *hypochlorous*, *chlorous*, *chloric*, *perchloric acid*, *potassium chloride*, *hypochlorite*, *chlorite*, *chlorate*, *perchlorate*), so consistent as to produce *periodic acid* (HIO_4). Even a layman uses symbols such as DDT, without realizing how precise and completely adequate the full name really is. Pure mathematics is language at its most perfect: here we have self-consistent systems of abstract terms in abstract relations.

Symbolic logic has the same kind of virtues. The fact that it is non-quantitative may make it a useful tool in the theory of linguistics, as in any scientific theory, where the rules and correctness of inference are at stake. The economy of conversational discourse, high as it is compared with such devices as gesture, the mapping (say) of chances by marking one of a thousand squares (which would have to be counted) in order to say 'one in a thousand', or of listing every object and every event separately, is as low compared with that of symbolic logic, as the use of Arabic as compared with Roman numerals (try to multiply CCCLXV by itself, and then 365).

Logic gets rid of the ambiguity and vagueness of 'natural' languages; there seems to be nothing to prevent its application to a systematic body of fact and theory, such as those with which linguistics deals, all the existing treatises on which yet fail in rigor, in clarity, and in comprehensiveness. Thus grammar does not recognize the converse function implicit in a comparative expression such as 'x is taller than y' except by means of correlates ('y is shorter than x') since the degrees positive, equative (as in Welsh), comparative, and superlative designate only increasing, not decreasing intensity. Similarly, a transitive verb and an adjective are logically both two-place functions ('$\hat{x}$ sees $\hat{y}$', is on a par with '$\hat{x}$ is-taller-than $\hat{y}$' - $^\frown$ means 'any'), but grammar fails to indicate that language is adapted also to many-place functions, and misconstrues language by not admitting the converse function. Again in

Much have I travelled in the realms of gold

the point of reference (R) coincides with the point of speech (S) but not with the point of event (E)—the line is not narrative, but a direct report—and all three points of time are required in a logical diagram, though conventional grammar is satisfied with two. The logical analysis of a future tense or a perfect tense does correspond to what we find to be historically the development of these tenses in some Indo-European languages, especially in their later forms, e.g. *manebo* 'I shall remain', or *je vais aller* in which *-b(o)* and *vais* are presents. A simple future, better a posterior present, is logically $S, R - E;$ the point of speech and the point of reference coincide. Punctuation becomes in logic a subclass of syntactical terms; the intensional referend of the subjunctive mood (for example in unfulfilled conditions), and sometimes of the indicative (if modified by an appropriate particle or marker) is on a par with the negative, and some languages actually have a negative conjugation. In fact a negative operates by selection, not by limitation. Logic is well equipped to cope with these and many other features of language, and some at least of its devices are also well adapted to mechanical coding devices.

If events are the real stuff of the world, and come part by part, then a progressive aspect is more satisfactory than a present tense, and logical analysis of process, rather than substance or form, is superior to structural analysis.

Linguistic symbolism usually goes far beyond concrete relations. Even the simplest spatial designations are symbolically imbued, as in *sinister* ('left-handed') and *dexterous* ('right-handed'). The greater the distance between symbol and phenomenon, the higher order the abstraction, but not necessarily the more universal. Nor is it true to say, with the philosophy of symbolism, that diversity of language means a diversity of the aspects in which the world is seen, notwithstanding the fact that modern scientific thought finds the structure of language uncongenial: for the scientist's purposes, linguistic symbols are inadequate.

Phonemes are classes of equivalence of speech-sounds; morphomes too, except when a morphome is also a word, are below the level of effective linguistic symbolism, which may be preserved in records as memory, as well as being communicable among contemporaries. But language, however inadequate logically or scientifically, satisfies ordinary, everyday requirements, even when it does not meet all possible criteria of good symbols. The criterion of simplicity would prove a delusion in ordinary verbal behaviour, where actual disturbances in transmission bring about a redundancy (i.e. greater complexity of distinctive features than is ideally necessary) that cannot be dispensed with. Economy, also a valid criterion, is prominent; and in certain forms of discourse the demand for elegance is usually satisfied, especially in structure; so is the demand for equilibrium, which is a guarantee of comprehension, and appears in such matters as number, frequency, size, and perspicuity of the symbols.

You are struck some day in May by the 'blueness' of the sky; but a physicist speaks of the wave length of light that you call 'blue' in terms of angstrom units (of which there are 10^8 in 1 cm.), from 3900A at the red end of the visible spectrum to 7600A at the violet end. The poet makes play with the sky's blueness. But the physicist who tells us that a rocket propelled by an exhaust, that, on the annihilation of matter, would consist entirely of light, would have a thrust powerful enough to drive a space-ship to the sky—at least to the nearest star—in something over four and a half years at a speed of about 600,000 miles an hour, has taken a flight of mathematical imagination to which the name of poetry is not to be denied. No poet has quite risen to this occasion: our modern cosmology, worthy of such a poetic genius, still seeks in vain. The scientific story is ready to supplant, the world over, local and temporary myths, the disruption of which by scientific language is not at all in itself impoverishing, since this language commands its own poetry, and, vastly more important still, a universality not hitherto developed in any other form of language. For science is a language as well as an activity; it is now in the range of pure science to bring up to date our outmoded verbalizations of the world about us. Its language has the property of leading to the deduction of whatever is implicit in the premises, and so to new discoveries. Some reconstruction of conversational discourse is bound to follow in time.

Hence all science is centred around language; from its own genre-style, its code and its symbolic systems, science is in a position to produce a creative style that is higher valued in the hierarchy of languages than other forms of discourse. Granted even that our concepts of the physical world are constructs, still this is a characteristically human procedure, and the current argument of seeing science and the humanities as somehow in conflict totally unjustified. Both science and poetry are symbolic forms, and the languages in which they are expressed redesign themselves, after some delay, at need. 'Reality' has been seen as flux, duration, relations, events, or atomized elements—but language accommodates all four, being the mould in which 'reality' is made more significant, whether expressed in the discourse of science or of religion. A scientific theory such as quantum mechanics clearly is not a mere recept from 'Standard Average European' language; the language itself needs to be remade in certain particulars.

From time to time attention is called to observations of the poets drawn from science, Shakespeare or Milton or Donne. But these are hardly relevant, beyond the observation that scientists do make the effort, and for the most part successfully, to coin new formations acceptable to the usage of the language, Greek more often than Latin, upon which they draw. Occasional lapses are found, like *telegram* instead of *telegrapheme*. These are trivial matters. The fundamental problem is to adapt language, which has been outstripped by physics, to the needs of science, to the needs of constructs for which linguistic symbolism is now totally inadequate. Huxley could and did define science as 'organized common sense'; now much of it begins to look like uncommon nonsense, which admits no correlates between its constructs and the so-called 'primary' data of sense impressions. Hence the scientists are called upon to wrestle with problems of language as well as of their own sciences. It is not at all like the linguistic problems of the poet or novelist; but much more like that of a solver of a many-dimensional crossword puzzle—any word may be tried, but only one will fit all parts in all directions. In the same way, not until a univocal linguistic expression was available could Heracleitus expound his theory of flux. Science does not seek to 'explain' nature, but aims at constructs whereby to symbolize it. This being so, language can never be wholly free from the possibility of error and deception. Or again, words are sometimes simply *not* there for connexions, for correlations which *are* there. Complete independence from language is not attainable; verbal guidance is needed to a very high degree. This need has long ago been satisfied in Euclidean geometry, algebra, and classical physics; but not for the constructs of modern theory.

The hypothesis that scientific method is fundamentally adaptable to the study of any part of nature is now widely accepted. Language is commonly thought to belong to the field of the humanities. But this is a survival from the nineteenth century, when the study of language, based upon the well-known languages of well-known and extensive literatures, chiefly Indo-European, with some attention to Semitic, Ugro-Finnish, Altaic, and Sinitic, was chiefly historical and comparative. There has been more recently some tendency to count linguistics among the social sciences, for obvious reasons. But scientific discourse, and especially symbolic logic, has become a problem in its own right, which natural scientists can hardly afford any longer to ignore. Moreover the basic question of the nature and validity of the distinctions commonly drawn between natural

and social sciences, or between scientific and humanistic ways of
knowing, is being actively debated. This much is clear, that the
study of language, whether scientific or literary, should proceed
from a point of view that need not be changed whenever a linguist
directs his interest into the field of another science. The linguistics
of today hardly satisfies this requirement. But it has taken some
steps toward satisfying it: the theory of molecular linguistics of the
twentieth century, and especially the introduction of the mathematical concept of function—that is to say, of the dependence of and
interrelation between linguistic phenomena, one to another, are
steps forward. The close association of spatial, temporal, and other
sensations, of colour and sound, smell, taste and touch, are inter-
related in memory and linguistically expressed through the media
of literary forms as well as of the sciences of physics, chemistry,
biology and the rest. It is difficult not to admit that there is a
fundamental unity here, even if it is more difficult to demonstrate
the unity. A clue may be found by approaching linguistic expression
as motor activity first and foremost. An utterance is a fragment
of nature, and there is no real gap between it and other fragments
in sequence. What is sought is a mutual accommodation of linguistics
with other positive sciences, indeed with all possible forms of knowing.
It has more than once been pointed out in recent years that 'every
proposition of a positive science refers to actions of men observed
by men', and there seems to be a creeping advance away from a mere
mixture of incompatibles, disorderly even in their very premises,
toward the construction of a unified philosophy, with full recognition
of the overwhelming role that verbalization plays in all scientific
theory. Some now forecast that the verbalizing will be done not by
the human nervous system, but by 'logical machines'; and we are
told that any sort of behaviour can be imitated by mechanism if
only the mechanism is complicated enough. Should this come about,
the errors and delusions that verbalization admits may at last be
completely eliminated. But when linguistics is reduced to constructs,
it becomes an abstract science, as far removed from natural language
as mathematics. Linguistics is a human invention, invented for a
particular purpose, that is for dealing with those features of language
in which linguists are interested. There is a dilemma in the circumstance that linguistic elements, the phoneme, morphome, and the
rest, are units in the laws of linguistics, but that these laws enter into
the operation of the phoneme or morphome or other element. Such
circularity is not so much 'inevitable'; it is a condition. Again the
laws of linguistics are not independent of temporal any more than
of linear conditions—language and its constituent elements are
always connected with their past history and with their future

course. The result is that descriptive method conceals a vast amount of complications, and even of ignorance. Notwithstanding the appeal of simplicity in scientific theories, there is a good deal of essential complexity. Language is emergent, and subject to a modified form of the hypothesis of continuous creation. Structural elements in a new configuration give rise to new properties which are dependent primarily upon arrangement, and this is certainly true of language. For this reason alone it is possible to look forward to greater efficiency in language, and to favourable developments of this unique power.

11 (p. 216): *Mandelbrot's Formula*

MANDELBROT'S formula is independent of the language considered. It is justified by quantitative results, the statistical structure of language. The bounded units are ranked in the order of decreasing frequency of occurrence; then the frequency p_n of the nth entity is given by the formula

$$p_n = \frac{P}{(n+m)^B}$$

where P, m, B are positive constants, m being significant when n is small, B when n is large. But m and B are of mathematical not empiric derivation; yet the formula represents quite accurately the statistical data obtained from a great variety of languages.

12 (p. 218): *'Information'*

THE amount of 'information' is measured by the logarithm to the base 2 (since the choices are binary) of the number of available choices. 'Yes' or 'No' is *two* choices (either/or), but one binary digit (1 or 0). If $m^x = y$, then x is the logarithm of y to the base m, e.g. $2^4 = 16$, that is 4 is the logarithm of 16 to the base 2, or $\log_2 16 = 4$. If you have two choices and then stop, that is one unit (yes or no), i.e. proportional to $\log_2 2$ (logarithm of 2 to the base 2) or unity, for $2^1 = 2$. Hence a two-choice unit of 'information' is called a 'bit' or 'binit' (binary unit). But why must a binary system of numeration (dyadic numbers) be used? Because it has only two digits (0 = no, 1 = yes). If we have sixteen choices, we have four bits ($\log_2 16 = 4$), if eight choices three bits, and so on, to the end of a word or message. Not only phonemes and graphemes, but also morphomes and words, and presumably (for it has not yet been demonstrated) meanings may be treated in this way, since (except at the extreme limits of frequency-distribution) meaning is multiple and each alternative of meaning may be presented as a 'yes' or 'no' question.

Now frequency of occurrence gives the probability of the amount of freedom of choice. If we have N symbols (graphemes, phonemes, morphomes, words, meanings) of the probabilities p_1, $p_2 \ldots p_n$ respectively, then the amount of 'information' H in a sequence is the summation of the terms of the form $-p_i \log p_i$ (negative because any probability is equal to or less than 1, and the logarithm of numbers less than one is negative), for the probabilities are known from the frequency of occurrence, and since these are governed by the structure of language, a general formula may be deduced: $H = -\Sigma p_i \log p_i$ (Σ is the summation). A refinement of the theorem takes account of long-range statistics, but does not alter the fundamental fact that negative entropy, that is a measure of orderliness, is a law of language, or rather of glossodynamics. In plain language it means that a linguistic status would, if its determinacy were 100 per cent as a consequence of absolute rigidity, be completely stable; but since it functions by variables which are selected by the sequence of symbols, language is metastable.

GLOSSARY

* means a form not actually recorded.

: This sign in Linguistics is used between forms which are set side by side for comparison or contrast, as *man: men*, or Latin *carus:* English *whore*, Latin *decem:* English *ten*.

The explanations that follow are to help the general reader. They are not intended as definitions, which in many cases would not serve this purpose. Terms not used in this book are not included.

ACTIVE *See* VOICE.

ADJECTIVE A word that attributes a quality, e.g. *good*.

AGGLUTINATIVE Said of languages in which the formative elements of words are merely juxtaposed.

ALLOPHONE A class of phonetically same segments, also called positional or contextual variants, e.g. the initial phonemes of *key: cool*, the differences in articulation being (*a*) induced by the following vowel, which is distinctive, and therefore (*b*) redundant. The initial phoneme is thus the same in both forms.

ALVEOLAR Articulated at the ridge behind the gums, as English *t*, but not French *t*, which is articulated at the teeth, i.e. dental.

ANTHROPONOMICS The science of *human* social relations.

APHASIA Inability to speak with normal symbolic control.

ASPECT Kind of action, e.g. progressive, as *He is dying*, or completed, as *He is dead*.

ASPIRATION The puff of breath that may accompany a speech-sound, e.g. after the *p* in *pin;* written ¹(*p*¹*in*).

BINARY Said of a system of enumeration which uses only two digits, viz. 1 and 0. Also called dyadic. Contrast denary (or decimal), which uses ten digits, 1 2 3 . . . 9 0.

BOUND *See* FORM.

BOUNDED A complete sequence, from beginning to end, as of phonemes in a word or morphome, of morphomes in a phrase or word, of words in a construct or sentence.

CASE The category of distinctive forms in declension, as actor (Latin *dominus*) and possessor (*domini*), often, as here, interdependent with other categories of NUMBER here (singular) or GENDER (here masculine).

CATEGORY A grammatical classification determined by function and form, e.g. tense in the form-class of finite verbs, combining the functions of action and time, as present (*see*) : past (*saw*).

CONJUGATION Variation in verb forms, e.g. *see, sees, saw, seen*.

CONSTITUENT The common part of any two or more complex forms or constructs, e.g. *un/gentlemanly: gentleman/ly: gentle/man*. Or *He | missed his bus; He| there | missed his bus; That poor fellow | on the corner | missed his bus*. From these the ultimate constituents are obtained.

CONSTRUCT A repetitive identity of order, e.g. of forms, as stem + suffix (*slow + ly*) or of words, as actor + action + goal (*The dog bit the man*). The former is a morphomatic, the latter a syntactic construct.

DECLENSION Variation in noun forms, e.g. Latin *domina, dominam* etc., *dominus, dominum* etc.

DISCONTINUOUS (of a morphome) A broken or repeated sequence, as French *ne . . . pas*, German *wenn . . . gleich*; or Latin *-arum . . . -arum* (often called grammatical agreement).

DISCRETE Separate, distinguishable.

ENTROPY Positive measure of disorder.

EPILEGMA Any unit of analysis of utterance, as word; hence (e.g. as in Eskimo) a corresponding part of a sentence-word.

ERGODIC Said of a sequence in which a reasonably large sample tends to represent the system as a whole. A 'once word' is the only (and often not a real) exception.

FORM A recurring identity of utterance, e.g. (pp. 39, 69, 113, 116, 119, 138, 146, 244, 248) *book, book-s, book-ish*. A form is said to be FREE if it may stand alone and still have meaning, BOUND if not, e.g. *kind: kindly:-ly*.

FORMANT A bound form (see that term) which is added to a root or stem, e.g. *-ie-* and *-tat-* in Latin *societat(-em, -is)*.

GENDER A grammatical classification of forms, usually in nouns, pronouns, and adjectives, fulfilling the same function and marked by agreement, e.g. Latin *bona femina* (feminine) 'a good woman': *bonus poeta* (masculine) 'a good poet', not a classification by sex, e.g. *bona domus* 'a good house' is feminine.

GLOSSEME Unit of signification (form, construct, syntagma, zero-element), e.g. *man, -ly, -s* in *cuts, kind*, actor + action + goal, stem + suffix, *sheep0* (zero) plural. The adjective is GLOSSEMATIC.

GRAPHEME A minimum unit of writing, not capable of subdivision, e.g. the letter *d* in *din*, or *g* in *dig*. The adjective is GRAPHEMATIC.

INFIX An element interposed in a sequence, e.g. *n* in *stand: stood*, or Latin *linquo* ('I leave'): *liqui* ('I left').

INFINITIVE *See* MOOD.

INFLEXION Variation of form as in conjugation or declension.

INTENSIONAL Conveying intent, connotation, implication or depth of meaning.

LINGUISTICS The scientific study of the phenomena of language.

METASTABLE Stable compared with all states differing only infinitesimally from a given state.

MOOD A grammatical category of verb forms, actually or formerly expressive of the speaker's attitude, e.g. inferring natural likelihood (*might*) or wish (*would that . . . !*).

MORPHOME A form which cannot be analysed into smaller forms, together with its corresponding meaning. Such minimum significant forms fall into classes, e.g. *boy* (noun), *think* (verb), *of* (preposition), *-ing* (suffix). A morphome-alternant is a selection in context, e.g. *wive-* (: *wife*) only before *-s*. Alternants belong to the same morphome. The adjective is MORPHOMATIC.

NEGENTROPY A negative measure of disorder, or a positive measure of order. The opposite of entropy.

NOUN A part of speech (see that term) that functions as a name e.g. *man, beauty, John*, or (better) see above pp. 38, 47, 48, 227, 233, on the names of objects and of events.

NUMBER A grammatical category that distinguishes by form between one, two, three, or more than three, of a kind, e.g. *boy: boys*, *amat* 'loves': *amant* 'love' or ἵππω 'two horses, chariot' are singular, plural, and dual respectively.

PALATALIZATION Said of consonants articulated against the soft palate, e.g. *k* in *cupid*.

PARADIGM A model of inflexion typical of the variant forms of a large number of words, e.g. in conjugation and declension.

PART OF SPEECH A summation of word-classes (i.e. words having the same function), e.g. noun, verb.

PERSON Grammatical category of distinctive forms expressive of speaker (first person), address (second person), or neither, e.g. *I go: you go* or *Go!: he goes, they go*.

PHILOLOGY In England the same as LINGUISTICS; elsewhere the study of literature.

PHONEME A grammatical abstraction to designate a class of equivalence of minimum speech-sound, e.g. *k* in *car, cat, can't, cool.* Contextual or positional variants, also called allophones (see that term), belong to the same phoneme, e.g. aspirated *p¹* in *put*, unaspirated in *spin.* The adjective is PHONEMATIC.

PHONETICS The study of the gross physiological and acoustic features of speech-sound.

PLOSIVE A consonant completely stopped, e.g. *p, t, k.*

POLYSYNTHETIC Said of languages in which the smallest bounded unit is a whole sentence.

PRETERITE *See* TENSE.

PRO-PRESENTATIVE The quality of language by which an utterance conveys meaning without an actual presentation of an object, quality, or event; or by which a referend may call up another referend or referends.

PRONOUN That of which the referend (usually a noun) is not disclosed in the clause in which it stands, e.g. *I, he.*

REFEREND That which is symbolized or referred to by a verbal symbol, e.g. the referend of *rain* is 'the moisture of the atmosphere condensed and falling in visible drops'.

SEMANTICS Branch of linguistics which deals with meaning.

SEMIOLOGY Science of signs.

SENTENCE A maximum syntactic construct.

SIBLING Akin by blood relationship, or common parentage.

SUFFIX An element appended at the end of a root or stem, e.g. the root *boil* has the suffix *-er* (agent or instrument) in *boiler.*

SYNTAGMA Arrangement of units in a syntactic construct.

SYNTAX That branch of linguistics which deals with the arrangement of syntagmata.

TENSE Time of action, as *he lives* (present) : preterite *he lived* or future *he will live.*

UNVOICED A phoneme pronounced without tension of the vocal chords (fleshy membranes in the larynx), e.g. *t.*

VERB Part of speech expressive of a state or action, e.g. *is, kills.*

VOICE A category of verb-forms that distinguishes between parties to an action, as active (the actor is specified) e.g. *Mrs Maybrick killed her husband, she fired a gun;* passive (the actor is suppressed or generalized) e.g. *Mr Maybrick was killed, a gun was fired;* middle, also called reflexive, e.g. *the gun fired* (itself).

VOICED Phoneme pronounced with tension of the vocal chords (see unvoiced), e.g. *d.*

WORD A bounded (i.e. complete, both at beginning and end) sequence of phonemes with internal statistical probabilities. Less exactly, a free-standing, recurring vocal feature together with its corresponding meaning, e.g. *quick, quickly* (but not *-ly*), *bláckbird* (but not *bláck bird*, which is two words). That is, there is an association of a given meaning (or meanings) with an ensemble of phonemes, adapted to a given grammatical function.

Note on 'ergodic'—By this term is meant that the statistical average of occurrence of a given element taken from a number of messages (and therefore over an undefined period of time) need not, for any practical purposes, be treated otherwise than as if the messages were being observed simultaneously; that is to say, in an author, Marlowe for example, as a message-source, usage has not changed during the period either of his creative writing or of our observation of it. In other words, historical change is not observable.

Explanatory note with regard to the map—The use of different colours, red and black, is to indicate roughly the interpenetration of languages belonging to different linguistic groups. The Atlas of linguistic maps, from which the map in this book is adapted, is that which accompanies the work of Wilhelm Schmidt, *Die Sprachfamilien und Sprachenkreise der Erde*, Heidelberg, 1926.

Corrigenda to map—*for* Sudanic *read* Sudanese, *for* Arauzanian *read* Araucananian.

INDEX

Same, 114, 141, 145; *see also* Identity
Same relations, 143
Same response, 119, cf. 8; *see also* Temperature, *Rain, raining*
Sampling, 112
Schizophrenia, 191
Science, 92
Scientific discourse, 165
Segmentation, 145
Selection, 115, 131, 142, 143, 144, 151, 169, 174, 196, 203, 207, 212, 219
Selection and variation, 224
Selective property of language, 153, 168, 207
Selective variation, v, 39, 168, 175, 179, 203, 236
Selectivity, 161, 218
Self-stabilizing control, 190, 218, 238
Sentence, 143
Sequences, 203
Similarity, 166
Single-handedness, 166
Solipsism, 226
Sound, 127
Sound waves, 111
Spectogram, 118, 128, 153
Spectrograph, 119, 120, 123, 125, 132
Speech, 106
Speech organs, 167
Speech Synthesizer, 133
Sports, 237
Stammering, 156
Statistical analysis, 136
Statistical averages, 196
Statistical investigation, 168
Statistical method, 73
Statistical properties of Language, 164
Statistical regularity, 11, 157, 170
Statistics, 43, 77, 98, 164, 168
Status, linguistic, 115, 116, 174
Stereoscopic vision, 166
Stochastic, 170, 218
Stress, 46

Structural analysis, 109
Structural linguistics, 145, 164
Structure, 122
Structure, of language, 225
Structure, of the universe, 225
Style, 116
Substitution (or commutation), 116, 137, 141, 145
Substratum, 51
Superstratum, 51
Suppletion, 139
Syllable, 134
Symbol, 161
Symbol and referend, 198, 203
Symbolic form, 105
Symbolic logic, 111, 209
Symbolic meaning, 198
Symbolism, 8, 117, 151, 160, 212, 219
Symbolism in modern poetry, 104
Symbolization, 167
Synchronic, 110
Synesthesia, 191, 192, 207
Syntactic dimension, 105
Syntagma, 115
Syntax, 142, 148
Synthetic speech, 158
System, in language, 38, 114, 147
Systematic symbolism, 196

Talking, 167
Techniques, convergence of, 131; *see also* Convergence
Telephone, 209
Telephony, 118
Temperature (*thermometer, hot, cold*), 66, 67, 80, 84, 102, 199-200, 230, 233, 236, 238; *see also* Identity, Same response (e.g. *Rain*, 8, 9) *and* Communication; cf. p. v (Preface)
Therapeutic power, in language, 190, 219; *see also* Self-stabilizing control
Thinking, 75
Thought, 213, 227
Transformation, 129, 132, 200, 208, 209

DATE DUE

NO 12 '63			
NO 13 '63			
DE 20 63			
FE26 '64			
DE2 '64			
DE16 '64			
OC 2'67			
JA3 '68			
AP 3 70			
MY 26 70			
NO1 71			
MY 25 '72			
OC 7 '75			
MY 23 78			
JA 24			
AP 26'88			
GAYLORD			PRINTED IN U.S.A.

Whatmough, Joshua

Language: a Modern

TITLE

Synthesis.

DATE DUE	BORROWER'S NAME
NO 12 '63	Edith B. Dowd
NO 13 '63	DeLong
DE 20 '63	
FE 26 '64	Anita Mosl
DE 2 '64	Brooks Mitchell
DE 16 '64	RENEWED
OC 2 '67	Arlene Arends
JA 3 '68	Sara Gillespie
AP 3 70	B. Christiansen
NW 18 70	Carrie Gem
MY 26 70	RENEWED
NO 1 71	winifred wise

DATE DUE	BORROWER'S NAME
NO 22	RENEWED
	RENEWED NOV 20
MY 25 '72	Lisa Pine MAY 14
OC 7 '75	Pam Shute SE 16 '75
MY 23 78	K. Hollander 6 OT
JE 13 79	RENEWED MY 30 78
JA 24 '84	Gary Albert JA 23 '84 139
AP 26 '88	MY 5 '88

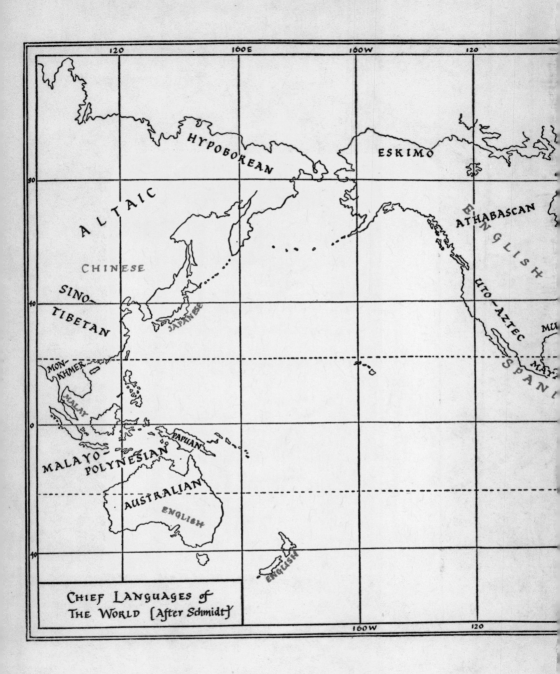

CHIEF LANGUAGES of THE WORLD (After Schmidt)